Gouache for Beginners

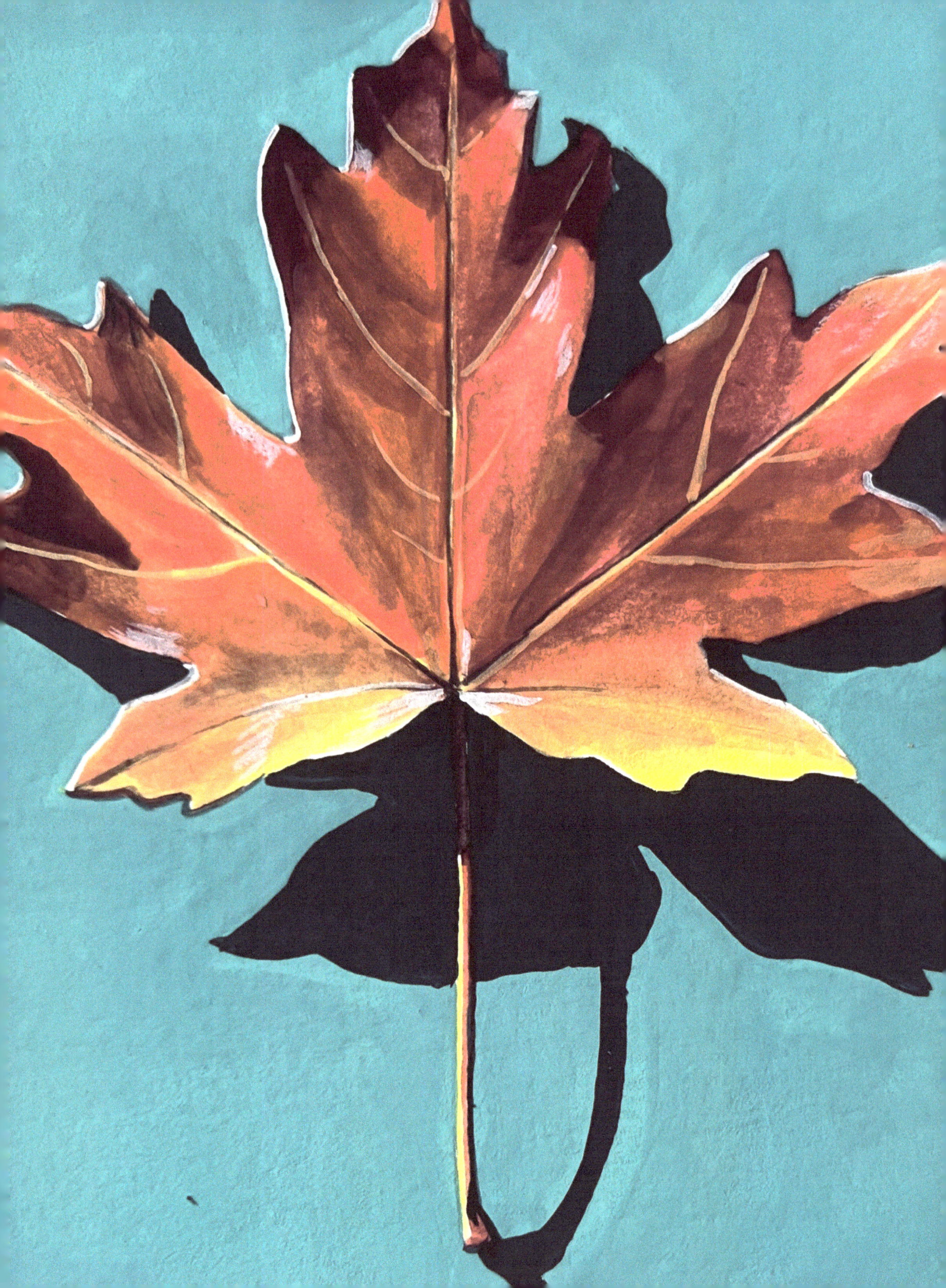

GOUACHE FOR BEGINNERS

Simple, stunning
& realistic projects

KATE JARVIK BIRCH

Walter Foster

ISBN: 978-0-7603-9348-2

Digital edition published in 2025
eISBN: 978-0-7603-9349-9

Library of Congress Cataloging-in-Publication Data

Names: Birch, Kate J., author.
Title: Gouache for beginners : simple, stunning & realistic projects /
    Kate J. Birch.
Description: Beverly, MA : Walter Foster Publishing, 2025. | Includes index.
Identifiers: LCCN 2024043888 (print) | LCCN 2024043889 (ebook) |
    ISBN 9780760393482 (trade paperback) | ISBN 9780760393499 (ebook)
Subjects: LCSH: Gouache painting--Technique.
Classification: LCC ND2430 .B57 2025 (print) | LCC ND2430 (ebook) |
    DDC 751.42/2—dc23/eng/20241019
LC record available at https://lccn.loc.gov/2024043888
LC ebook record available at https://lccn.loc.gov/2024043889

Design and page layout: Kelley Galbreath

Printed in USA

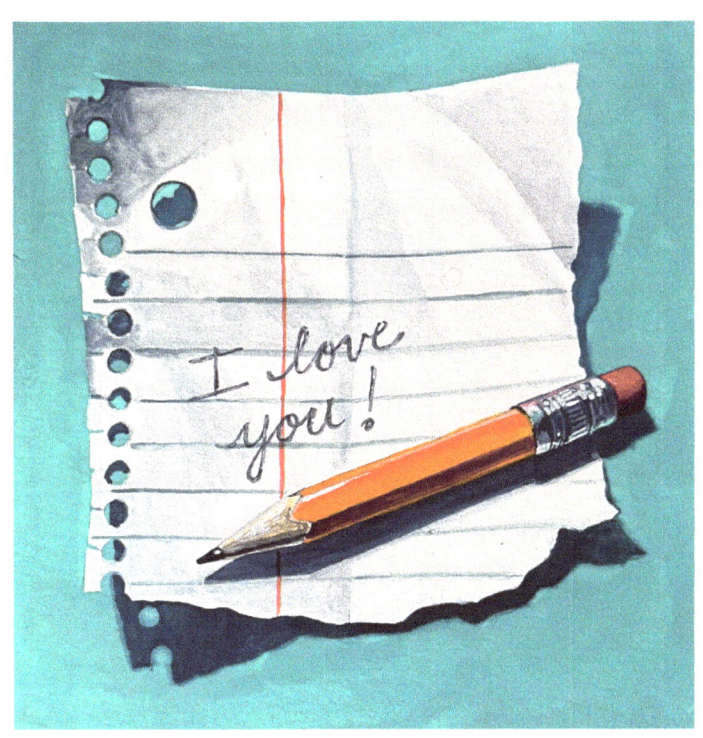

Thank you to my love, Daniel,
for always making me see the world
with fresh eyes.

CONTENTS

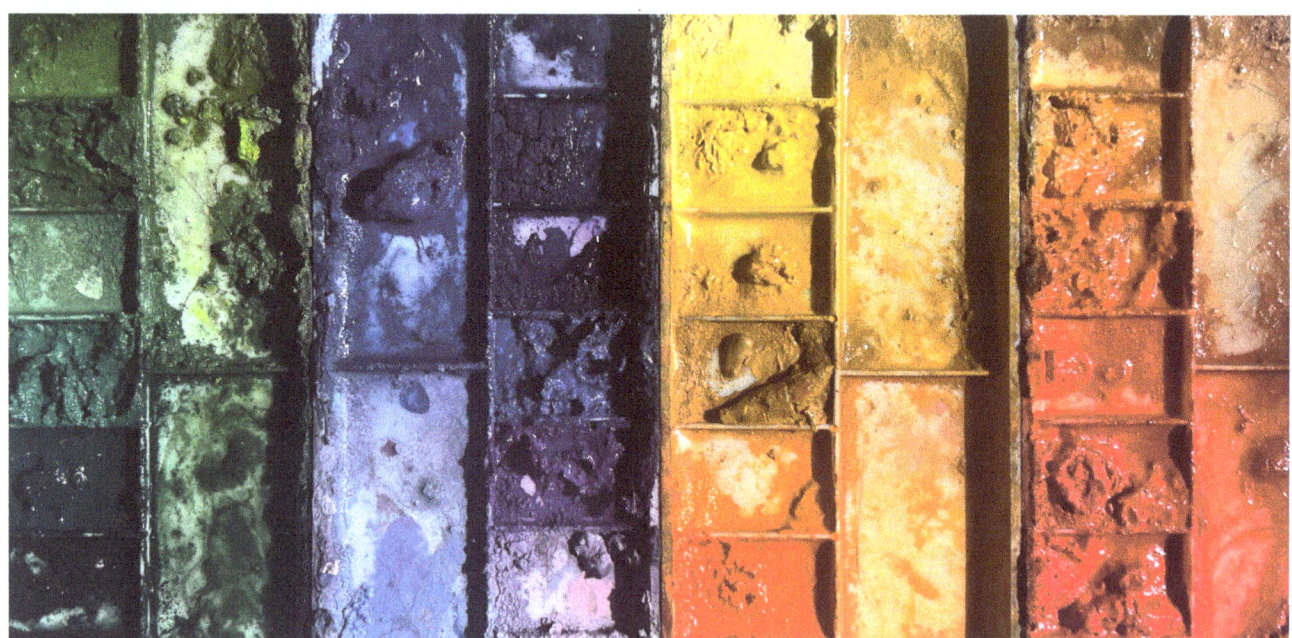

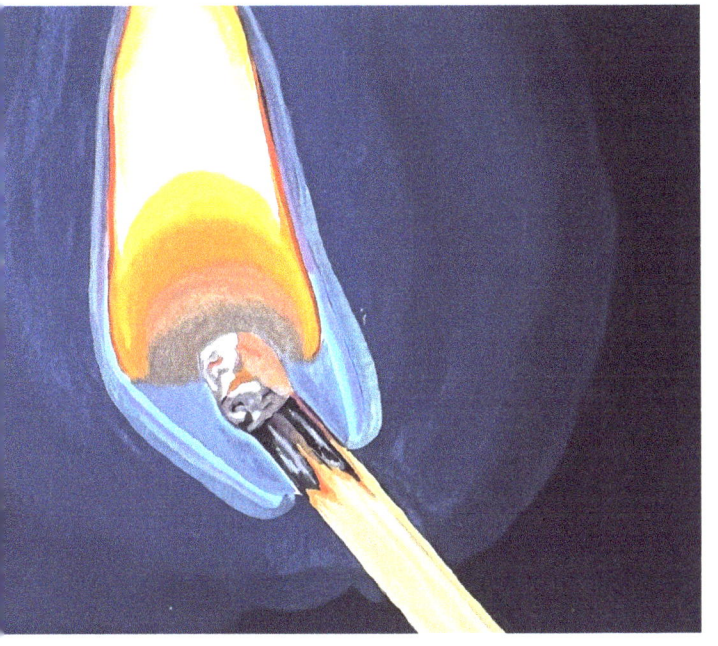

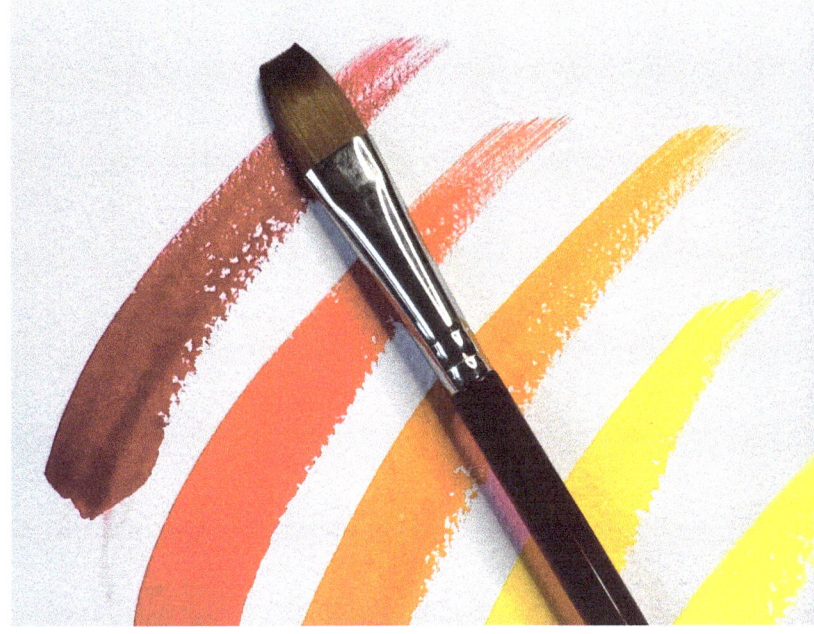

55 FIVE
The Projects

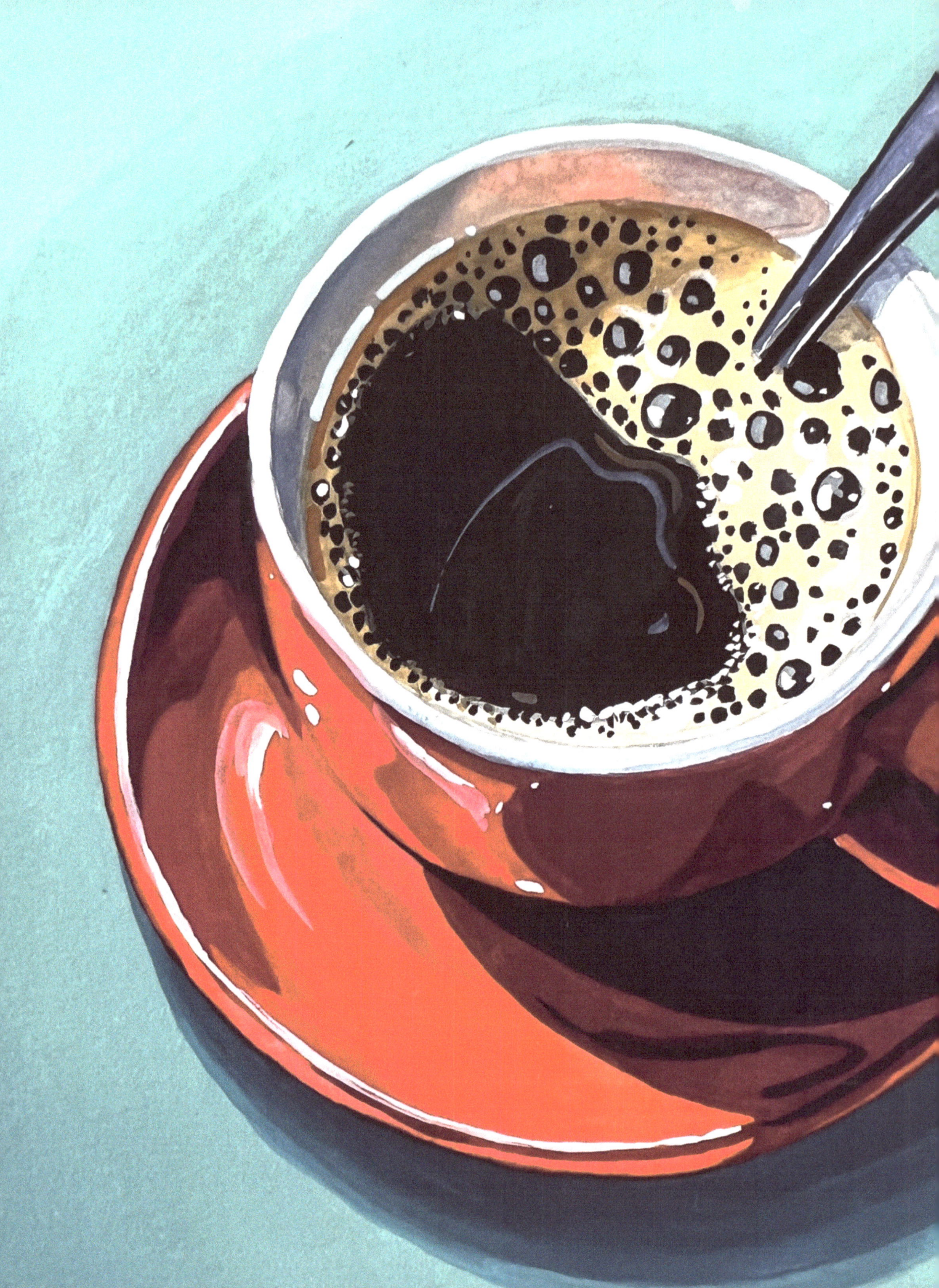

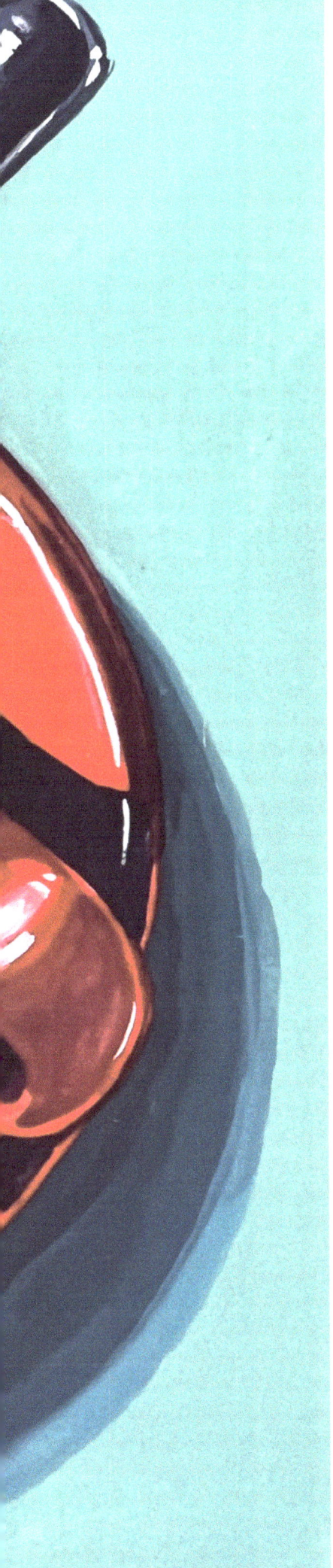

Introduction

I was one of those kids who could spend hours at the kitchen table with a box of markers and a stack of blank pages, coloring pictures of horses and fancy ladies in ball gowns. From the moment I could pick up a pencil, I remember people complimenting my artistic skills and, as a person who likes praise a bit too much, I absolutely ate it up.

I sometimes wonder what percentage of artists had a similar experience as I did growing up. Was that little boost to my artistic ego at age six . . . seven . . . eight . . . enough to encourage me to foster and nurture my talent? I don't actually believe that we're blessed with innate talents. What I do believe is that anyone who wants to be an artist CAN BE, as long as they're willing to put in the work that it takes to find their unique voice. Some of us, the ones who started early, were fortunate enough to get a head start at a time when our inner critics were a little bit more forgiving and our grasp of what was "good" art was certainly less refined.

I'm a firm believer that excitement and desire, not talent, are actually the most important qualifications for mastering anything. Skill will come with time and practice, but if you lose the spark and the passion too soon, you'll never see your true potential.

All this is to say, you've already got everything you need inside of you to succeed. It just takes persistence. I've been on my own art journey for many decades (more than I'd like to admit), and my study with gouache has been almost as long. I'm happy to share some of the secrets I learned along the way, from my favorite brushes and kinds of paper to the best consistencies to mix your paint. When I started working with gouache, I had trouble finding instruction on how to use it to make fine art. Hopefully, the time I've spent over the last couple of decades has worked out most of the kinks and this book will make your journey a little easier. My hope is that this book will be the jumpstart I can give you to free up some time for the most important part of growing your career: creating!

My Story

Even after ALLLL those drawings of horses and ball gowns, I didn't think about art as a career choice until my first year in college. I began college planning to go into elementary education. I was excited to add a drawing class as one of my electives, which seemed too impossibly fun to count toward my degree. I showed up to class with my freshly sharpened pencils and my new sketch pad, smiling like I'd pulled off a bank robbery. That excitement, right there, should have been my first indication to pay attention and listen to what I really wanted to do with my life.

It didn't come as a surprise to me that I excelled in class. I was in there with people who had never drawn before and there I was, a girl who'd already been doing this since she was a kid. When my professor pulled me aside after class one day to say how impressed she was and that she thought I should consider changing my major, her words greatly affected me. It was as simple as that . . .

I had my children when I was really young, so my time in college was punctuated with raising three kids, but I did go back to get that degree in painting and drawing. Of course, this made it a bit more difficult to find time to paint, but when you're excited about what you're doing, you find a way.

That doesn't mean there weren't hiccups. Because my house was fairly small, and I had my easel and paints set up in the family room, there were some . . . accidents. The most terrifying one I remember happened when my youngest daughter had just turned two. One morning I woke to her standing beside my bed with what looked like bright red lipstick smudged around her mouth and dolloped through her hair, making it stand up straight in front. I sat bolt upright in bed, knowing full well I didn't own any red lipstick, but I did have a lot of cadmium red oil paints I'd been using the day before.

In school, my teachers all made it a point to tell us how poisonous our paints were and that because of this, we should avoid contact with our skin whenever possible and wash our hands thoroughly after each paint session. Frantically, I called poison control who (a little too calmly) told me to give her a glass of milk to drink and keep an eye on her. That was it.

Needless to say, the oil paints got moved to higher ground and, to this day, I still prefer watercolors, particularly gouache, over any other medium. While I still wouldn't recommend eating your paints (no matter your age), water-based paints are, on the whole, quite a bit less toxic than oils. Much of this has to do with the solvents for both mixing and cleaning oils, which are obviously not necessary when using gouache, which can be diluted and cleaned with water.

I was actually first introduced to gouache during a typography class in college. I wasn't expecting to fall in love with the medium. We weren't even using it in a particularly artistic way. We'd been told to buy a tube of black gouache to render a few lettering projects, but the moment I mixed that paint with water and started painting it onto the matboard we'd been assigned to use for our project, I fell in love. I loved the creamy consistency and the way it looked almost like velvet when it dried. I liked it so much I decided to see if I could incorporate it into fine art.

For more than two decades, I've sold my art at festivals, galleries, and to art publishers. I've done illustrations for books, and I've seen my art on television. All the while, my love for gouache has grown. Over the years, I've seen it accepted by the art world as more than just the step-sibling of oil paint. It's finally recognized as a legitimately beautiful and well-loved medium. Now it's my turn to pass this amazing medium on to you. It's my hope that you'll love it as much as I do.

What Is Gouache?

When I tell people I paint with gouache, they inevitably ask me, "What is gouache?" The easiest explanation I give is that it's opaque watercolor. While that's a perfectly acceptable explanation, it's definitely an oversimplification.

To understand what gouache is and why it's opaque, it helps to understand what the paint is composed of. All paints are made of pigment and binders. What sets both gouache and watercolor apart is the water-soluble binder, gum arabic, which is most often used. Because of its adhesive qualities, gum arabic adheres to paper fibers when it dries, but can be reactivated with water.

Because the basic components of gouache and watercolor are very similar, we have to think of them on a more microscopic level. The pigments in watercolor are much more finely ground so that when thinned out with their binder and water, more paper shows through between those particles of pigment.

Gouache, on the other hand, is quite a bit coarser and more of that pigment is packed into the binder. The result is that less of the paper shows through the paint when it's placed on the paper, resulting in a richness and vibrancy that makes gouache unique.

This isn't to say that some colors of gouache aren't more transparent than others, or that you can't choose to thin it out in areas if you choose. But how gouache is applied, versus how traditional watercolor is applied, is quite different, especially when you're thinking about how whites or lighter colors are used.

In traditional watercolor, the white of the paper works as the white in the painting. Thin layers of paint are built up over the paper in progressively darker layers. Gouache, in contrast, uses white or lighter colors mixed into the paint to create lighter portions of the painting. In areas of pure white, paint will still be applied, instead of leaving the paper to show through.

Gouache is also special because of its beautiful matte finish when it dries. With so much more pure pigment and less binder than watercolor, gouache doesn't have the shine that other mediums have. This does make your painting a bit more fragile than other mediums. You'll want to avoid rubbing the surface of the painting to prevent unintended marks.

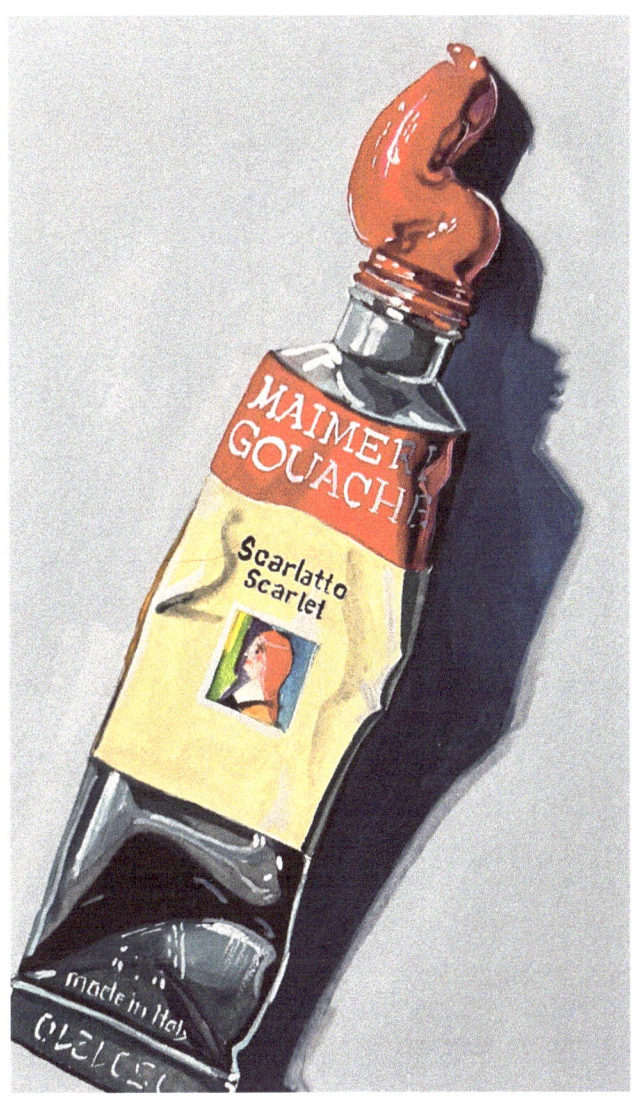

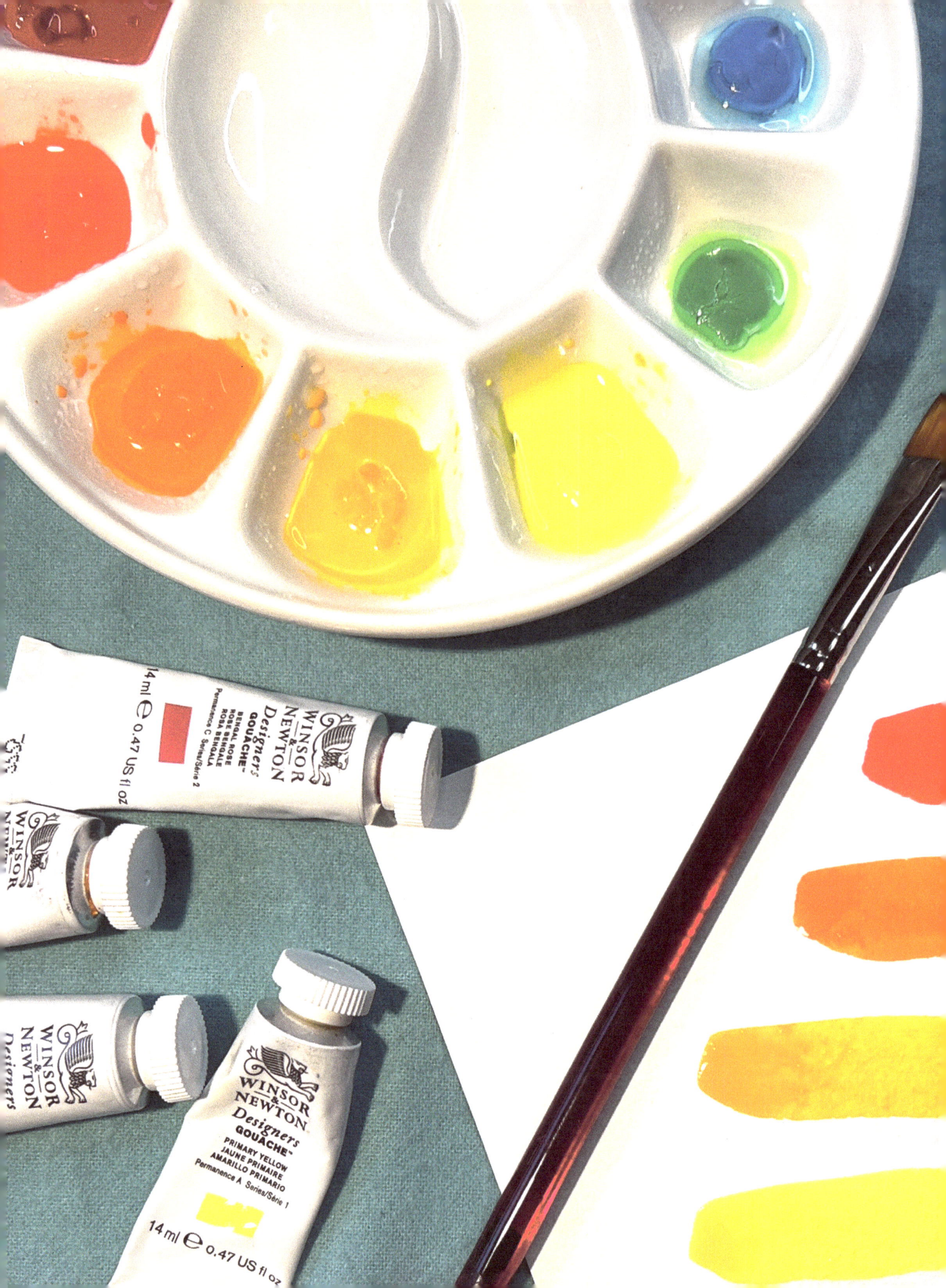

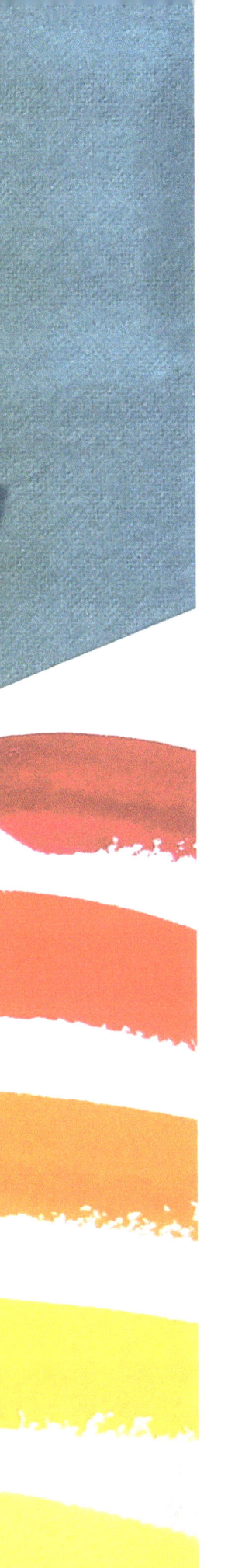

ONE

TOOLS & MATERIALS

I don't know about you, but for me, visiting an art store can be both a transcendent experience and an *expensive* one. I'm a sucker for art supplies! So, I'm going to do my best to not go overboard in this book with the supplies I'm suggesting you buy to get started in gouache. Of course, you're welcome to buy more than I suggest, but these supplies will definitely be plenty to get you started.

One of the best ways to decide which supplies you need is to think about what purpose the tools you're getting need to fulfill. Are you looking to experiment and practice? Maybe you don't need to get the most expensive paints and archival papers. Are you working on paintings for a gallery show or a commission? Now might be the time to spend a bit more.

Remember that just because one artist loves a certain kind of brush, or swears by a specific kind of paper, it doesn't mean that you'll love those same things. One of the great joys about art is discovering *your* favorites, whether that be a tool, a paint, or even a technique. There's no "right way"; there's simply what's right for you and your art.

Paint

Because this is a book about gouache, it seems fitting that the first (and arguably most important) supply we cover should be paint.

There are a few things you need to know about the types of gouache you're likely to come across at your art supply store or online. First, I need to point out the difference between acrylic gouache and traditional gouache. Acrylic gouache utilizes an acrylic binder, making it permanent and not water-soluble when it dries. In my opinion, acrylic gouache acts so similarly to acrylics that I hardly consider it gouache, and I really don't use it in the same ways I use traditional gouache. For the purposes of this book, we'll be using only traditional gouache.

Because traditional gouache is water-based and water-soluble, even after it dries, you can manipulate and blend it. I also prefer the appearance of traditional gouache, which dries with a matte and velvety finish that can't be replicated in acrylic gouache.

Tubes vs. Pans

As you're shopping for paints, you'll probably notice gouache is sold in both tubes and in kits with pans of paint. We'll be using a palette and often mixing new colors within our palettes. Because of this, as well as the higher-quality paints you can find in tubes, I recommend buying gouache in tubes, either in a set or in the individual colors you'll use most often.

An inexpensive gouache I often recommend to students is Arteza. It comes in a kit with twenty-four or sixty colors. If you don't mind spending a bit more money, other brands of gouache I like are Utrecht Artists' Gouache, Winsor & Newton, Maimeri, and Holbein. There are many other brands I've never used, and if you don't mind investing in paints, I encourage you to try many brands until you find the one that suits you best.

Suggested Colors

I know it's tempting to go out and buy every color available, but unless you've won the jackpot recently, you might want to be a bit more selective. Following is a list of colors I enjoy and use frequently. It may not be possible for you to get all these colors, but as long as you've got a reasonable selection of the primary colors (see page 36) and black and white, you'll be able to mix a lot.

- **Yellows & Oranges:** Pale yellow, lemon yellow, dark yellow, ochre, pale orange, orange, red-orange

- **Reds & Pinks:** Hot pink, bright red, red, dark red, blood red, maroon

- **Greens:** Yellow-green, bright green, turquoise green, veridian green, dark green, green-black

- **Blues & Purples:** Lavender, purple, pale blue turquoise, bright blue, dark blue, blue-black

- **Blacks & Browns:** Black, brown-black, dark brown, tan, light brown, umber

- **Gray & White**

Storing Your Paints

Because you'll only use a small amount of paint at a time on your palette, you'll want to find a good way to store your paint. I like to keep mine organized in drawers based on color, but you could also throw them all into a big box and call it good if you don't mind doing a bit more searching when it's time to refill a color. In the next section, I'll share suggestions for organizing and storing your paint in palettes.

Tip

Not all paint brands use the same names for colors, but you should be able to find something close to these suggestions.

Palettes

Finding the palette (or palettes) you enjoy working with is as much about personal preference as choosing what kinds of shoes you like wearing. Are you going for comfort and ease, scale and cost, or maybe appearance? Palettes can be as diverse and different as high-performance tennis shoes and flip-flops and there are about as many to choose from in a range of costs. Here are a few things to consider.

What to Look for in a Palette

Because gouache is a water-based medium, you're going to be mixing paint in lots of different consistencies, and the most important quality you want in a palette is separate reservoirs to hold your colors. Without these small basins, your paints will mix together into a muddy mess.

Besides these reservoirs, you also need an area for mixing colors, because you're never going to have all your colors premixed and ready. You're going to want to be able to pick up small amounts of paint with your brush to mix with other colors on this flat and large portion of your palette.

For me, I also include accessibility as an important characteristic in my palettes. I paint on a medium-sized desk without a whole lot of excessive space for my palettes. I want to be able to move my palettes around easily so that the colors I'm working on are right next to me. This way I can avoid reaching and stretching across wet paint. My sleeves thank me.

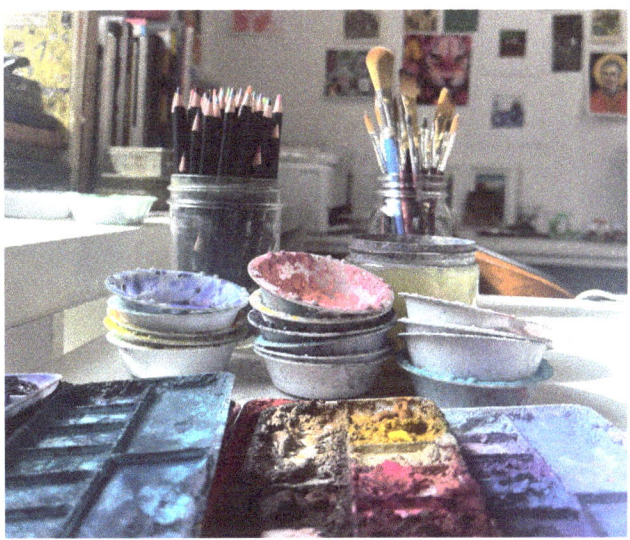

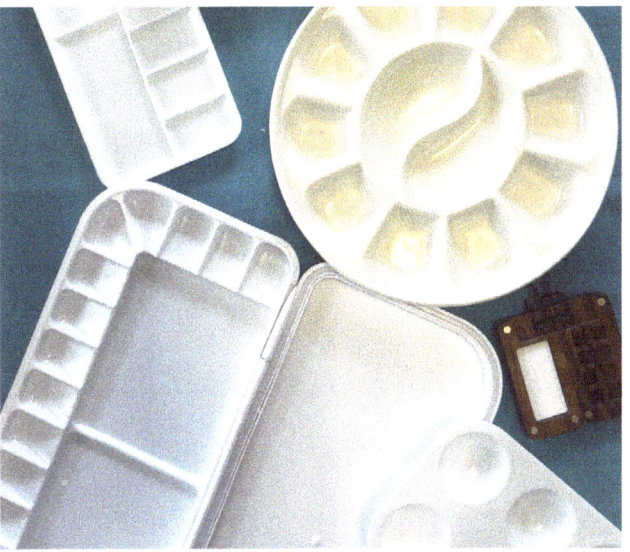

Types of Palettes

Palettes can be made from a variety of materials.

PLASTIC

Because plastic palettes are easy to come by, and usually inexpensive, they're a great choice for figuring out what you like to use and how you like to set up your colors within your palettes. Every once in a while, I'll choose to set up a whole palette in a very specific mix of colors (all skin tones, for example), and because a little plastic palette only costs a dollar or two, I can afford to play around with more options.

I also like to have some stand-alone small plastic bowls that hold a larger amount of colors I want to use a large portion of without remixing. I'll often use these little bowls to mix a large amount of background color.

Plastic palettes do come in larger sizes, many with lids that can keep your paint free from dust and pet hair (yes, this is a problem I suffer from when using my smaller palettes without lids).

One of the drawbacks to plastic is that some paints may stain the palette.

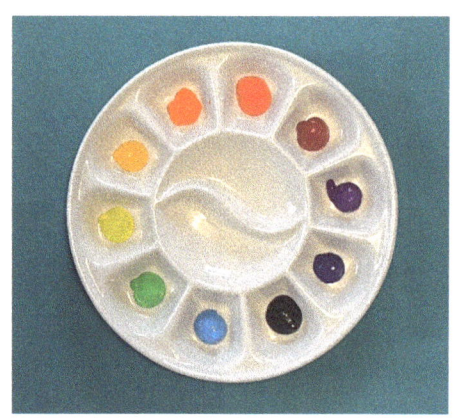
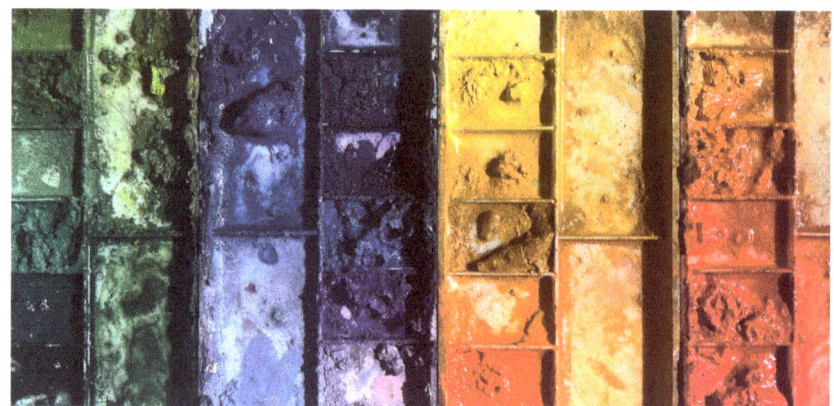

CERAMIC

Ceramic palettes are easy to clean out and can often be quite pretty. Ceramic palettes are definitely more pricey, but if you're careful with them, they can last forever.

Because ceramic is much heavier and bulkier than plastic, these palettes will be a bit trickier to switch around on your desk and aren't great for travel.

WOOD

It's definitely more unusual to find a palette made from wood, but there are a few available. Often these palettes still contain small plastic tubs for the individual paints, and the wood acts more as a container. They can be quite attractive, but aren't all that practical. The wood is porous, and even the most careful artist will get a fair amount of water on the wood while working.

METAL

Like wooden palettes, most metal palettes also have plastic inserts. And just as wood is susceptible to damage from the water, metal is also vulnerable to corrosion.

Arranging Your Palette

The way you arrange your palette is very much based off your own personal preference and is often informed by the subjects you paint. You might only work with a limited palette, in which case, you don't need every color. That said, the following suggestions are for people who plan to use the whole range of colors.

If you used one of those cheap watercolor sets in school as a child, it will come as no surprise how quickly colors can turn brown and muddy when allowed to mix

You can tell I use my palettes a lot!
But because I keep the warm and cool colors separate, the colors don't get muddy.

with colors outside of their color family. Because of this, I suggest setting up your palettes in color families. Warms with warms, cools with cools. Maybe you'll want to play around with this and come up with an arrangement that makes more sense to you, or maybe you'll see the utility in this setup as well.

Storing Your Palettes

I'm probably the worst person to be giving this advice, because if you came to my house and looked at my palettes, you'd probably find equal parts pet hair to paint. I know, it's gross, don't judge me! Because I paint every day (sometimes multiple times per day) I leave my palettes out on my desk at all times. The benefit of this, besides accessibility, is that they air-dry fully between uses. I've never had an issue with mold or spoiled paint because of this.

Many palettes have built-in lids, which is great for keeping your paints free of dust (or pet hair), and if you choose to use one of these, I'd recommend letting your paints dry fully before closing up your palette to prevent any extra water from staying trapped inside. If your paints dry completely, you can easily rewet them before each use and they'll have a very long life. Because gouache is so thick with pigment and less binder, it will fully dry out quite quickly.

Brushes

Not all brushes are created equal. If you've painted in other mediums, you might be tempted to use the brushes you already own, but oil and acrylic brushes are less than ideal for painting with gouache. Because their bristles are often course enough to handle thick paint, they don't handle gouache ideally. You're going to want a brush designed with thinner, more delicate bristles and an absorbent body to hold plenty of water.

You've probably guessed by now that watercolor brushes are the best choice for painting with gouache. But that still leaves you with enough choices to overwhelm you. In this section, I'll suggest my favorite kinds of brushes and what they're good for. In my own paintings, I actually use a rather small range of brushes. Of course, I encourage you to experiment and find the kinds of brushes you enjoy most.

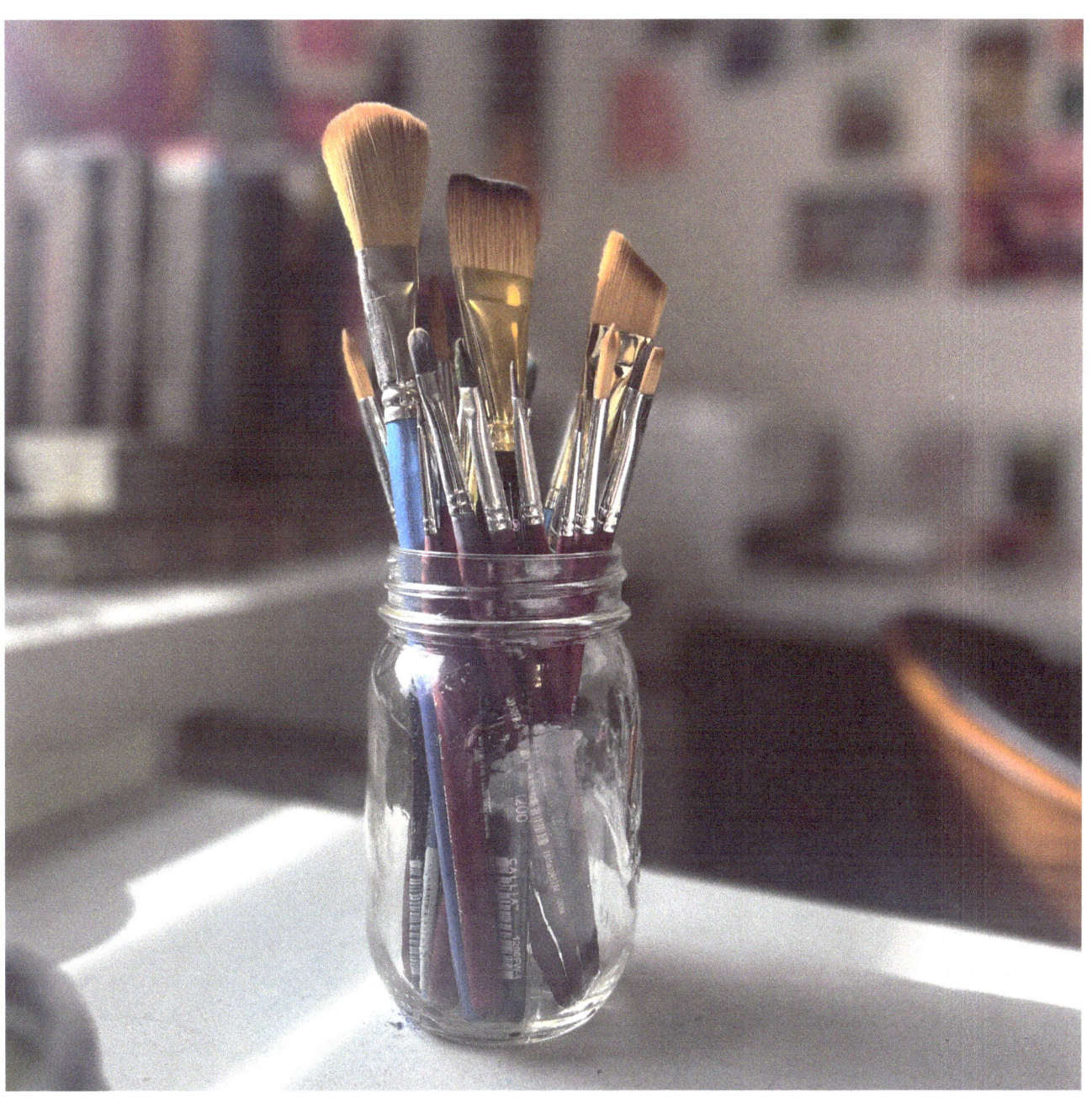

Natural-Hair vs. Synthetic Brushes

When you start shopping for brushes, you might notice a huge difference in price between the natural-hair and synthetic brushes. Natural-hair brushes are made from animal hair, often sable. These brushes are often considered superior to synthetic brushes because of their ability to hold more water and pigment. This is due to the makeup of each individual hair, which has tiny ridges. Some say that natural-hair brushes also hold their original form better than synthetic brushes.

Because of the large price difference between synthetic and natural brushes, I definitely recommend starting with synthetic. Get the hang of your materials and your brushes, and if you decide to splurge and try natural-hair brushes, you'll be able to judge the difference better for yourself.

The Anatomy of a Brush

Understanding the sections of your brush can be helpful when getting to know how to use it. Shown here,

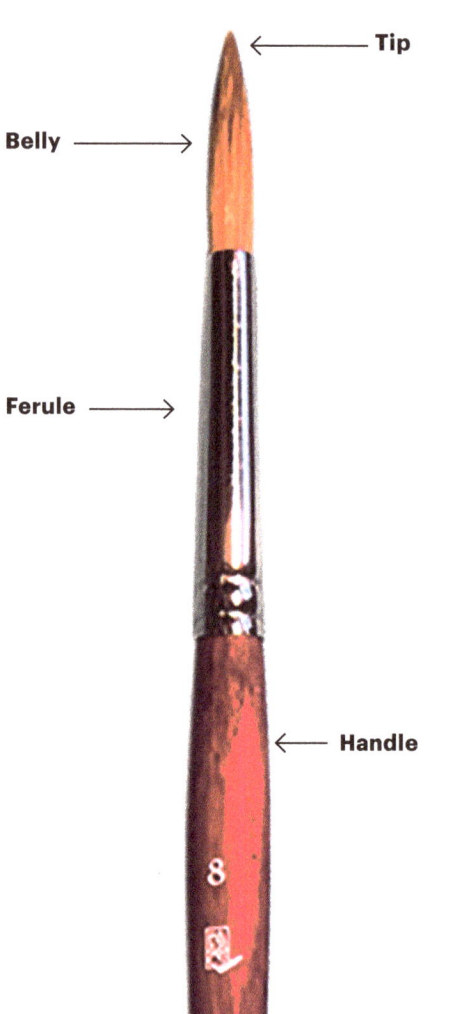

you'll see a diagram explaining the makeup of your brush's body. This sort of common terminology can make it a little bit easier when discussing painting.

Types of Brushes

Here are the most common types of brushes I use when painting with gouache.

ROUND BRUSHES

Most artists consider round brushes to be the most versatile and commonly used brushes. Because of their round bodies and pointed tips, they're useful for creating a variety of brushstrokes, from very thin to quite thick, depending on the size of the brush. I really love small round brushes and use them for detail work more than any other kind of brush.

RIGGER BRUSHES

The rigger has a similar shape to the round brush but longer bristles to hold more water and pigment, allowing you to create longer thin lines without having to reload your brush with paint. The drawback is that you lose some of the control you can get with shorter-bristled round brushes.

FLAT BRUSHES

When it comes to flat brushes, there are a couple different kinds to choose from and they do slightly different things. When set side by side, you'll immediately be able to notice the difference in the length of the bristles between a long flat brush and a short flat brush (which will sometimes be referred to as a "bright").

The long flat brush will hold more paint and have quite a bit more give in its bristles, making it feel looser in its mark making. I personally like the control I get with the more compact bristles in the short flat brush.

ANGLED FLAT BRUSHES

With characteristics very similar to standard flat brushes, the angled flat has bristles cut at an angle, which makes it ideal for pulling long, straight, thin lines of paint. It can also be used to pull on strokes of paint varying between thick and thin lines with more squared edges.

Tip

Belly

Ferule

Handle

8

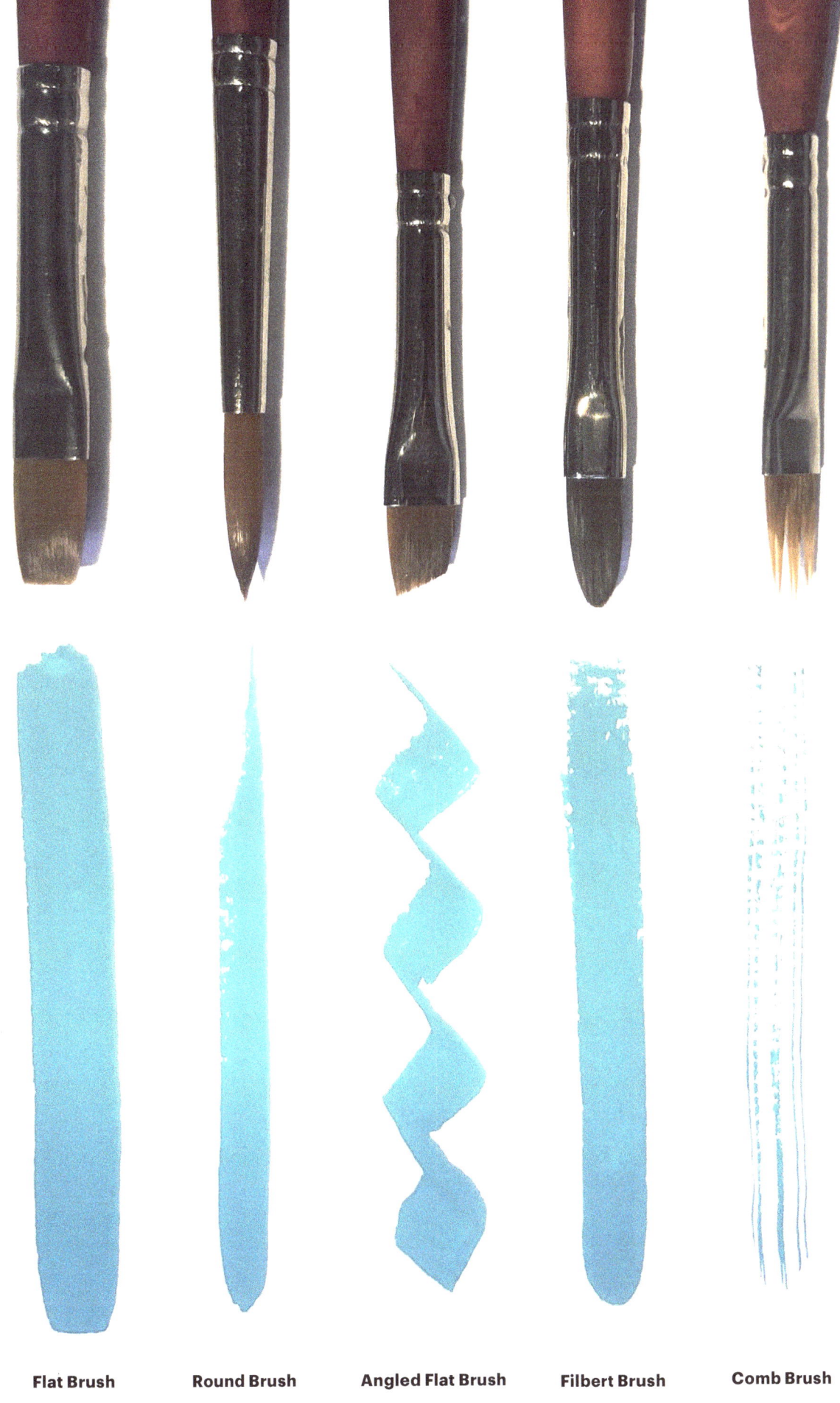

Flat Brush **Round Brush** **Angled Flat Brush** **Filbert Brush** **Comb Brush**

FILBERTS

The kind of brush I use more than any other is the filbert. With their flat bodies and tapered and rounded tips, I find them to be useful in almost every part of the painting process, whether it be laying out large background color, or filling in smaller, more delicate shapes. When brushed with its flat belly down, the brush can create a nice wide shape to fill in broad areas, or, when flipped on its side, can draw a fine, crisp edge.

The filbert is said to have been named after a filbert nut because of the similarity in their shapes.

COMB BRUSHES

As its name suggests, the top of a comb brush has staggered bristles that give it the appearance of a comb. You can find comb brushes in flats and filberts. While these brushes might not be commonly used, comb brushes are excellent for producing many fine strokes at a time. These brushes can be ideal for detailed areas of fur or grass. I find they work best when not overly wet.

Cleaning Your Brushes

One of the great things about gouache is that it's entirely water-soluble, making cleanup so much easier than some other mediums. While it's definitely ideal to wash your brushes after each use, it's inevitable that you won't always be able to. At least make sure that they've been left to dry either flat or upside down on a paint drying rack. Avoid leaving your brushes in your water, as this can cause them to bend and distort. Prolonged time in water can also make the bristles splay.

Some people prefer to only use water to clean their brushes. This is sufficient much of the time, but I like to give my brushes a good wash with soap after using particularly strong colors (like phthalo blues or greens). There are many different soaps that will work when cleaning your brushes. I like The Masters® Brush Cleaner, which can be found at most art retailers. This cleaner is great because it also conditions your brushes. But I've been known to save a little money and use a gentle dish soap, like Dawn®.

To wash your brushes, simply rinse them under cool running water, squeezing the excess out from base to tip until the water runs clean. I often take my brush and wiggle it back and forth along the palm of my hand while pulling back. This helps to work out the paint that might be stubbornly wedged deep inside the brush.

After your brushes are clean, pat them dry, being sure not to scrub them too harshly. Then, while still damp, reform the bristles so they dry in a way that holds their shape.

Avoid putting your brushes away standing up while they're still wet. Excess water can drip down into the ferrule and loosen the glue or even soak into the wood of your handle.

Paper

Although some people paint with gouache on other surfaces, a good-quality watercolor paper is the best place for you to start because it's made expressly for water-based media. Don't be fooled into believing that simply choosing watercolor paper is going to be the only choice you'll have to make, though. There are many kinds of watercolor paper on the market and some are definitely better than others.

Paper Texture

First, you need to decide which paper texture to paint on. The two main options are cold pressed and hot pressed.

COLD PRESSED

Cold-pressed paper is probably the most common type of watercolor paper used by artists working in watercolor and gouache. As it says in the name, cold-pressed paper is made by pressing wet fibers (usually cotton or cotton and cellulose) onto unheated cylinder mould machines. These rollers are covered in felt, which gives the paper a slight texture called "tooth."

The fibers of cold-pressed paper are less tightly pressed than the fibers of hot-pressed paper, making it more absorbent and quicker-drying. Because of this, more of the pigment will settle down into the paper and can often give a more uniform color when it dries.

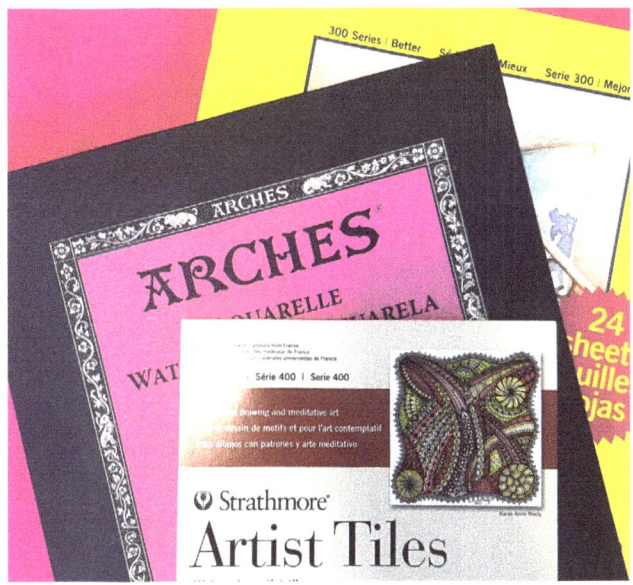

HOT PRESSED

Unlike the cold-press process, hot-pressed paper is pressed tightly between heated cylinders that are not covered in felt. This gives the paper a smooth and more compact surface. Because of the lack of tooth, hot-pressed paper can be ideal for highly detailed paintings. This lack of tooth also allows the paint to sit more on the surface of the paper as it dries and colors often appear a bit more vibrant.

Paper Weight

When choosing your paper, you'll notice it is labeled with weights in pounds and usually comes in four sizes: 90-,

140-, 200-, and 300-pound. This refers to the thickness of the paper—the smaller the number, the thinner the paper. It seems like an odd measurement, but it refers to the weight of the paper when measured in 500-sheet bundles. I prefer to not go under 140-lb. paper because the sheets will buckle much more easily when saturated and aren't very durable if you try to lift off any paint.

Cotton vs. Cellulose

The easiest way to determine the quality of a paper is to know the content of its materials. The highest-quality papers are made from 100 percent cotton. The cotton doesn't contain acid, making it last longer and less prone to yellowing. Cotton is also more absorbent than cellulose and will hold pigment better.

Cellulose (wood pulp) is quite a bit cheaper than cotton and is often mixed with cotton to make a good-quality product.

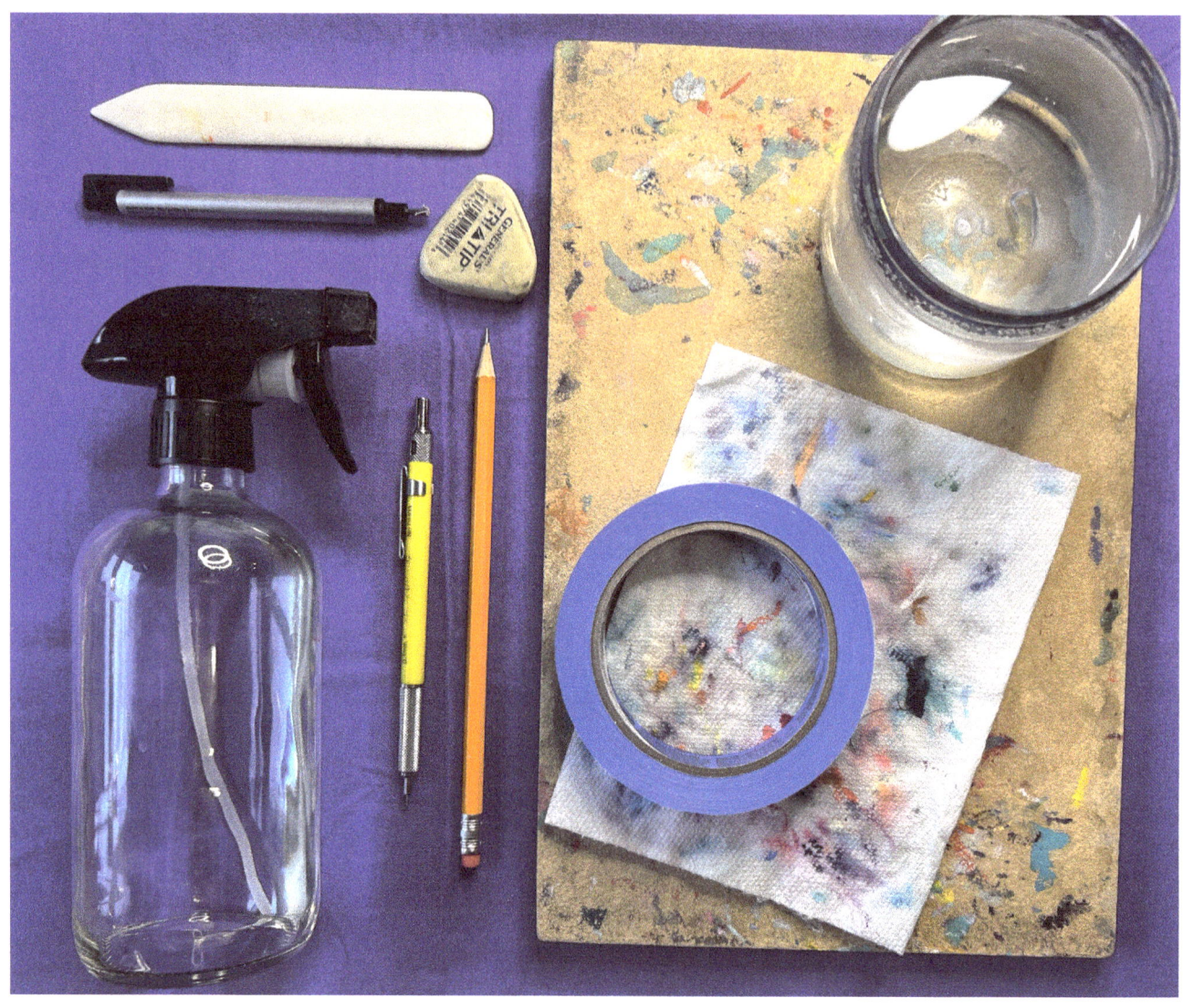

Miscellaneous Supplies

Even though we've gone over the supplies that are specific to gouache, there are still a number of items that you'll need to gather before you get started. Many of these items you might already have around your house, so grab a basket and set out on a little scavenger hunt.

Pencils

Because I begin all my paintings with an underdrawing, having a great pencil is key to beginning a great painting. The pencil you choose is very much a personal preference, but I'll give you a few things to think about when choosing your pencil.

I almost exclusively use mechanical pencils for my underdrawings. Although I wouldn't use a mechanical pencil if I was making art exclusively with graphite, I love it for sketching in the base for my drawings. This is mostly because I can keep a fine, uniform line and never have to worry about sharpening. In choosing my lead, I like a very fine tip (usually 3mm) and try to use a lead that isn't too soft or too hard. My lead is H, but you could also use a standard HB, which is equivalent to a #2 pencil.

If you would like to use a traditional pencil, I recommend using a lead that isn't too soft or too hard. If your lead is too soft, it will leave quite a bit of material on your paper and the graphite will be more likely to be

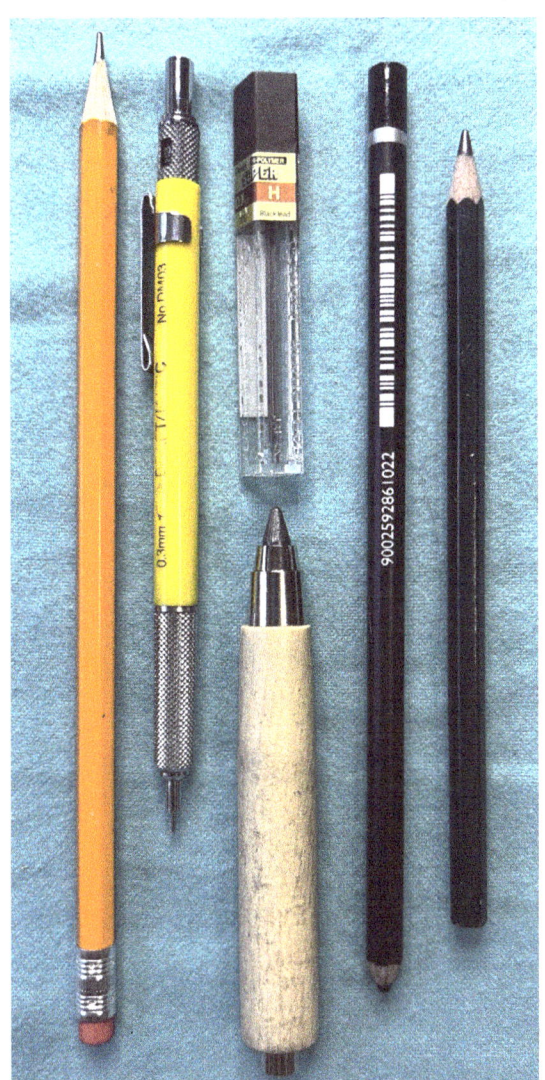

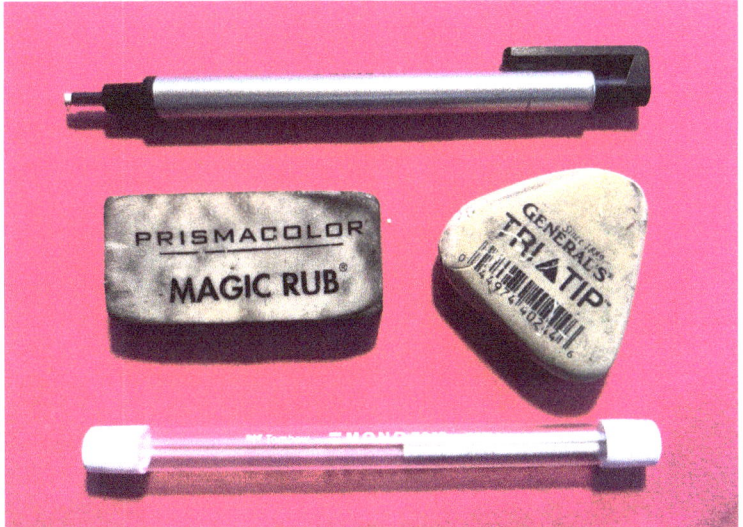

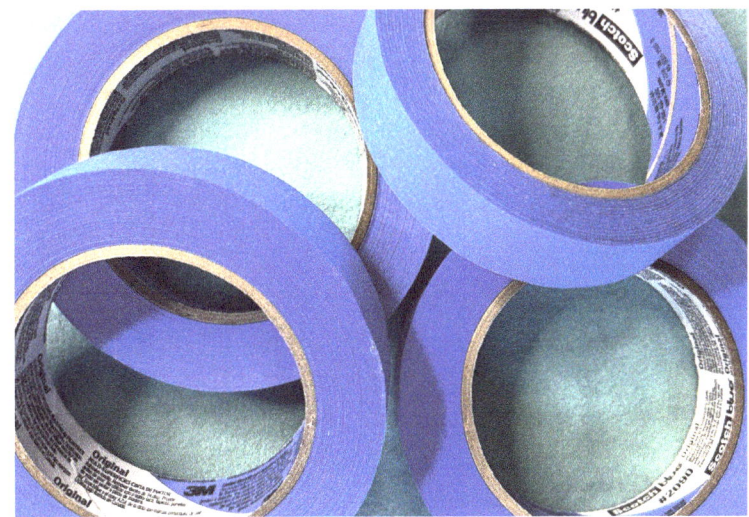

picked up with your brush while painting, leading to the possibility of discoloring your paint.

I also recommend avoiding pencils with graphite that's too hard because sometimes, in an effort to get the lines to show up dark enough, artists can end up pressing a bit too hard. Too much pressure with the pencil can emboss the paper and leave marks that are impossible to remove.

Erasers

There are so many different types of erasers to choose from and if you have a favorite, chances are it's going to work just fine for correcting changes on your underdrawing. I happen to prefer mechanical erasers because I like having a bit more precision and have found they

don't leave too many shavings to clean up. If you're going to be erasing larger swaths of paper, I recommend a good soft, white eraser.

Masking Tape

You'll be using masking tape to adhere your paper to your painting surface. Adhering your paper to a board is done to prevent buckling and warping. It also allows you to move your painting around easily as you're working on it.

There are special kinds of masking tape made particularly for painting. Whichever kind of tape you choose, you want one that can keep a tight seal between the paint and the paper (to avoid leaking under the edge). as well as a tight seal between the tape and the board, to prevent it from peeling off too easily.

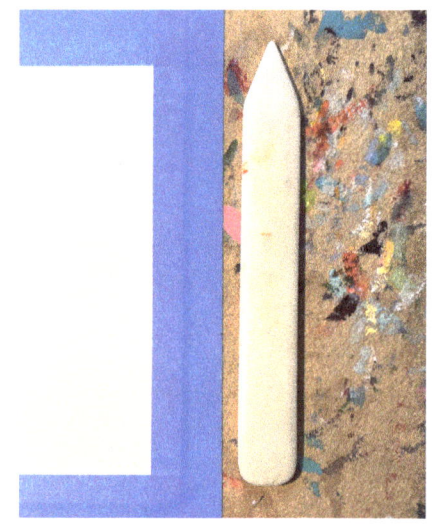
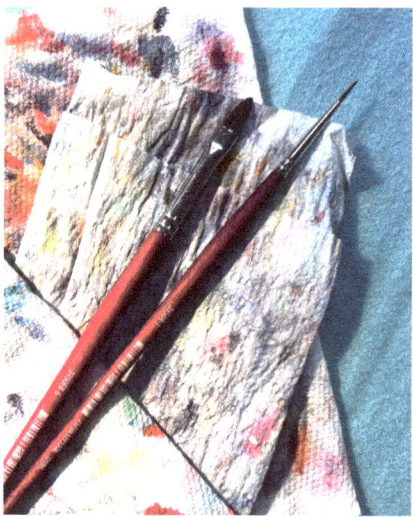
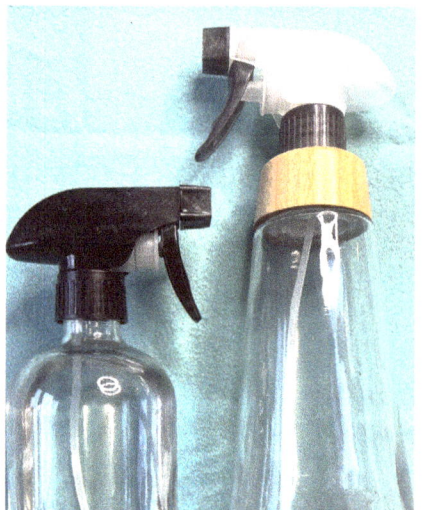

While there are plenty of kinds of artist tape available, I'm quite fond of the blue painter's tape you can find at your local hardware store.

Art Board

There are multiple types of board you can adhere your paper to while painting. The reason I recommend using a board, as opposed to taping your paper down to your desk or work area, is that you can move it around easily. Because of this, you'll want to consider the size, shape, and weight of your board.

Art supply stores often sell hardboard panels in a huge variety of sizes that are perfect for this purpose. You can also go to your hardware store and find pieces of MDF that you can have cut down to any size (or sizes) you like.

Bone Tool

As far as tools go, this is one I've been using for the least amount of time but find invaluable. Bone tools, or folders, are made for folding, creasing, and burnishing paper or leather. I use them to firmly attach my tape to my paper after affixing it to my board. This leaves me with a nice crisp edge after removing the tape.

Water Bowls

I've been known to use mason jars, glasses, mugs, you name it to hold my water, but I mostly use plastic jars with lids from my local art store. This is mainly because of my tendency to get the other containers mixed up with things I drink out of, and, I promise you, rinsing your brush in your coffee is almost as annoying as drinking paint water.

I recommend using two water bowls. One is for the first rinse to get the majority of paint off your brush, while the second allows you to get mostly clean water on your brush and will help prevent contaminating colors as you paint.

Paper Towels

You're definitely going to want a bunch of disposable towels to clean your brush off after rinsing between colors. I use the cheapest paper towels I can find. The most important quality they need is absorbency, and I've found that even inexpensive towels can last for weeks.

Spray Bottle

Another tool I couldn't live without is my spray bottle. You'll need to rewet your paints every time you paint (if not multiple times), and a good spray bottle with a nice mist makes this process quick and easy. I've been through many spray bottles over the years and find that something medium-sized serves me best. Too small of a bottle has to be refilled too frequently, whereas a bottle that's too big can be unwieldy. My current favorite holds 16 oz., which I've found to be an ideal size.

Setting Up Your Workspace

Even if you don't have a designated space to paint, you're going to want to give yourself enough room to comfortably have all your materials within arm's reach. I don't use all my palettes at once, so I pull out the ones I think will be appropriate for whatever I'm painting that day.

The size of the art board you're using will determine how much room you need on your desk. Make sure you'll be able to turn your board in any direction, to make it easy for yourself to access any part of your painting.

I paint directly from photos off my computer, so I always leave room for my computer in front of me.

You'll find the placement of things is unique to you. Even though I'm right-handed, I actually keep my paints on my left side. I've found this has been helpful in preventing me from dipping my arm or sleeve in my paints as often. The main point of your setup is to make everything easily accessible to you, so as to make your painting as seamless and easy as possible.

I choose to work directly on my desk at my workspace. Because I predominantly work quite small, this works for me, as the image isn't overly distorted by working flat; but if you're working on a larger piece, you might want to work at a drafting table or on an easel so that the piece you're painting isn't too foreshortened. Regardless of how you work, it's helpful to step back and view your work from many angles as you go to get a good sense of how it actually looks.

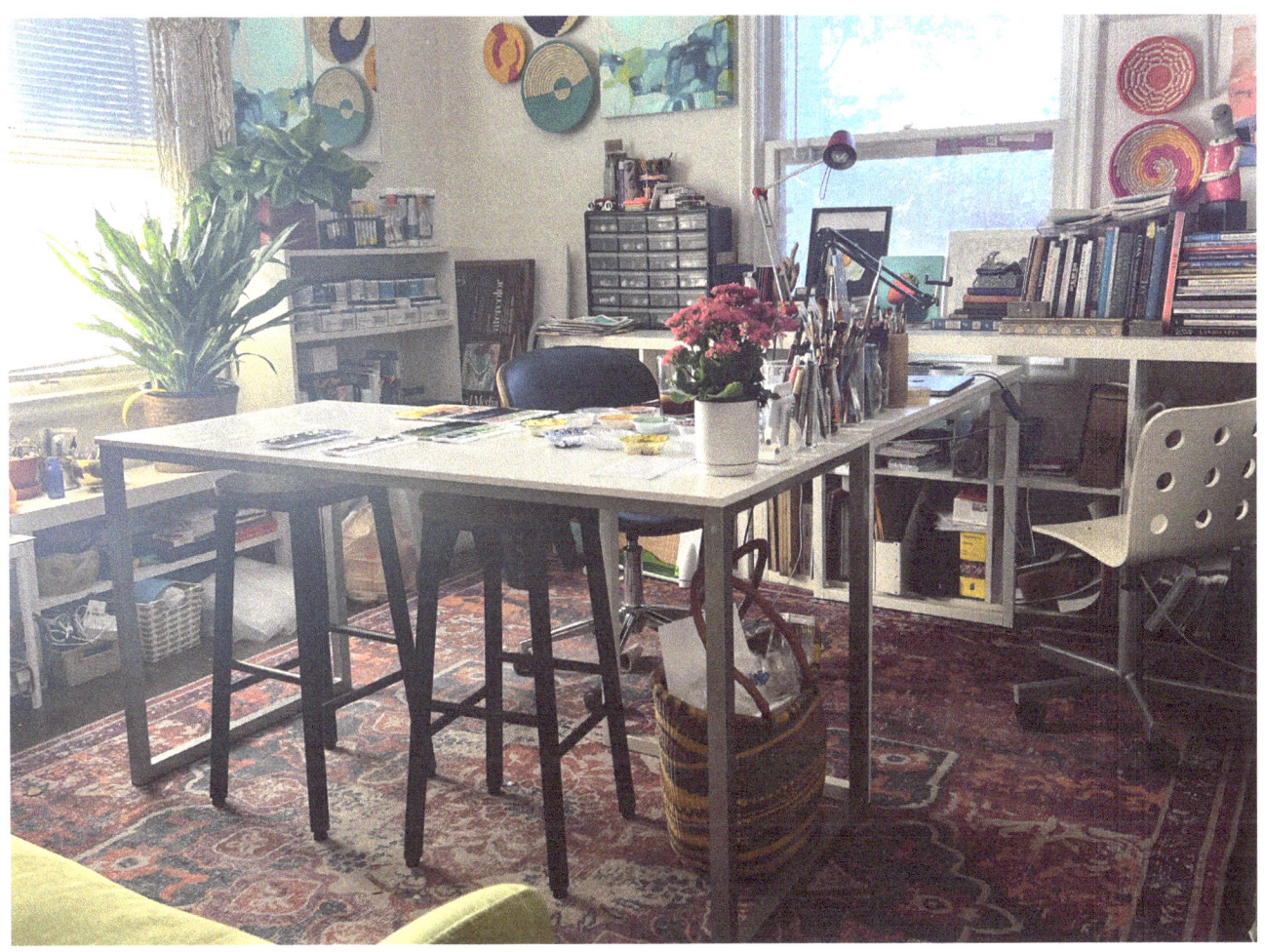

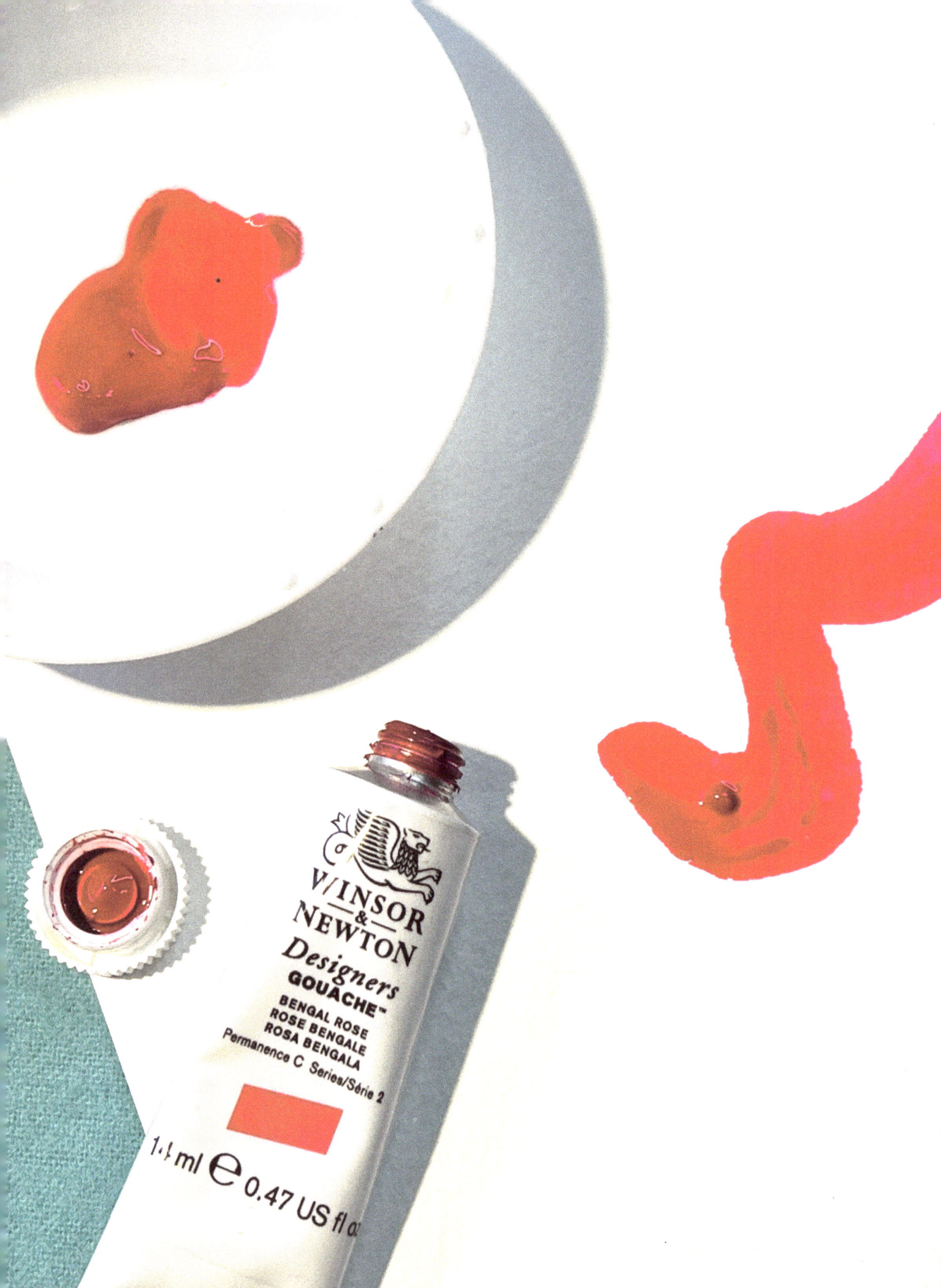

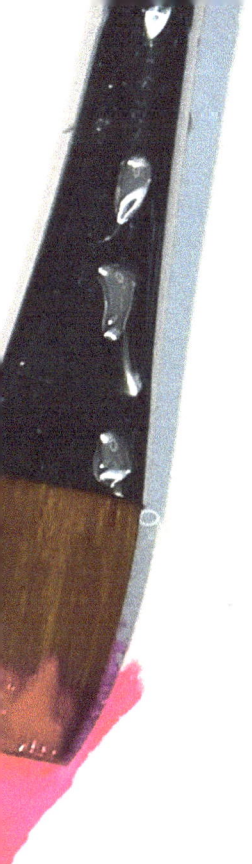

TWO

GETTING TO KNOW GOUACHE

If you're as impatient as I am, you'll want to dive right in to making art. But before you start your first painting, I think you'll find it invaluable to get to know your paint (and your tools) first. To give yourself as much of a head start as possible in creating gorgeous artwork, let's make sure you have a good foundation to build on.

In this section, we'll lay the groundwork for any good painting by learning to understand the paint and how it handles. You'll play around with different brushes to get the muscle memory of mark making in your own hands so you understand what each brush is capable of and how best to use it. You'll also test out layering with different colors and consistencies of paint. Using your paints, and other supplies, is the best way to get to know them and to figure out which techniques work best for you. So don't be afraid to experiment and just have fun. It's only paper after all!

Opacity & Viscosity

If you've ever worked on any digital images, you're probably already familiar with the term opacity. In essence, opacity is how see-through something is. Because gouache is an opaque watercolor, it's naturally going to be less transparent than traditional watercolors, but there are ways to adjust the opacity through changing the viscosity of your paint. The thicker the consistency of your paint, the more opaque and less transparent it will be.

I find the best way to think about the viscosity of my paints is to compare them to different liquids. Because different brands of paint mix their pigments with varying amounts of binder, the paint that comes out of one brand's tube is a different consistency than the paint that comes out of another brand's tube. To make sure we're communicating in a way we can all understand, I'll speak of paint as the consistency of water, milk, heavy cream, and (softened) butter.

To try out this concept, pick one color you'd like to work with. Start with a color that's a bit darker, such as red, blue, green, or turquoise.

Step One: Butter

Squeeze a coin-sized amount of your chosen paint color into your palette. Without adding any water to your color, take a medium-sized filbert or flat brush and dip the tip of it into your paint. Don't dredge your entire brush in color. You'll only need the top quarter to third of the brush to have paint on it. Now, on a blank sheet of watercolor paper, drag your paint in a straight line across the top of the page. See how far you can go until the paint runs out.

Step Two: Heavy Cream

Add a small amount of water to your paint (be conservative here, because it's much easier to add more water than to add more paint). Now work the water into your paint, stirring gently and smoothly so as not to splash or rub the thick paint too deep into your bristles. Keep stirring until the water is incorporated into the paint, thinning it down to the consistency of heavy cream. If you need to add a bit more water to get to the consistency of cream, remember to be prudent.

Before moving on, thoroughly clean your brush. It can be helpful to have a stir stick or a pallet knife to mix your paint instead of using your brush to prevent waste. Mixing with a brush can suck up paint in between the bristles and can be hard to wash clean.

Step Three: Milk

You're moving toward a more fluid consistency. As you've done before, keep adding a bit more water to your mixture until it reaches a milky consistency. You'll notice when you brush it across your surface that more white from the paper shows through. If there are dark pencil marks on your paper, they might be visible at this consistency. It's still possible to layer paint in this milky consistency, but you want to make sure the first layer has dried completely before layering on top to prevent any damp patches from being picked up by your brush, leaving a splotchy area.

Step Four: Water

I'm sure you've got the hang of this by now, but there's one more paint consistency I'd like you to test out. It can be helpful to know just how thin you can get your paint while still adding color to your page. Notice how much of the paper shows through when your paint is thinned down to the consistency of water. When you look through the marks you made with each level of viscosity, you'll see that the color of the paint appears to change from a darker, more intense hue to a lighter, less intense hue.

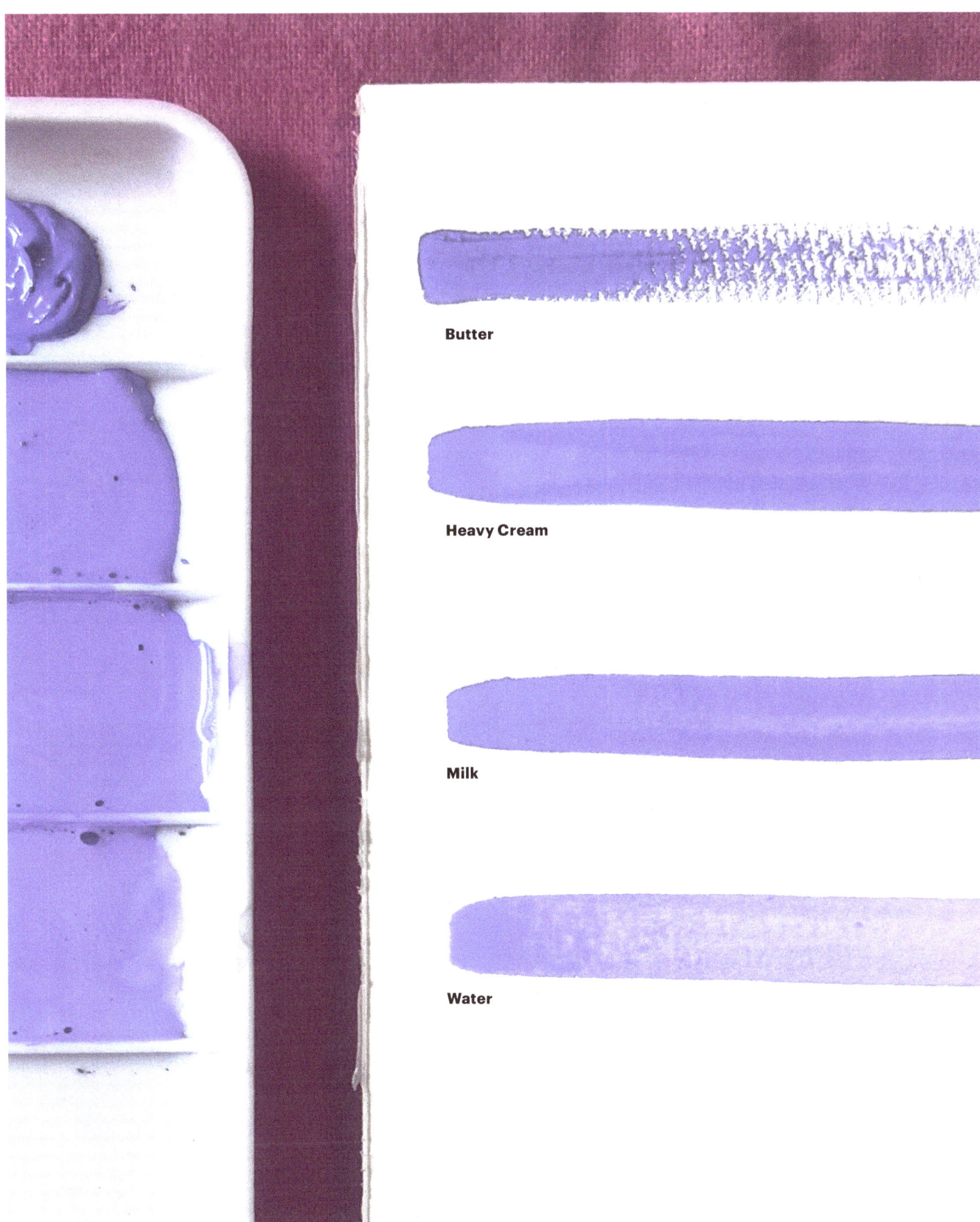

Butter

Heavy Cream

Milk

Water

Applying Paint

Now that you have a good understanding of how to change the opacity and viscosity of your paint, you can move on to layering. Gouache is usually layered less than traditional watercolors, which can be built up layer upon layer. That's not to say that you won't be layering with gouache, but as a general rule, you don't want to apply more than four or five layers. Because of gouache's thicker pigment, you'll find that trying to layer more than this will lead to muddy colors.

Building up thin layers of paint is called "glazing" and can be used to add depth of color to your paintings. It can also be used to correct colors in sections where the color matching in the first layer feels off.

A good rule when layering is to work from *thin to thick*. When starting with a thin layer, less paint absorbs into the paper, leading to more opportunity to add upon it. The thicker the paint, the more the paper will get saturated, leading to paint sitting on top of the paper. When too much paint builds up, it can lead to cracking or flaking.

Wet-on-Wet vs. Wet-on-Dry

If you try to add a layer of paint before the previous layer is fully dry, you will experience blending and lifting.

To illustrate this, try painting a square of yellow on your paper. Before allowing the paint to dry, drag

Wet-on-Wet

Wet-on-Dry

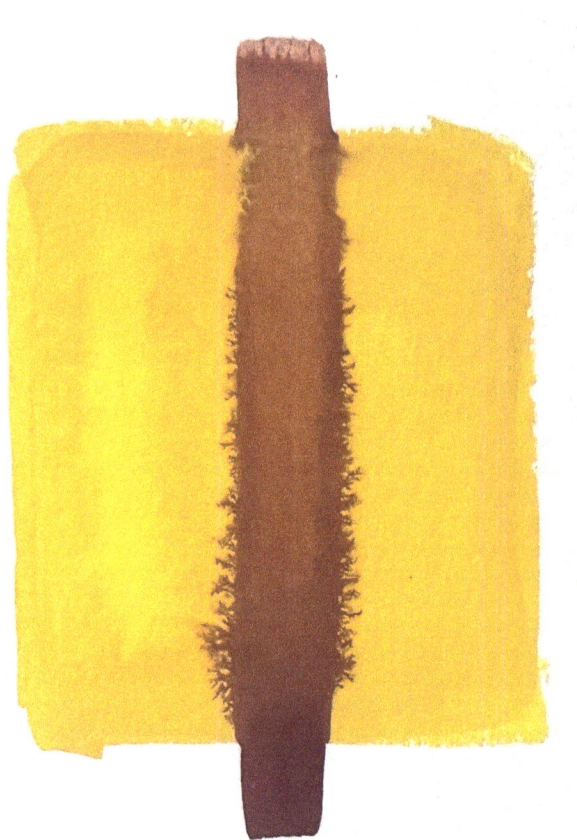

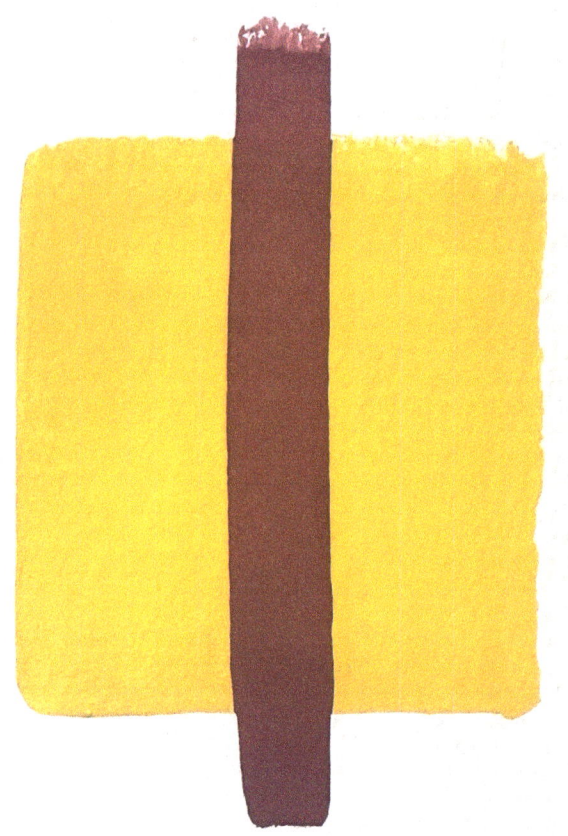

a stroke of red across the square. You'll notice that the edges of the red brushstroke bleed into the yellow, causing the colors to mix and swirl. This technique might be useful if you're attempting a loose blending of colors, but you'll have far less control over the end result. The watery effect that is left behind after the paint dries is frequently seen in traditional watercolor, and although I don't utilize it much in my own paintings, you might want to experiment with it more in your own art, as it's a truly lovely benefit of using water-based paints.

Now try this same technique, but this time, allow the yellow square to dry completely before adding the stroke of red. See how the edges of your red line hold their shape?

From here, you can experiment with the consistency of the paint you're layering. To practice, paint a few solid squares (you can use any colors you choose). After your squares have dried, paint three stripes of a different color across the surface, varying the consistency from watery, to milky, to creamy. Notice how the opacity of the top layer affects the color of the painted square.

Drybrushing

For the most part, you're going to use a well-wetted brush while painting with gouache. Drybrushing, however, can be an effective technique when you want to add

Watery, milky, and creamy consistency

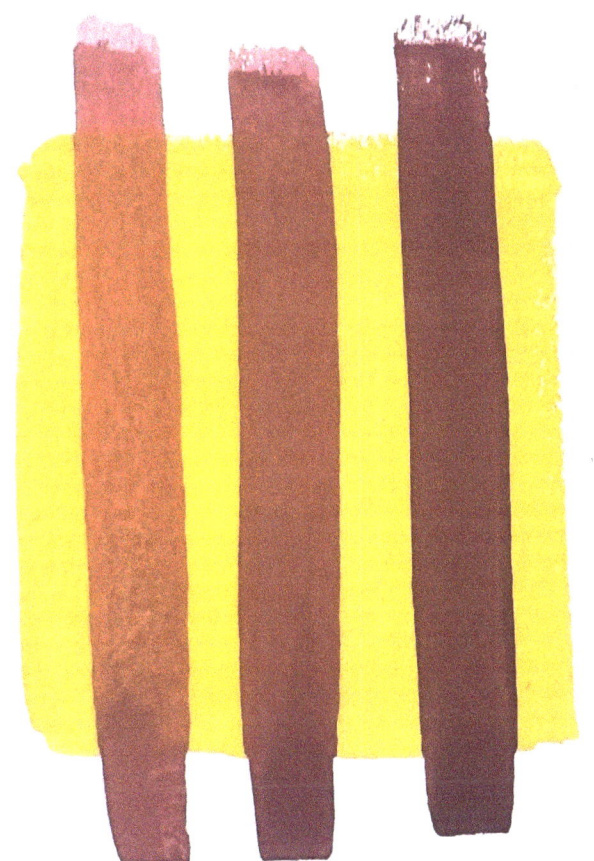

Drybrushing

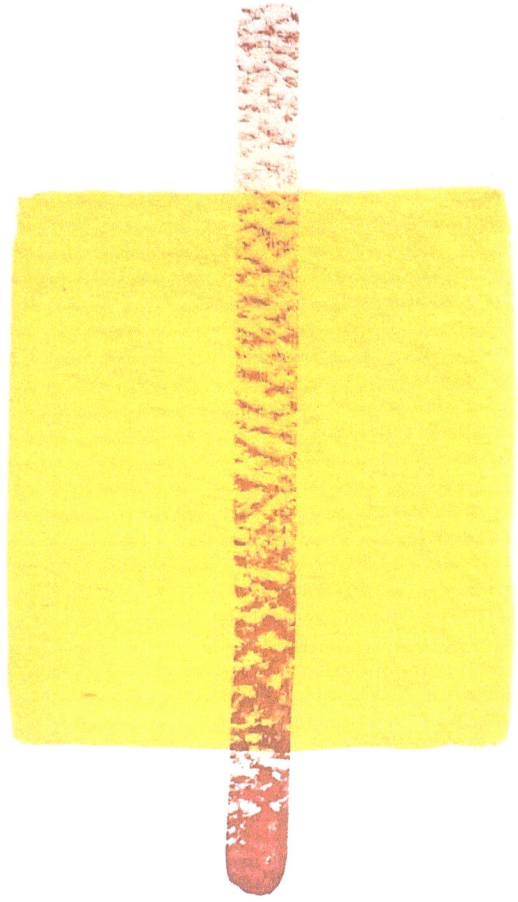

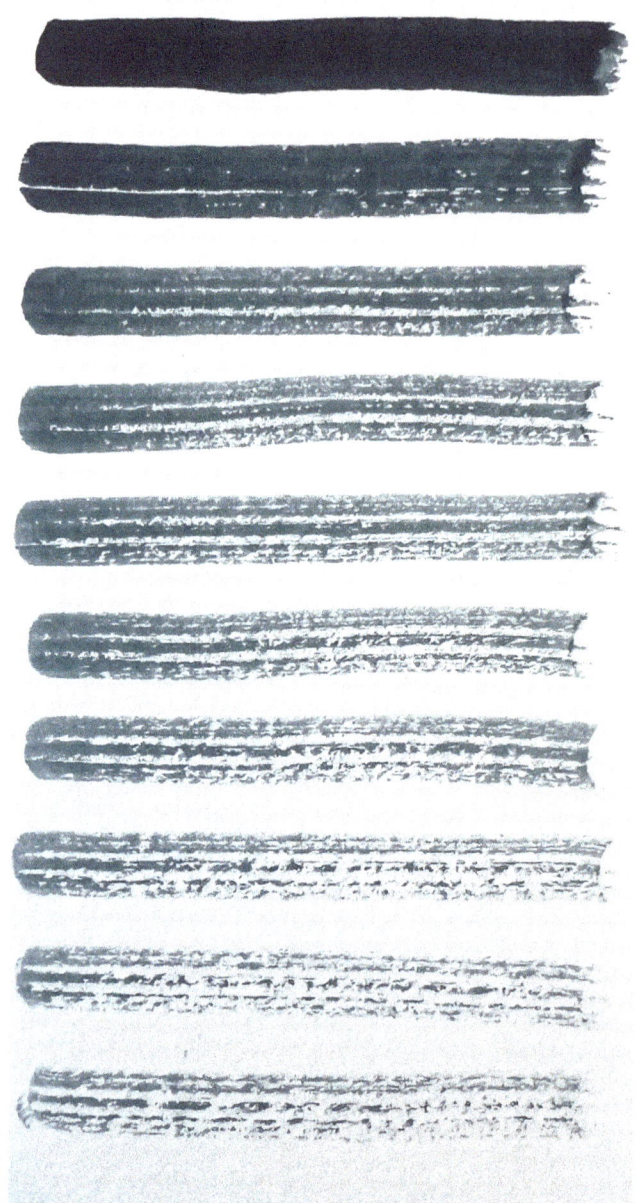

FROM TOP TO BOTTOM: As the paint on my brush is used up, the brushstrokes became thinner and sketchier.

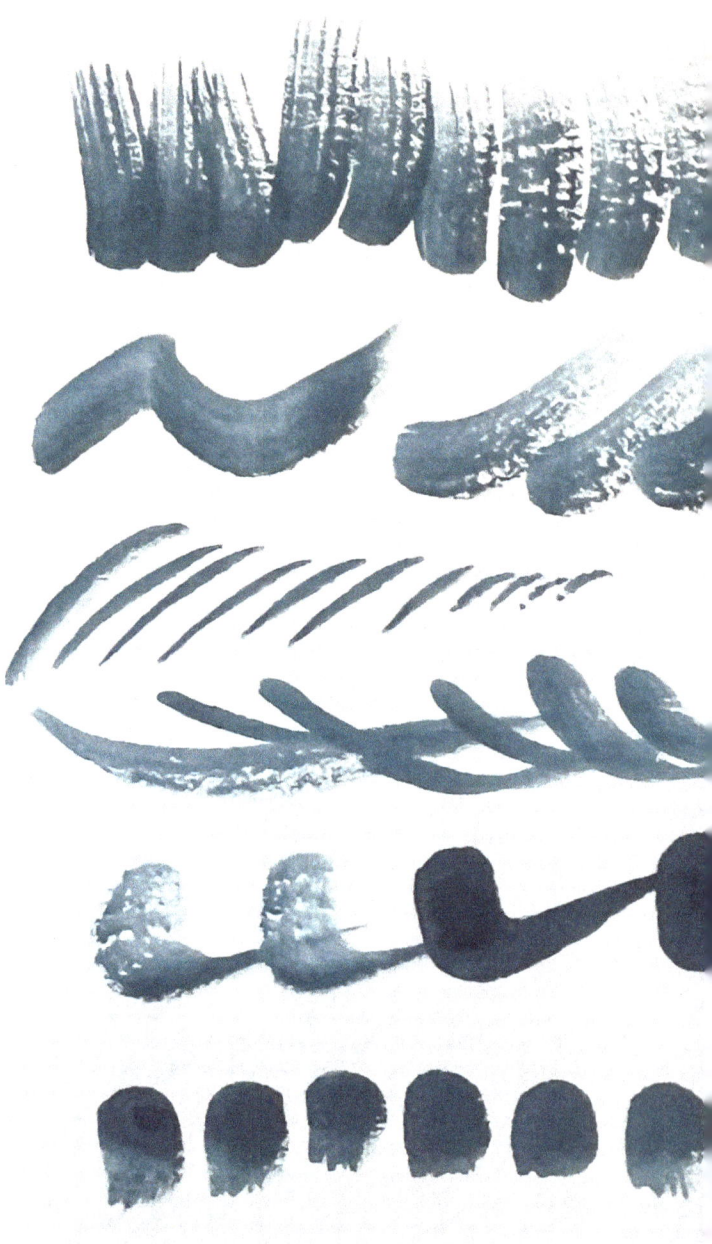

ABOVE: By varying your brush, the consistency of the paint, and the direction of the stroke, you can create a wide range of marks to use to create different effects in your paintings.

texture to objects, like fabric, metal, or hair. Because the bristles of the brush are relatively dry, the individual strokes are much stronger and more apparent because the edges of the paint aren't softened and blended by the water.

To achieve this technique, wet your brush then dry it on a paper towel, leaving just a small amount of moisture. Being spare with the amount of paint you use, dip the very tip of your brush into creamy or buttery paint. (Note: You don't want your paint to be too watered down

here because it won't be viscous enough to hold any shape.) Now try dragging your brush lightly across your paper a few times, noticing the way the brushstrokes change as the paint is used up.

For a painterly effect that includes more exaggerated brush marks, this technique can be a powerful tool. Remember that because you're using thick paint when drybrushing, you'll want to save these layers until the end of your painting.

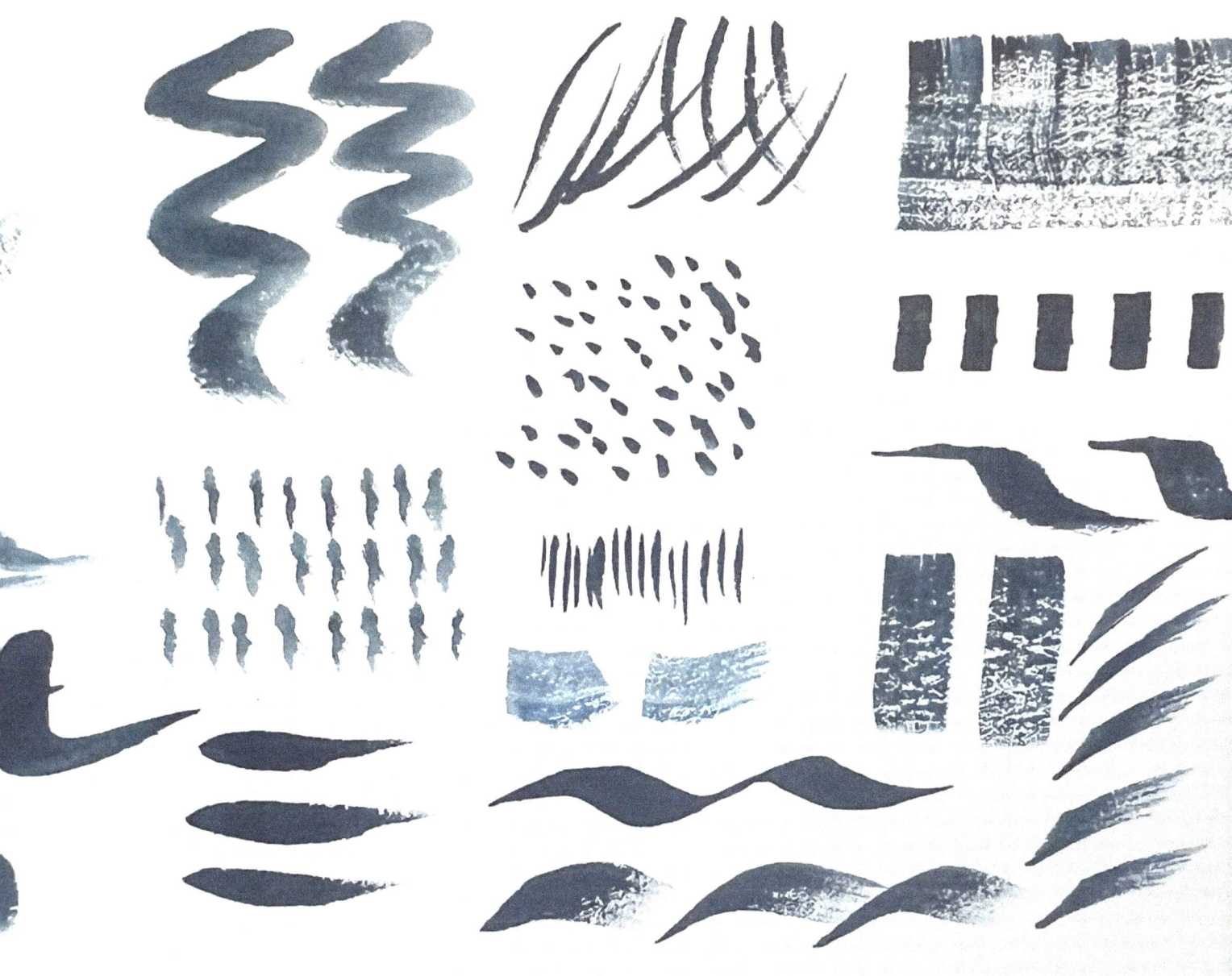

Mark Making

The style of painting you're creating determines the mark making you'll use. You may choose to use gouache in a graphic manner, filling the shapes of your image with smooth, flat planes of color, or you may want to paint with gesture and movement, highlighting the expressive strokes of the brush.

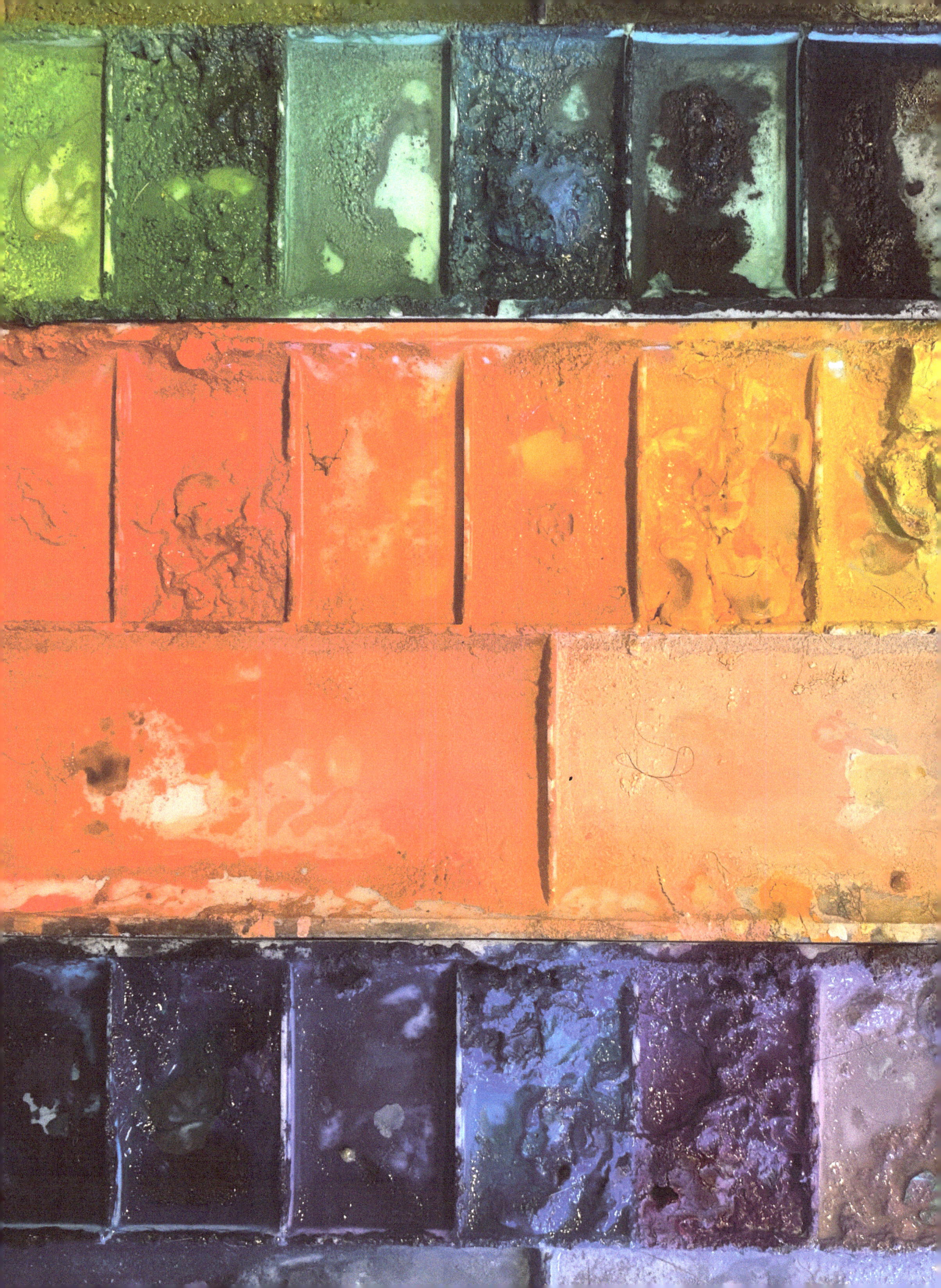

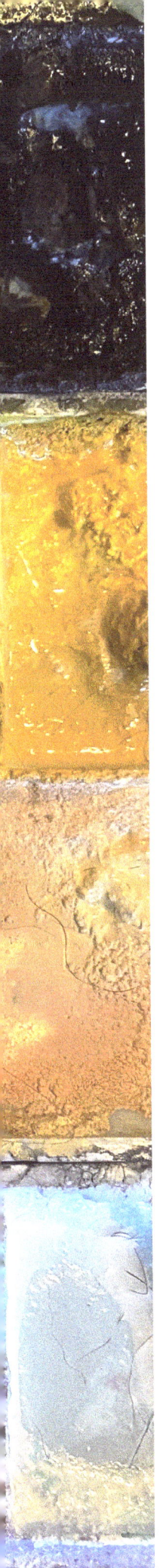

THREE

COLOR BASICS

Occasionally you'll use a color straight out of the tube, but most of the time, you need to be able to mix your colors. Although it's possible to buy a wide range of colors, it's definitely not necessary. With a bit of color theory you'll be able to create thousands of colors.

We won't delve too deeply into color theory in this book, but it's helpful to have at least a basic understanding of color. It will save you quite a bit of headache to know how colors react side by side, as well as what happens when you mix them together.

When you were in grade school you likely learned a little bit about colors. You probably learned the basics of the primary colors—red, blue, and yellow—and which of them you mix together to get basics like purple, green, and orange. You may have even learned about the color wheel and complementary colors. While these basics are fairly correct, color is more nuanced than what you got in elementary school.

In this chapter, we'll take a look at the color wheel and how colors relate to each other, learn a few helpful terms, and explore value with a sample project that will help you understand light and shadow.

The Color Wheel

You've probably heard color referred to in different ways. Likely you've heard of RGB, which has the same colors you learned about in that original color wheel (red, blue, green). But you've also probably heard of CMYK: cyan, magenta, yellow, and key black. These are the colors you'll know if you've ever had the pleasure of filling your printer ink. When using a limited palette, a wider range of colors can be made with the CMYK palette, especially when it comes to the variety of purples you can create.

The best way to understand how these colors combine is to make your own version of the two colors wheels (one using red, blue, and yellow and the other using cyan, magenta, and yellow). This way, you'll see the difference between these colors for yourself.

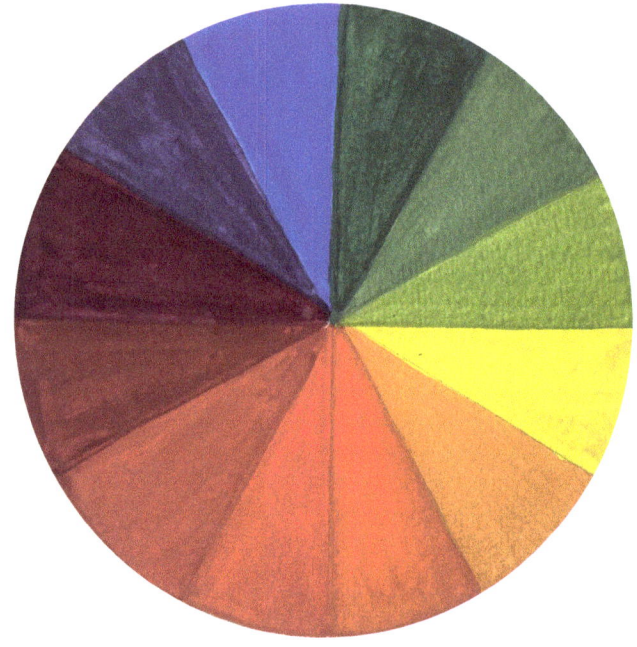

Color wheel using yellow,
blue, and red as the primary colors.

1 To create your standard color wheels, draw a circle and divide it into twelve sections. First paint your primary colors, leaving three blank spots between each one. Paint one wheel using yellow, red, and blue and one using yellow, magenta, and cyan.

2 To mix your first variants (secondary colors), mix equal parts yellow + blue, yellow + red, and blue + red (or yellow + cyan, yellow + magenta, and cyan + magenta).

3 To fill in the remaining slots (tertiary colors), combine these newly mixed colors with your primary colors, filling in the remaining spots next to your colors on the color wheel.

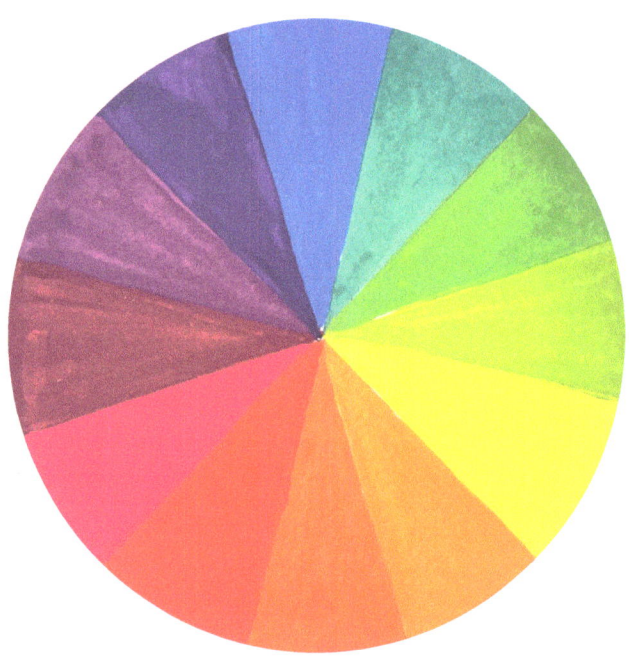

Color wheel using yellow, cyan,
and magenta as the primary colors.

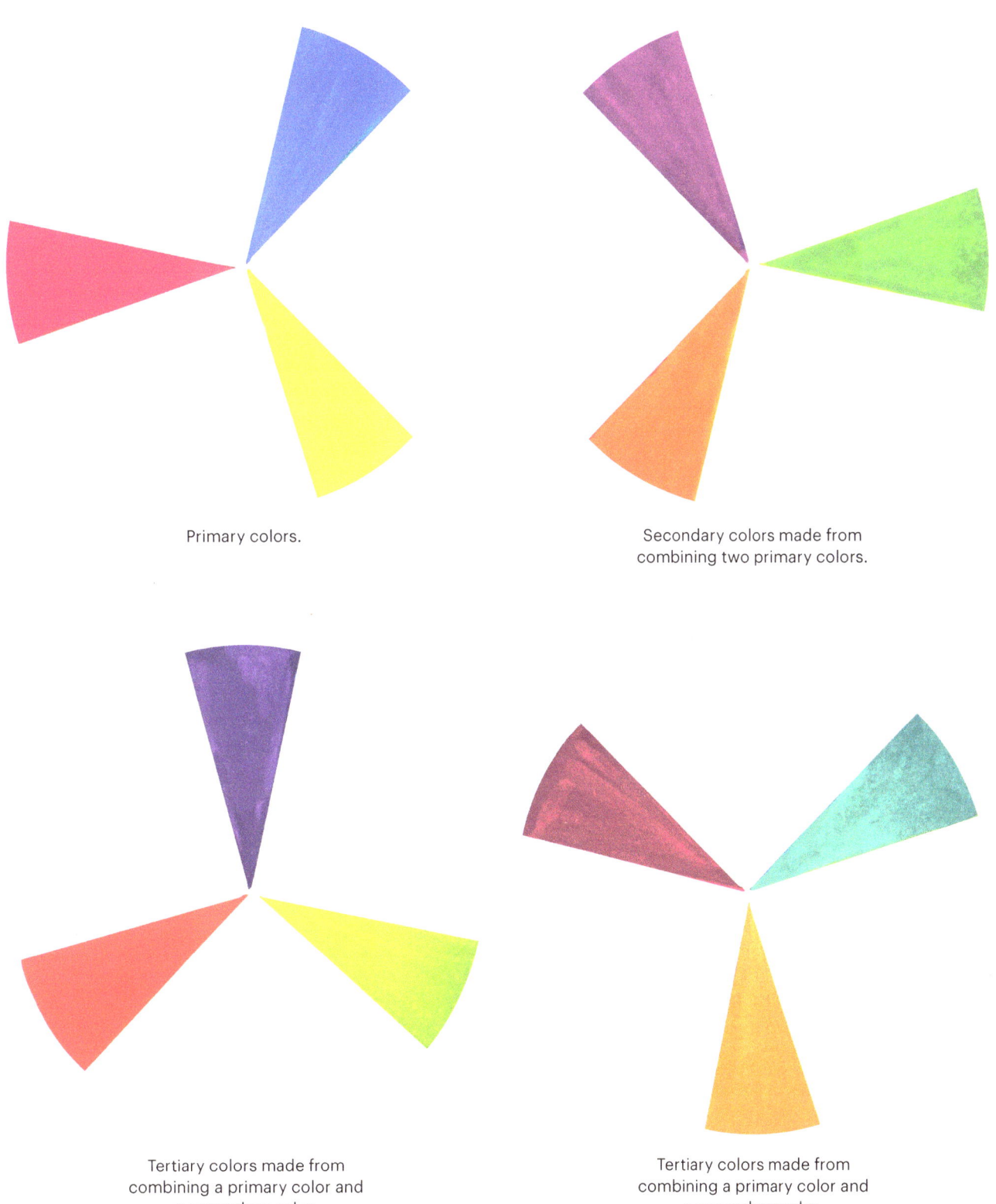

Primary colors.

Secondary colors made from combining two primary colors.

Tertiary colors made from combining a primary color and a secondary color.

Tertiary colors made from combining a primary color and a secondary color.

Helpful Terms

Sometimes the terminology used when speaking about art can be a bit overwhelming. In the following section, I'll go over some commonly used terms that you'll often hear referenced when speaking about color.

Hue

The term *hue* refers to the purest version of a color without any white, black, or gray added to it. It can be a bit confusing to distinguish the difference between the words "color" and "hue," because a lot of people use these terms interchangeably, but the simplest way to explain hue is to think of it as the color family the color you're using would fall into on the color wheel. If you had to explain the color in the simplest term, would you call it yellow? Orange? Green? A lot of the straight-out-of-the-tube colors you'll find at the art store fall into this category.

Tints, Tones, and Shades

The easiest way to expand the variety of a hue is to add black, white, or gray.

SHADE

A shade of a color is the darkened version of it. If you moved your color wheel from direct light into a shadow, the colors would change, wouldn't they? And the darker the shadow, the darker the color becomes. You can achieve a wide range of shades depending on how much black is added to your original hue. Pick a few colors to experiment with and notice how different they look when mixed with varying amounts of black.

TINT

In opposition to a shade, a tint is created by adding white to your hue. And like shades, tints can range from nearly white, to almost the pure hue depending how much white is added. As with shades, tints are only considered

Shades

Tints

Tones

tints if one of the pure colors from the color is mixed solely with white.

TONE

If you read the sections about shades and tints, I bet you can guess what makes a color a tone. Yes, gray! Any hue can be made into a tone by adding black *and* white in any varying degree. Adding gray to a color lessens the brightness of that color, in essence dulling it.

The range of tones you can create is almost endless, and using them along with tints, shades, and (sparingly) pure hues will bring much more dimension and complexity to your paintings. As you study the world around you, you'll notice that most of our surrounding world is composed of one of these variants of color.

Warm & Cool Colors

Even if you haven't given a lot of thought to warm and cool colors, you probably intuitively understand how they affect the art you view. For instance, warm colors, with their fiery hues, can make a piece of art feel bolder, while cool colors are naturally more soothing. Imagine a doctor's office. The walls are usually painted in soft blues or greens. This is because they are trying to give

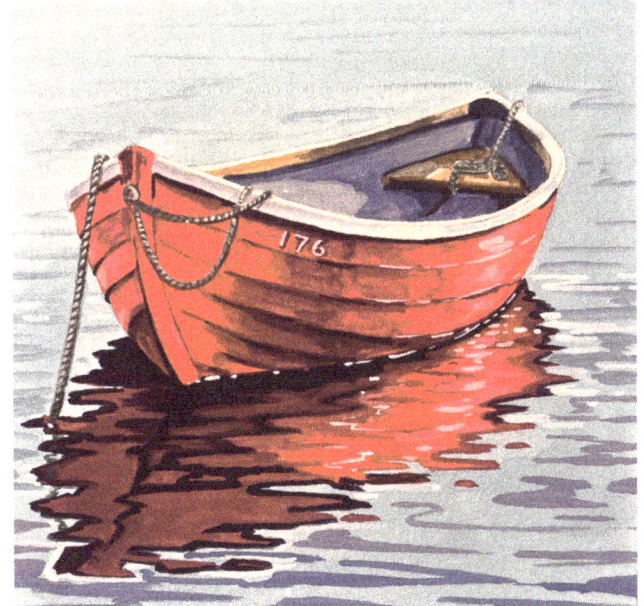

TOP RIGHT: Here I painted a similar subject with a cooler color palette (DIREX) and a warmer color palette (DIREX). **BELOW RIGHT:** You'll notice that the oranges contrast with the complimentary blue fabric, making the oranges pop off the page.

the room a subtly reassuring feeling. The colors you choose for your art can have similar affects.

The placement of colors can also be used to portray distance, especially in landscapes. Objects in the foreground will appear brighter (using warm colors), while objects in the distance, affected by the atmosphere, will appear cooler. Notice where you use warms and cools, and place them intentionally to elevate your art.

Another way to play with cool and warm colors is to deliberately place them side by side to create visual tension. Imagine the way a vivid orange sunset pops against deep indigo mountains or how a bright clementine stands out against a blue background. In contrast, imagine how a painting of the sea with predominantly blues and greens will feel cohesive and soothing.

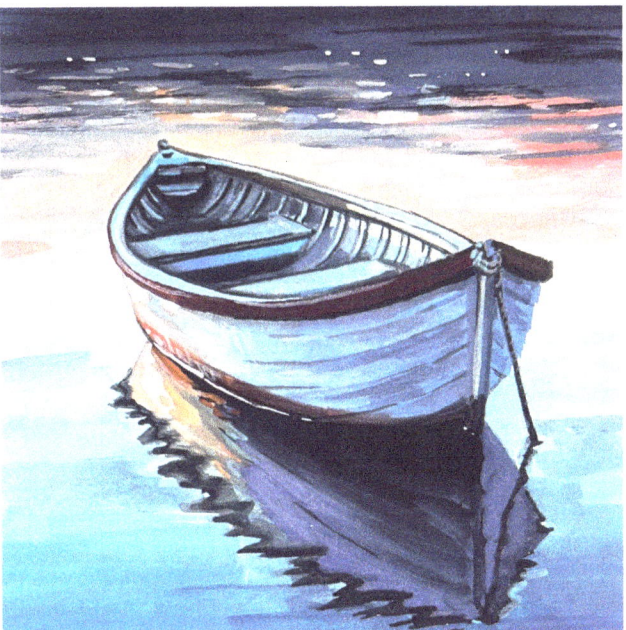

Complementary Colors

Complementary colors sit directly across from one another on the color wheel. The act of getting dressed in the morning has most likely introduced you to the idea of complementary colors. You've probably noticed the way a certain yellow shirt really pops when paired with something purple. In fact, you might not choose to put these colors together because when sitting side by side, they seem to enhance one another, making the yellow seem even more yellow-y and the purple seem even more purple-y.

This is because complementary colors offer high contrast to one another. Because they sit across from one

Tip

The science of color and how it affects us is fascinating. If you'd like to learn more, there are entire books devoted to color you can read, or you can simply search "science of color" online.

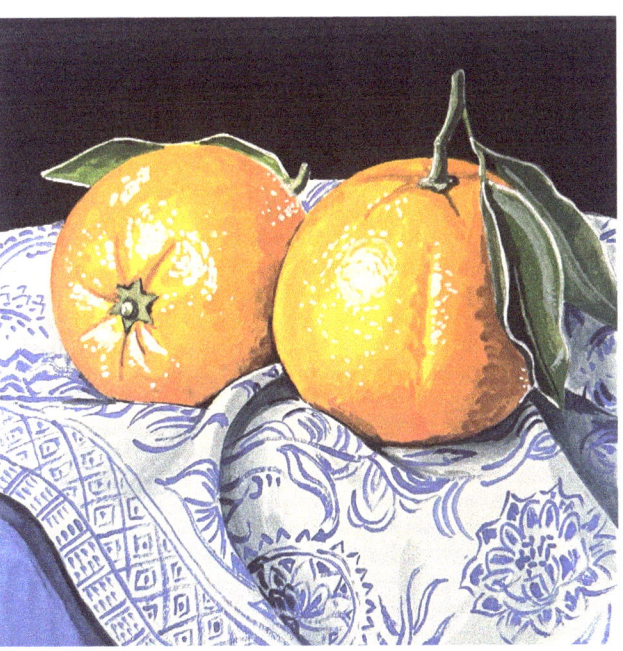

another in the color wheel, one of the colors will always be cooler and one will always be warmer. While these colors might look beautiful when sitting next to one another, the effect of mixing them reduces the brightness of the colors. One of the most interesting ways to create complex colors is to add a bit of its complement.

other on the color wheel, they feel much more related to one another, and when placed side by side in your painting have a pleasing, harmonious effect. Because these colors have a hue in common, they can be used to create beautiful color schemes to great effect.

Analogous Colors

In contrast with complementary colors, which sit across from one another on the color wheel, analogous colors sit next to one another. Because of the nearness to each

BELOW: This image of strawberries on a red background is an example of a predominantly analogous color palette. Because the painting uses mostly a range of reds, oranges, and pinks, the strawberries don't pop in quite the same way that the oranges in the previous image do, but the harmonious palette can be a bit more soothing.

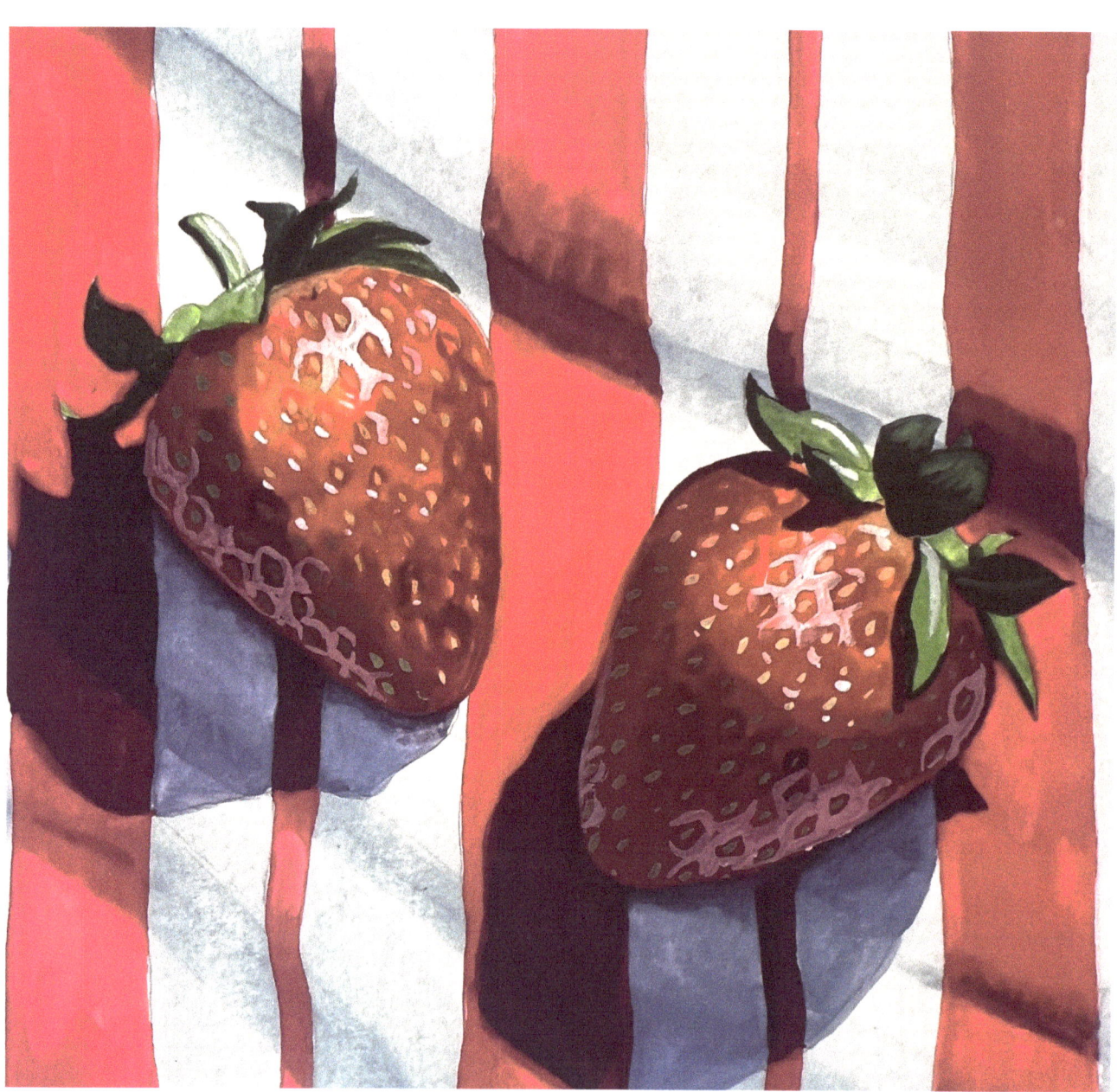

Value

The simplest definition of value is light and dark. One of the reasons artists often start their study of art by using pencil or charcoal is because being able to recognize and understand value is a fundamental skill. Color can bring a piece of art to life, but value gives it dimension.

It's almost always the case that brighter or lighter points in a painting appear to come forward, while darker points appear to recede. Deftly using a range of values between these points of light and dark can give your painting the illusion of depth.

To begin to understand value better, as well as find ways to verbalize it, we're going to start by creating a value scale. This is basically a range of values from the lightest (bright white) to the darkest (pure black).

Begin by sectioning your paper into eleven rect-angles. Paint in the first and last rectangles with pure white on the left and pure black on the right. In between, try to make a gradation of values by mixing black and white together to make shades of gray.

Imagine you're giving these shades of gray a percent-age value: 10 percent will be almost white with just the smallest hint of black and conversely, 90 percent will be such a dark gray that it almost appears black, but not quite.

Stepping down from the extremes, see if you can make the grays meet in the middle with a value of 50 per-cent. Take a good look at the example before you begin to make sure you understand the concept.

It might take a couple tries to get a value scale you're happy with, but it can be a valuable tool when you begin painting.

You may want to experiment with two different ways of mixing your values. You can try mixing a middle value by combining black and white (you probably won't use equal parts to get a middle value). From there, you'll add either more white to move toward the light end of the value scale or more black when moving to the dark end. Conversely, you can start on the extreme ends of the value scale (10% and 90%) and work your way toward the center.

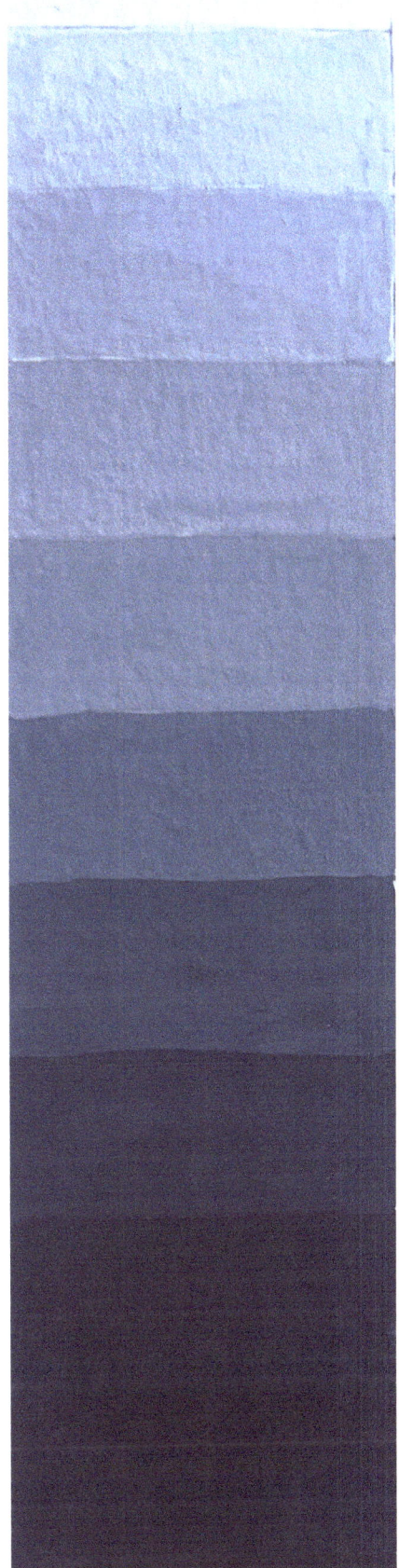

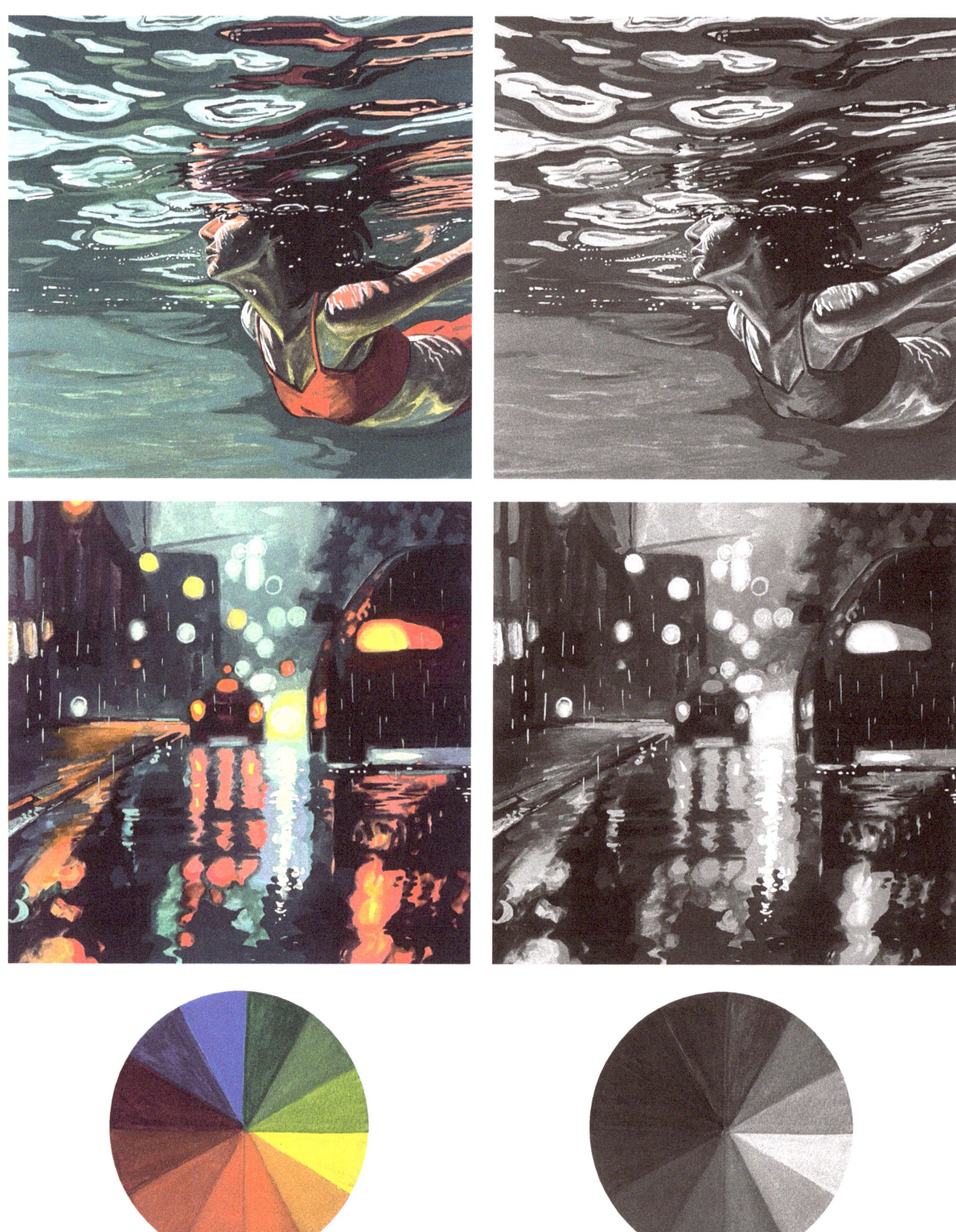

Here you can see two examples of my paintings
turned into value scale images.

Color vs. Value

One of the easiest ways to understand how the value scale and color relate is to take a few of your favorite color photos and turn them into black-and-white images. Now place these images side by side and really look at what happens to each individual color when it's translated into gray. Do any of the values surprise you?

Now that you've created your own color wheel, you can also use this trick to better understand your paint colors. Take a black-and-white photo of the color wheel and try to give the colors a number from the value scale you just created.

Value Study 1: Sphere

Painting a black-and-white value study of a sphere is a great place to start understanding light and shadow and how they interact on an actual shape in space to create the illusion of a three-dimensional object. As

you'll see in this step-by-step painting, different parts of the sphere react differently to the light. Here are some things to look for:

HIGHLIGHT

This is the part on the sphere where the light hits directly. It will be the lightest point on the painting.

MIDTONE

As you might guess from the name, these are the midtone values that are not hit directly by the light and are not in complete shadow.

CORE SHADOW

This is the place on the sphere where the light source is completely blocked. If you imagine the sphere as the earth, the core shadow would happen after the sun has set completely and no more light reaches it.

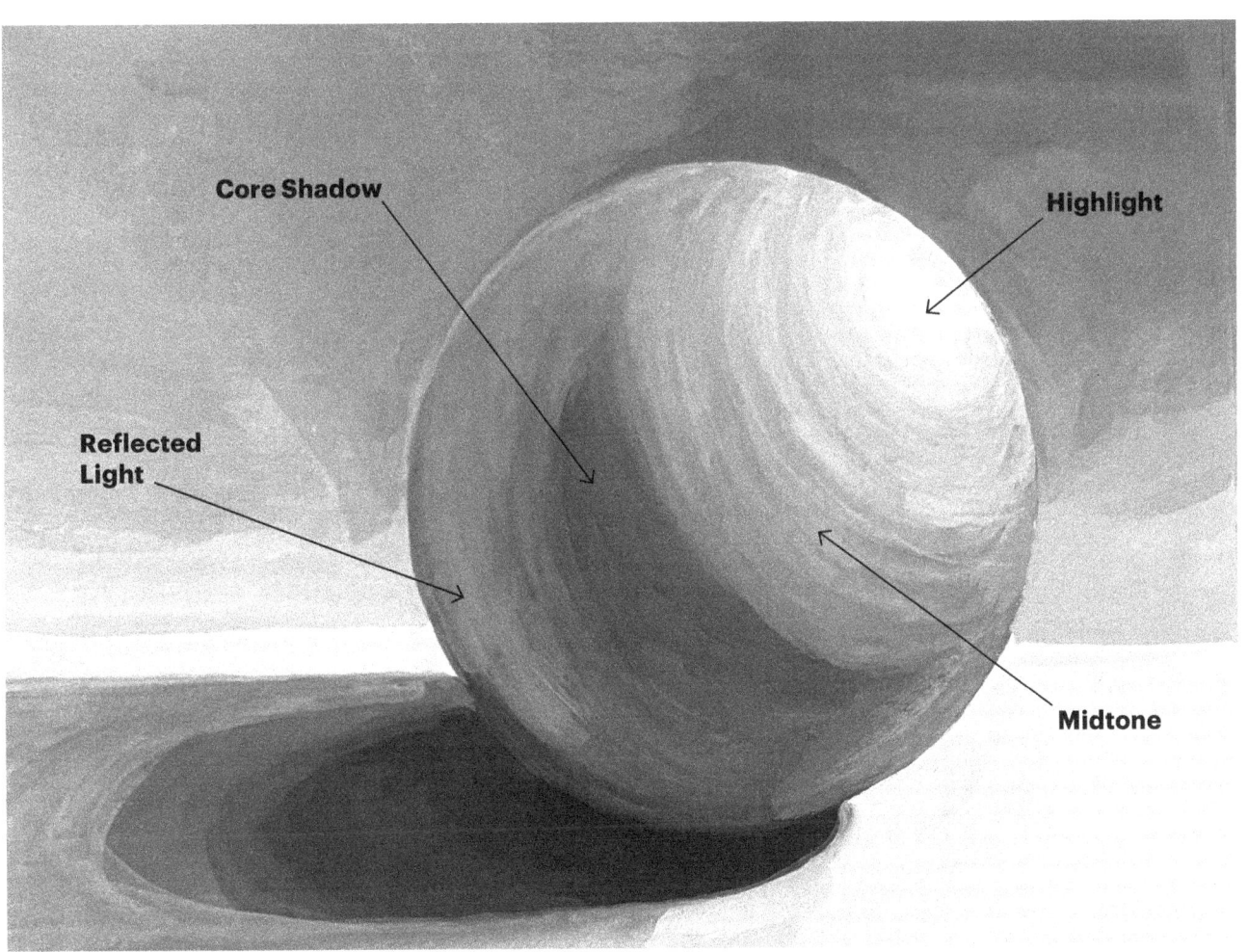

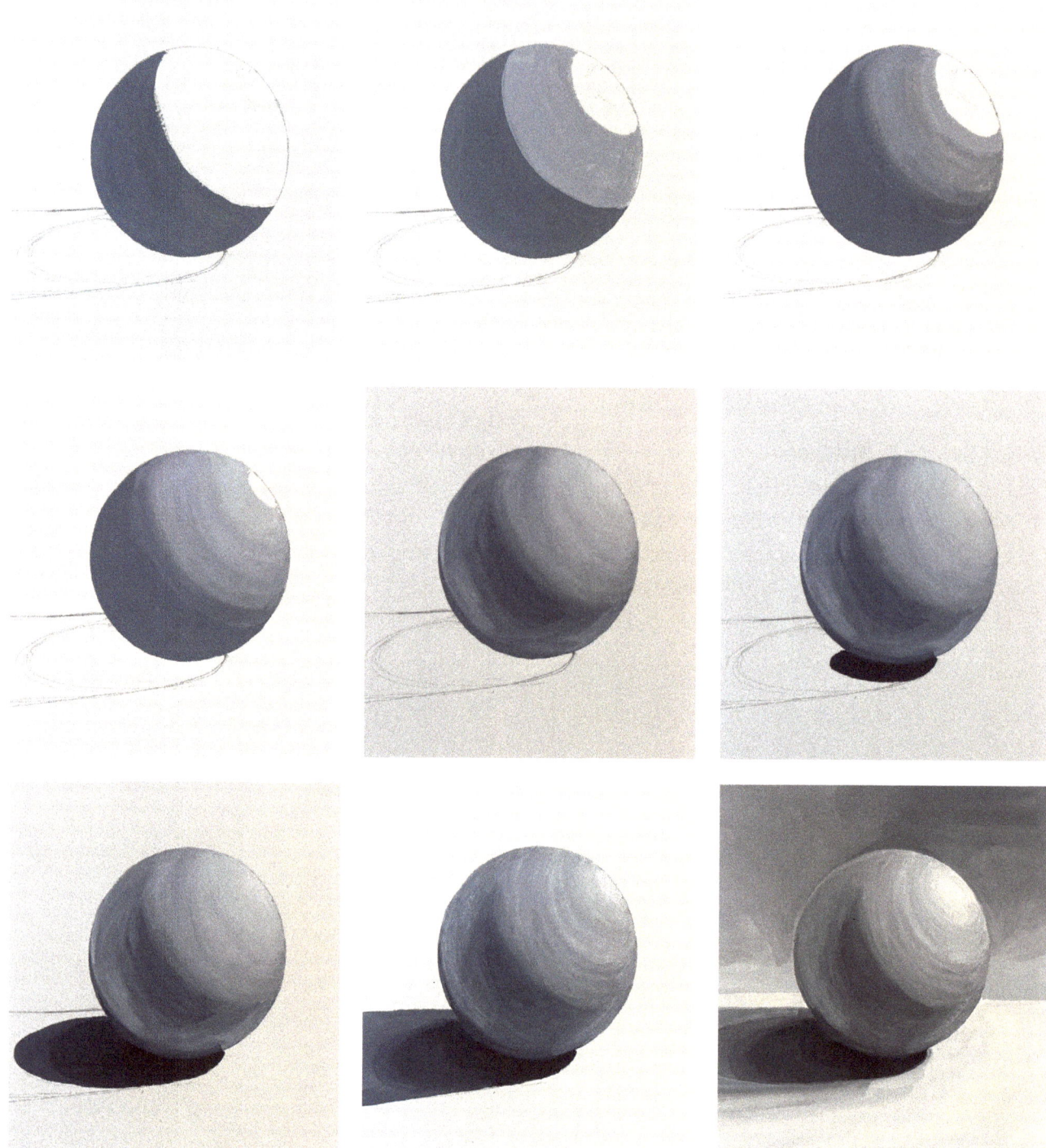

REFLECTED LIGHT

This is the light that shines off nearby surfaces and bounces back onto the sphere.

CAST SHADOW

Because your sphere doesn't just float in space, the cast shadow grounds your sphere to the surface that it sits on. You'll notice that the shadow is darker the closer it is to the sphere, where the surface is completely blocked from the light source.

Try painting your own value study to help you understand how light and shadow interact and how to depict them in your art.

Value Study 2: Shapes

Try painting three different shaped objects with differing values in *one* painting. This is a great way to compare how light affects them all differently. You'll notice subtle variances between them that can help inform your future color paintings.

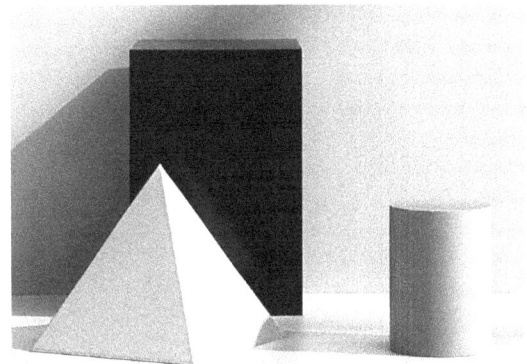

Reference photo

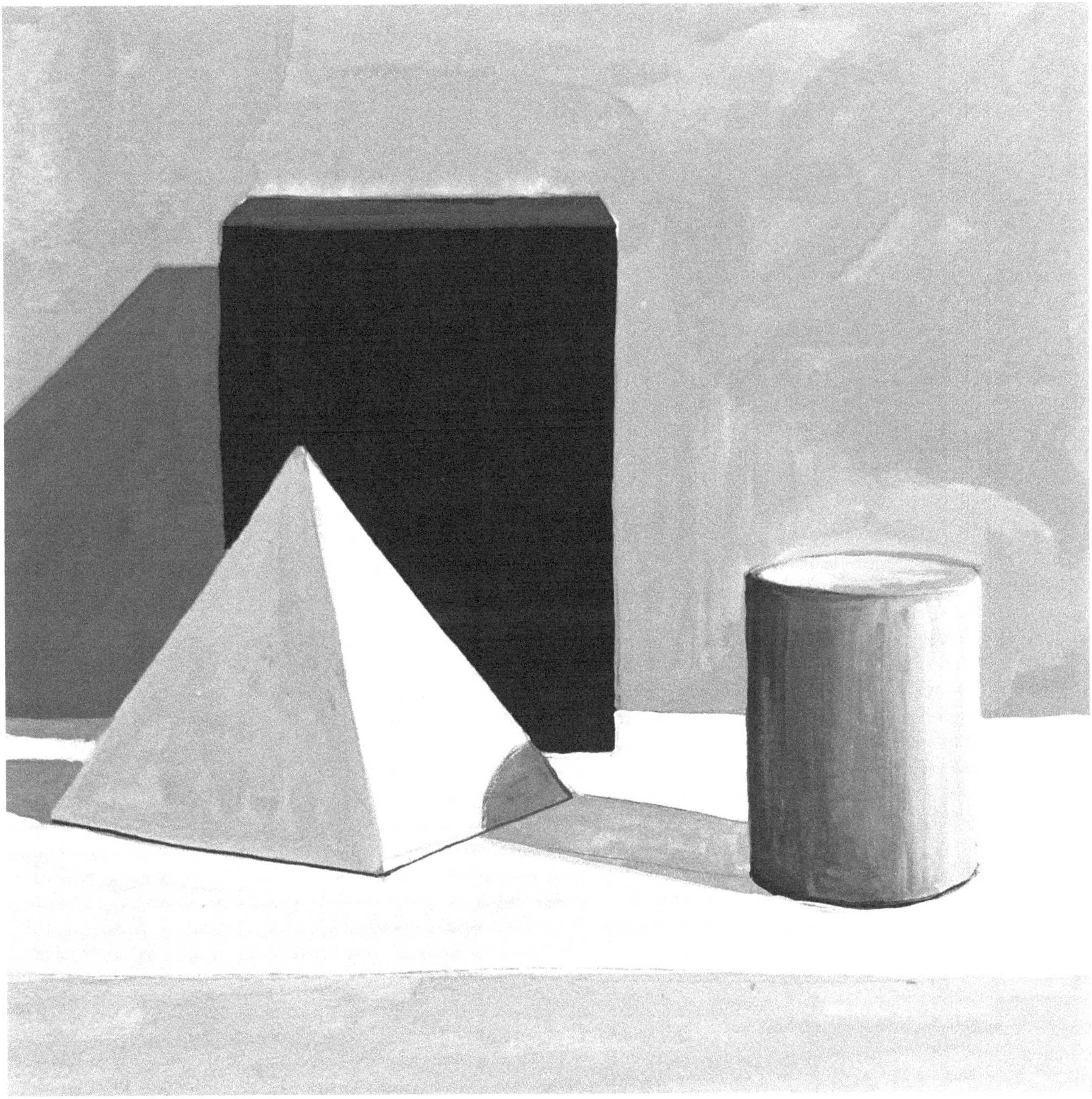

Painting

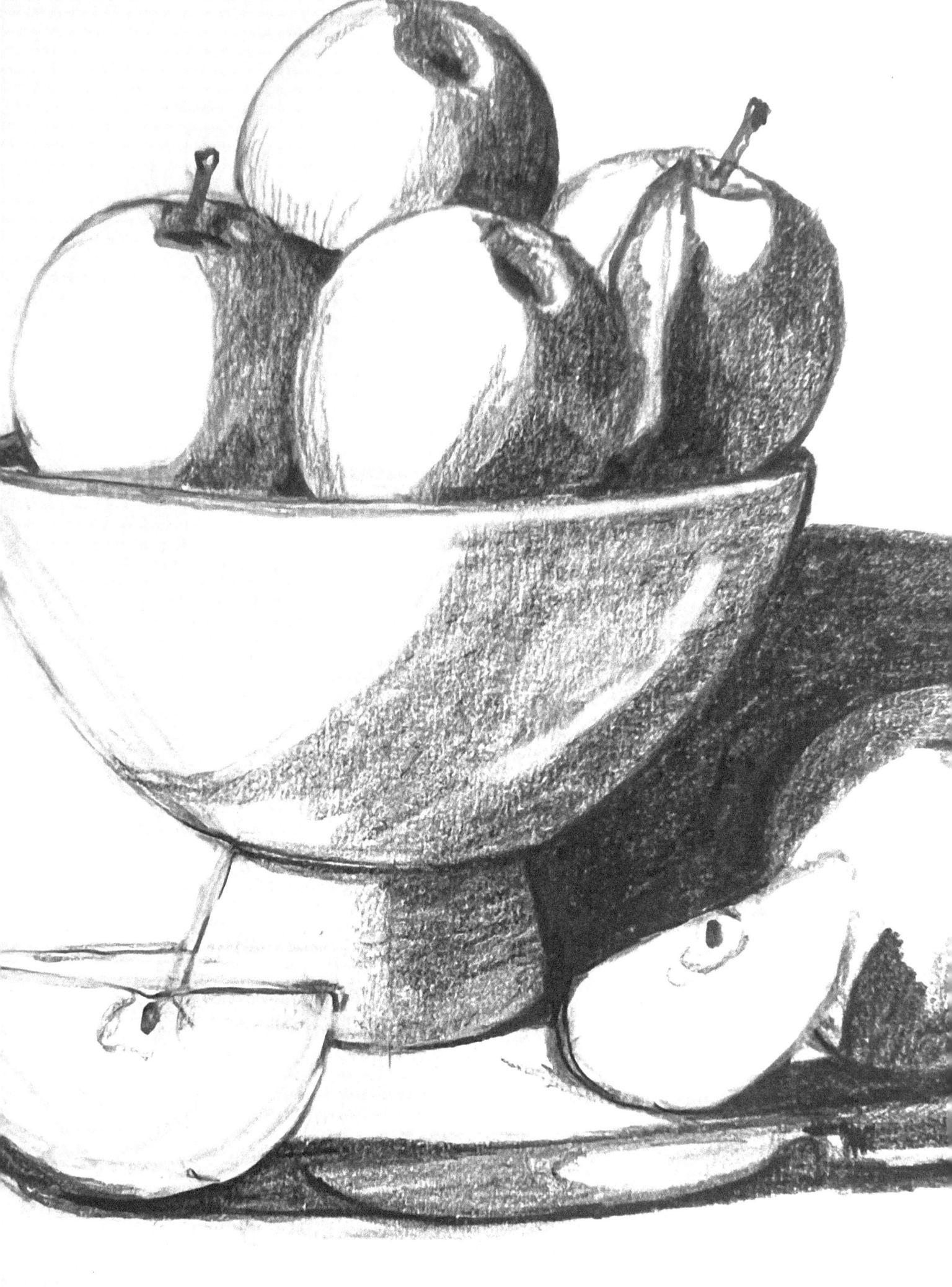

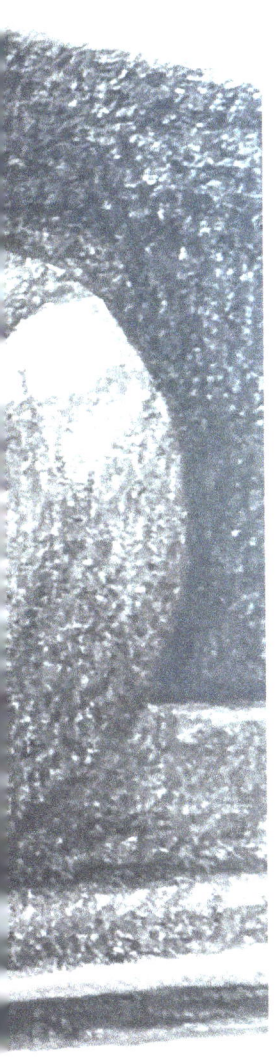

FOUR
DRAWING TIPS

It might seem strange, in a book about painting with gouache, to have a section about drawing and composition, but these skills are fundamental to creating a good painting, so I wanted to give you a few guidelines to think about before you move on.

Most people start drawing at an early age, but it isn't until you begin to understand shape, proportion, and contour that your drawings really start to look like the objects you're trying to recreate. It's not necessary to master your skill for drawing before you move on to painting. In fact, these skills will naturally inform one another. But it's helpful to keep in mind that the more time you focus on the basic fundamentals of drawing, the more lifelike your paintings will be. Giving yourself a strong foundation in drawing will free you to focus on the parts of painting that are unique to the medium.

Shapes

It seems so basic, but the entire world really is made up of shapes both two-dimensional and three-dimensional: circles, spheres, squares, cubes, triangles, and pyramids. The list could go on and on. But learning to see those basic shapes inside of more complicated ones can be the key to drawing.

When I was little, I was obsessed with horses AND drawing, so it was no surprise I inevitably wanted to learn to *draw* horses. In the library at my school, there were a few how-to books about drawing animals, and I made a point to check them out over and over again. One of the first things I learned about drawing animals was that a complicated creature, like a horse, could be broken down into shapes: a circle for the snout and a bigger one for the head, with a couple of lines connecting them; a long rectangle for the neck, a larger circle

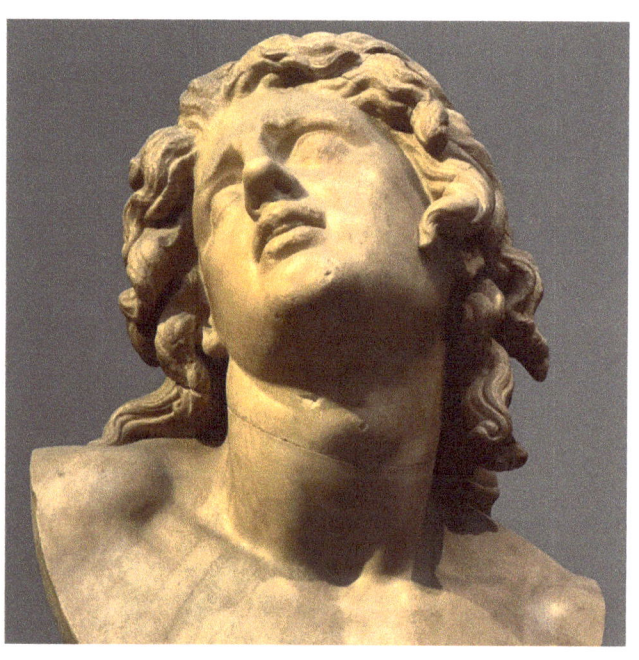

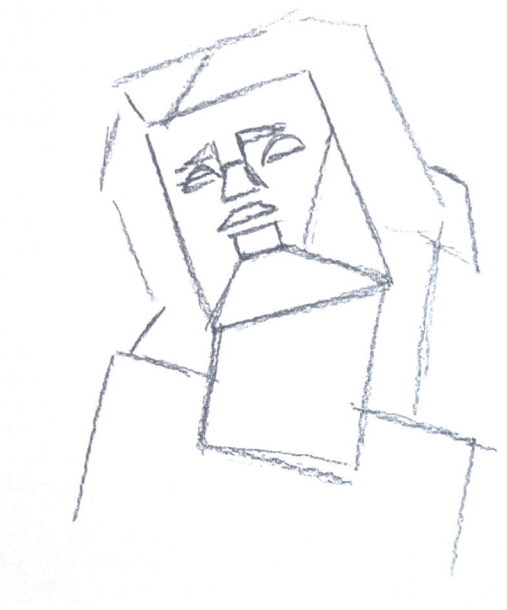

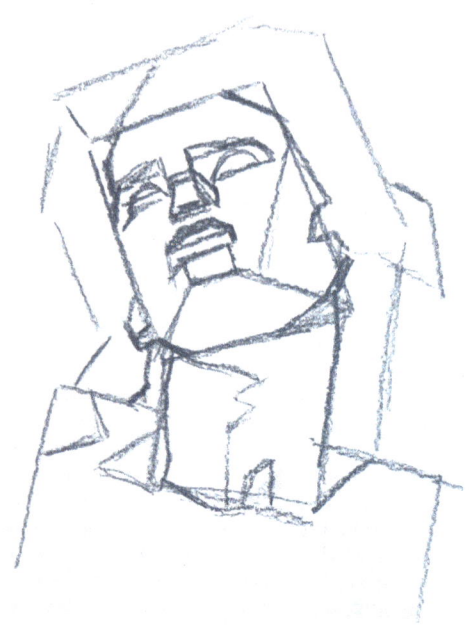

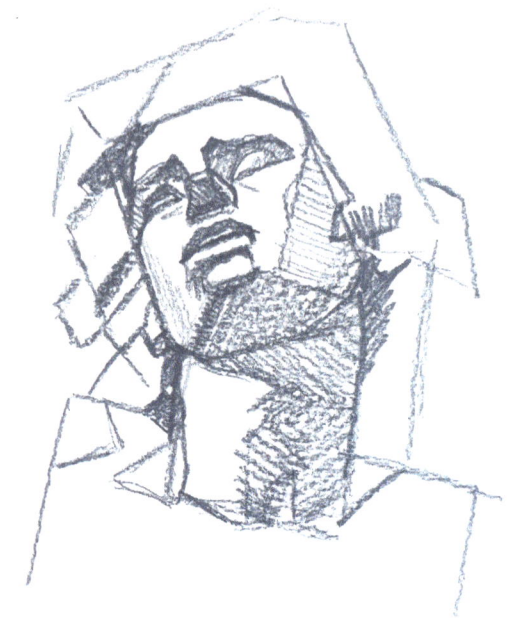

near the withers, and another for the rump. You get the idea. I won't bore you with more.

But what I didn't realize as I learned to draw horses this way, was that for the rest of my life I'd be able to break down complicated forms into simpler shapes. It still informs the beginning stages of my drawings to this day.

BELOW: Here's an example of a complex subject and how it can be broken down into simple shapes.

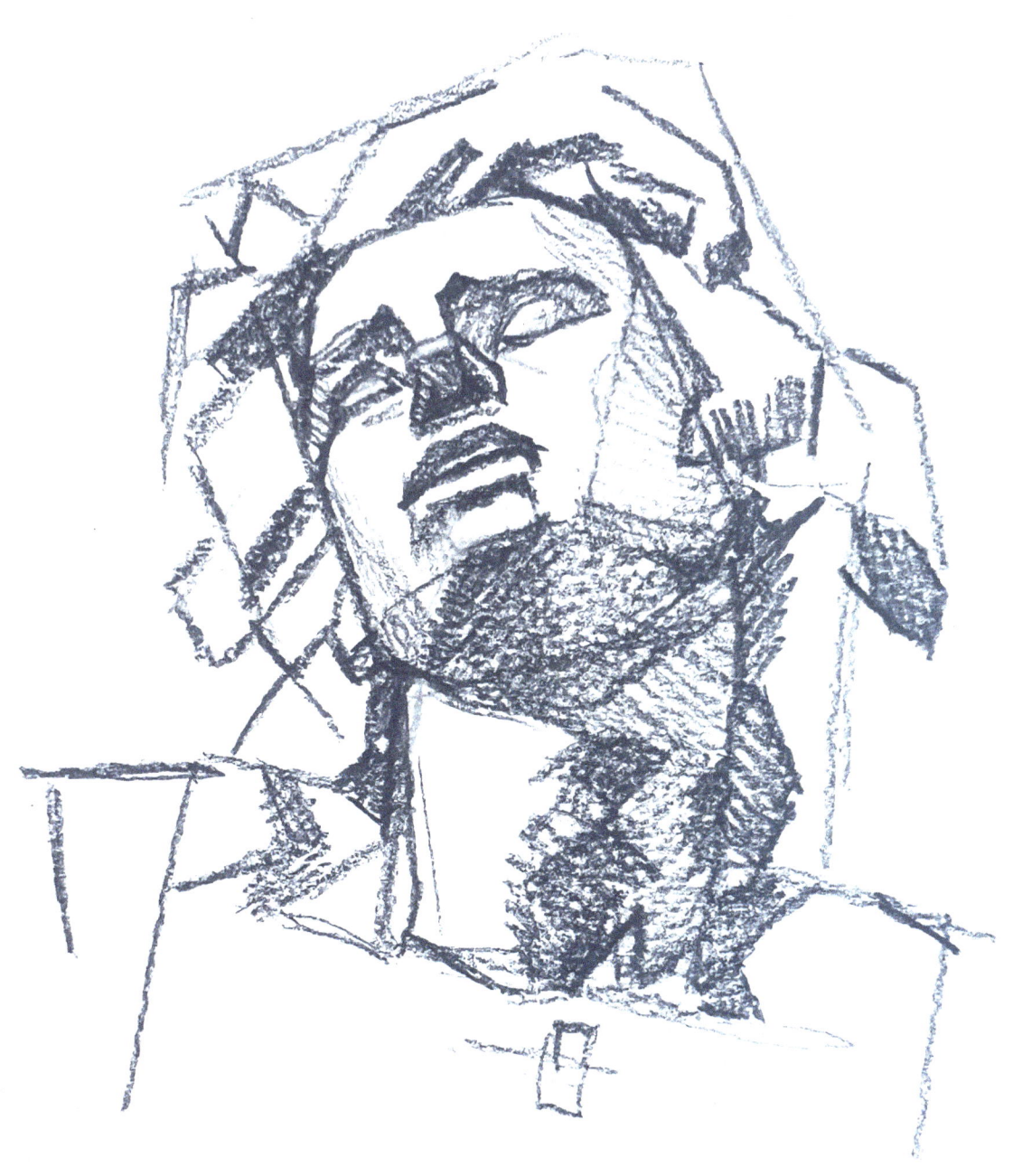

Proportions

Getting an accurate relationship between the objects in your art is a crucial part of the drawing process. The relationships between the shapes, sizes, and positions of your objects orient the viewer and help them understand your art.

One of the reasons caricatures often look so funny is because the artist has played with the proportions of the subject's features. While you can definitely experiment with proportions, it's important to understand how to portray them correctly before you start breaking the rules.

Measuring

Our eyes are really good at guessing the size of things, especially in comparison with other objects, but we're not always great at translating that to paper. One of the ways to get the proportions correct is to start with simple shapes (like we just discussed on page 48) and then compare the sizes of those shapes.

Let's say you're drawing a plate of lemon slices and you want to get the placement and proportions correct. You'll want to start by blocking in the major shapes. After they're blocked in, you can measure the height and length of the slices in comparison with one another by using a ruler or a piece of paper or even the length of your pencil. This works well if you're using a reference photo because the image that you're working from won't change. For example, if you measure the length of the top lemon, you might assume that all the slices will be equal, but depending on where it is in the photo, the length will change. If it's closer to the viewer, the bigger it will be in proportion to the other slices.

Take a moment to measure the slices in the reference photo. Now you can compare those measurements to the forms you've blocked in on your page.

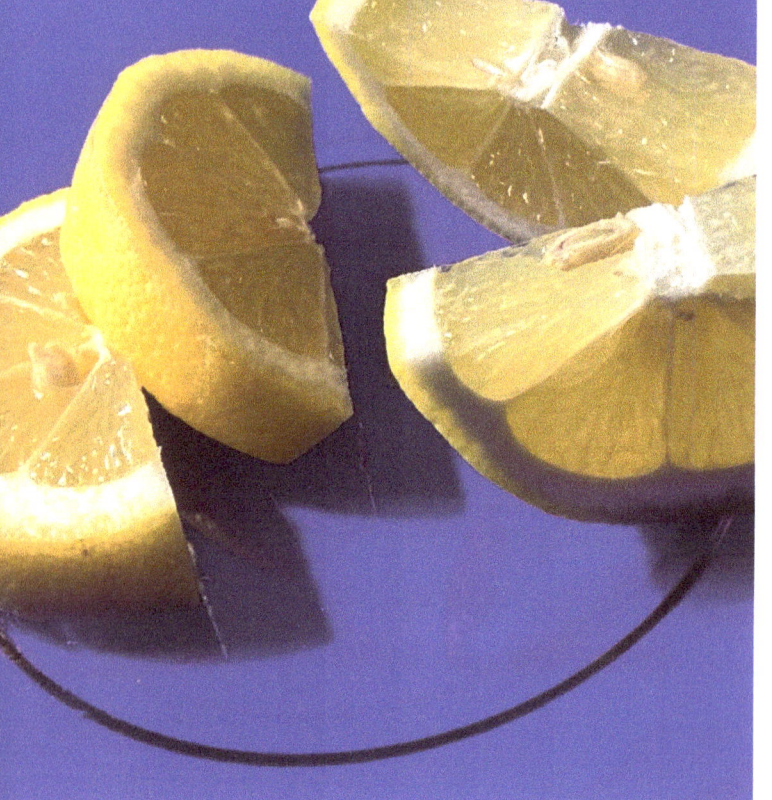

Negative Space

Another great way to measure is by noticing the "negative space" between objects. What shape do those negative shapes make?

Getting the placement and proportions of these shapes correct at the beginning of your drawing will really help your drawing—and later your painting—fall into place.

Once you're content with the placement and proportions of your objects, you can draw them in more permanently.

OPPOSITE: As you can see, start by using the simplest shapes to block in the bowl and apples. Focus on getting the placement and size of the items just right. Don't worry about the details at this point. Often, beginners will dive right into the details but will become discouraged when the composition isn't quite what they'd envisioned. A primary focus on placement within the composition will alleviate those problems.

With each progressive step, focus more and more on refining the image and adding more details. This way, the image grows together, like a fuzzy photograph coming into focus before your eyes.

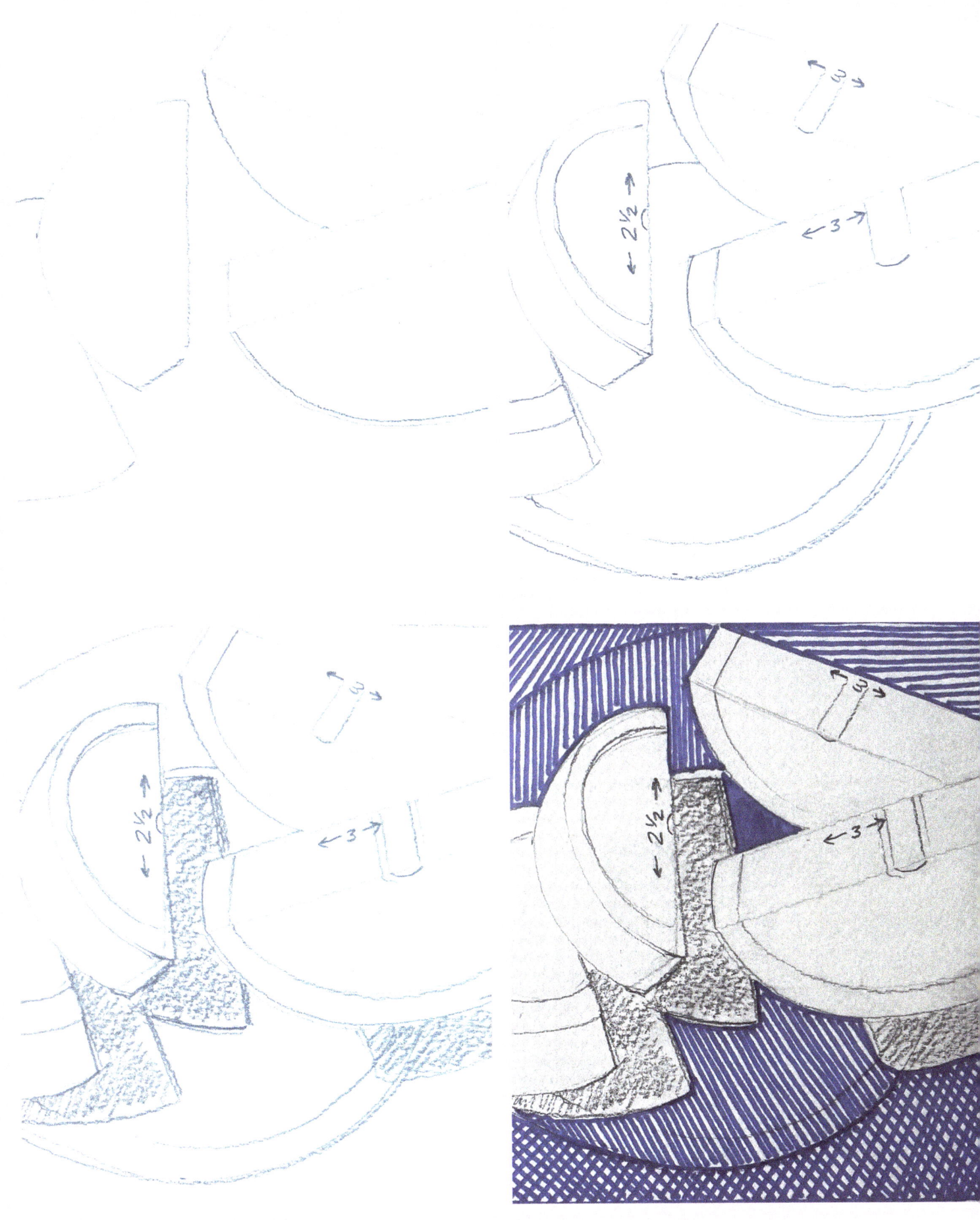

Contour

I once had a professor explain contour to me this way: Imagine you're a small ant marching your way around the outside of an object. As you march, you leave a small black line behind you. This line is the contour. In other words, the contour marks the edge of the form or the outline.

In drawing, there are a few different kinds of contour. While they can all be helpful to practice, we'll focus on cross contours.

If I asked you to imagine a globe, like the kind you'd find in a classroom, you'd probably imagine (besides the

Cross contour lines follow the shapes of your subject and create volume.

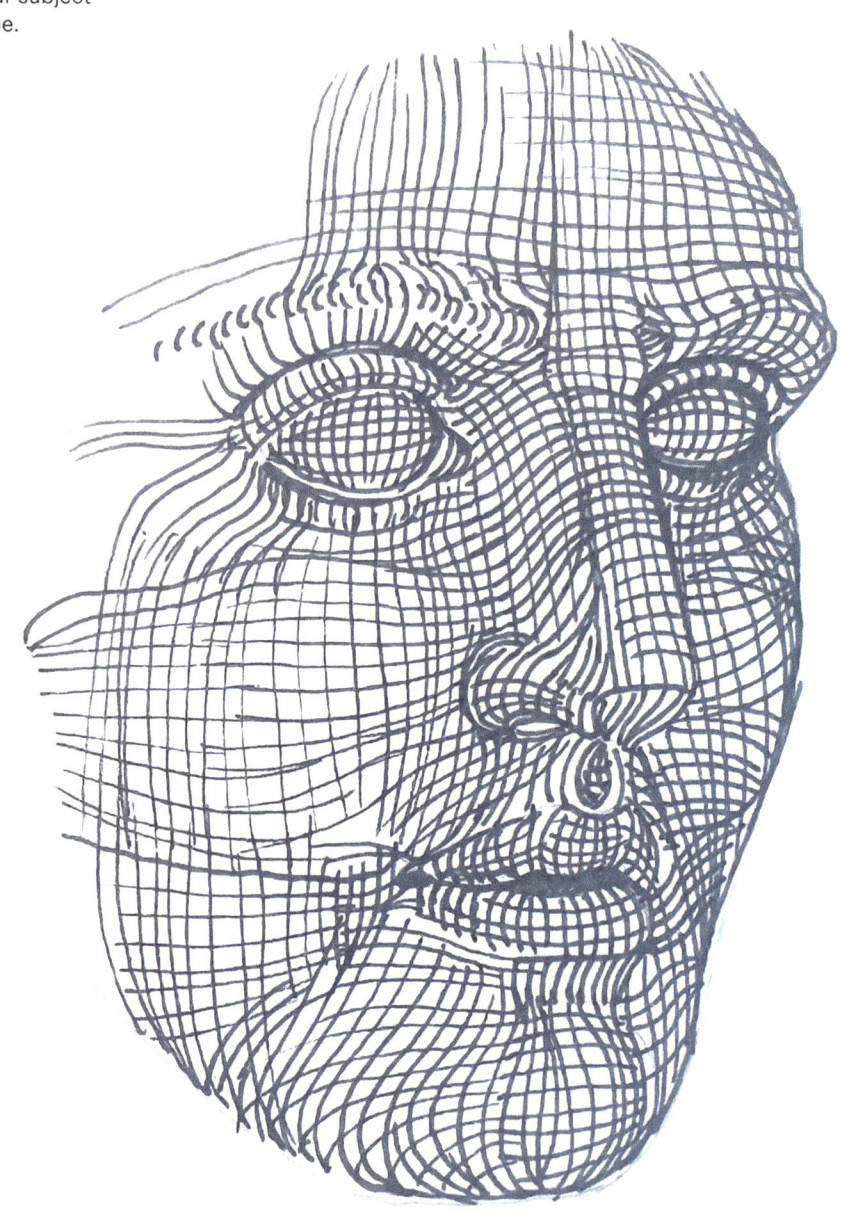

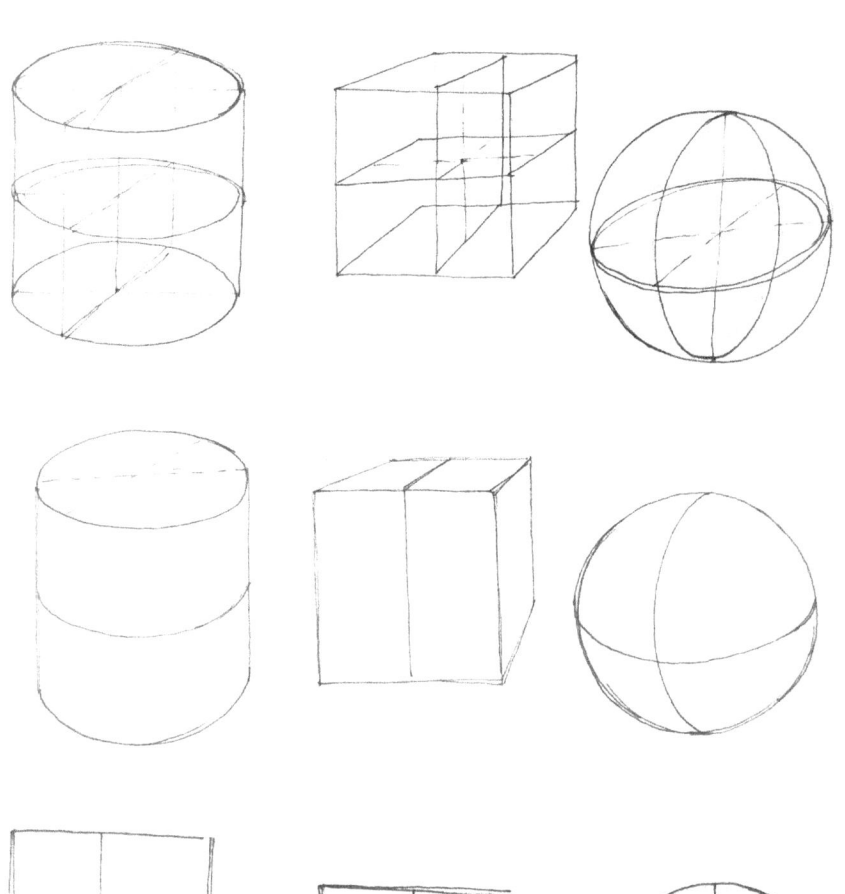

When drawing a three-dimensional form, it can often be helpful to image the path the line would take if the object you're drawing was transparent, like in these examples of a cylinder, cube, and sphere.

Here are some examples of what these objects would look like if they were not transparent.

And here are some examples of what these objects would look like if they had no dimension at all and were completely flat.

continents and oceans) the longitudinal and latitudinal lines that run up and down and side to side.

One of the easiest ways to understand cross contour lines is to take note of that globe. Imagine trying to draw those latitude and longitude lines . . . you wouldn't just draw straight lines, would you? The lines would follow the curve of the globe's sphere. This is exactly what cross contour aims to do.

When it comes to adding dimension to your art through line making, cross contour lines are the most effective at creating form.

See how much information these lines provide to the viewer? Find a few objects around your house to practice with.

Tip

If your mind is having trouble grasping how to translate the contour into lines in your painting, you can always try drawing on your object with a permanent marker to give yourself real lines to follow. This trick works well on fruit.

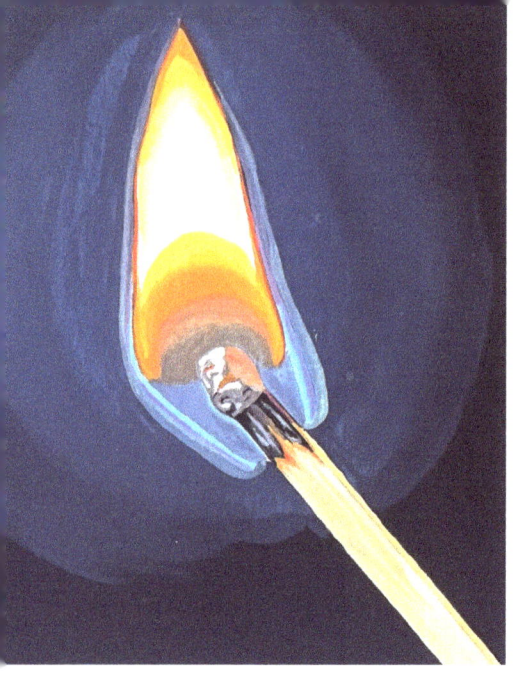
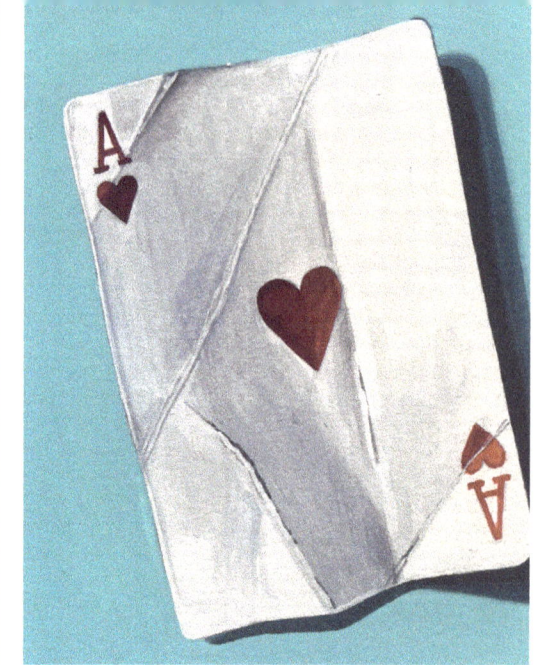
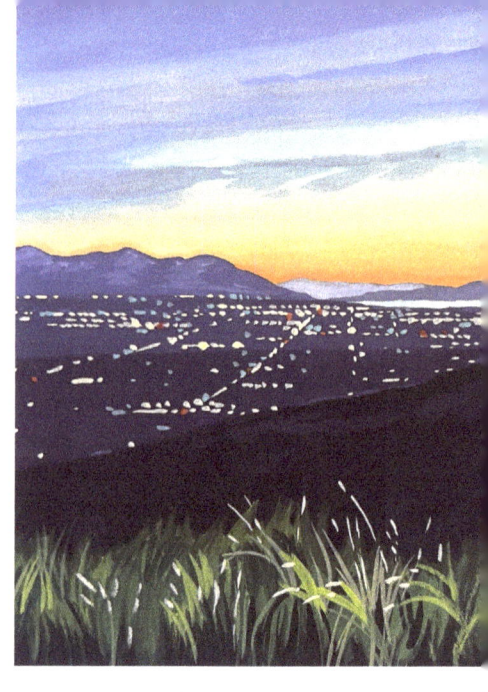
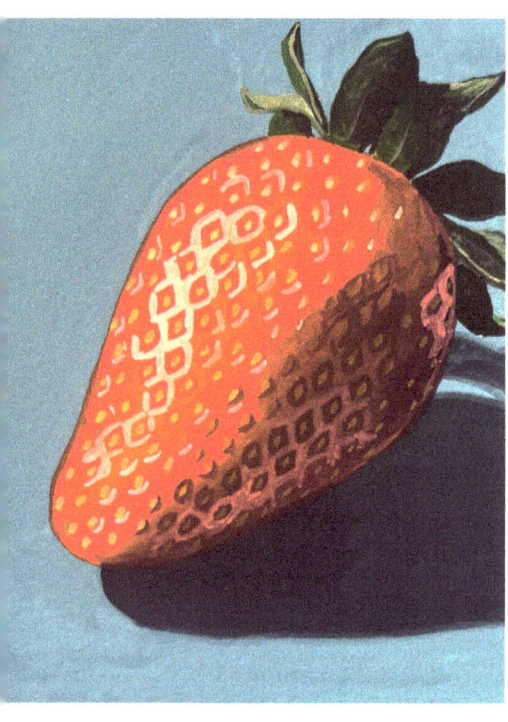
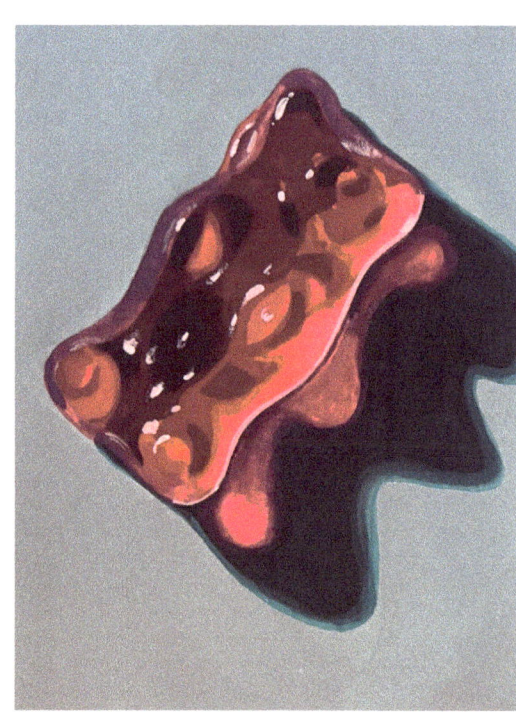
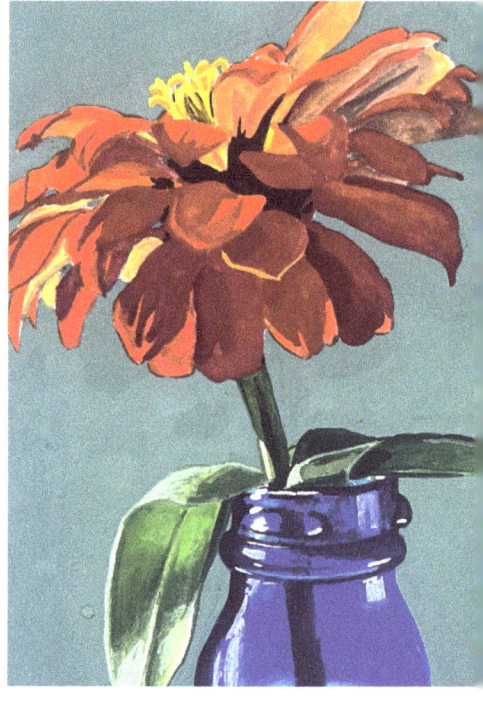
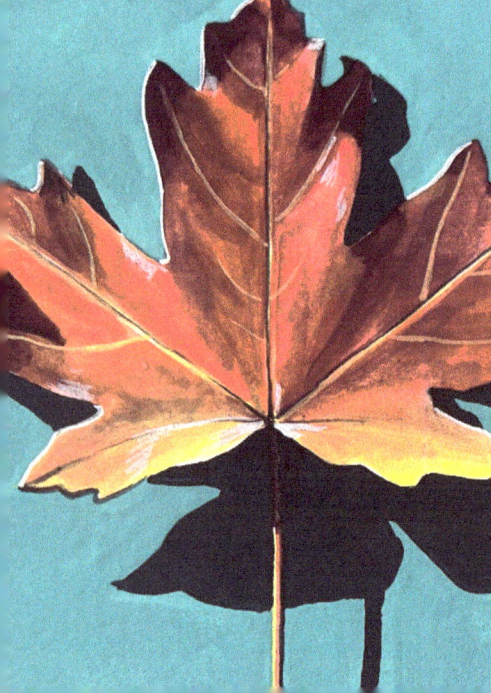
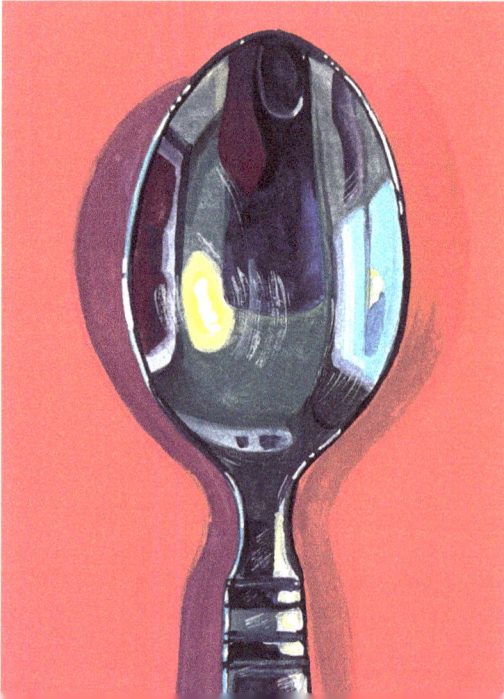
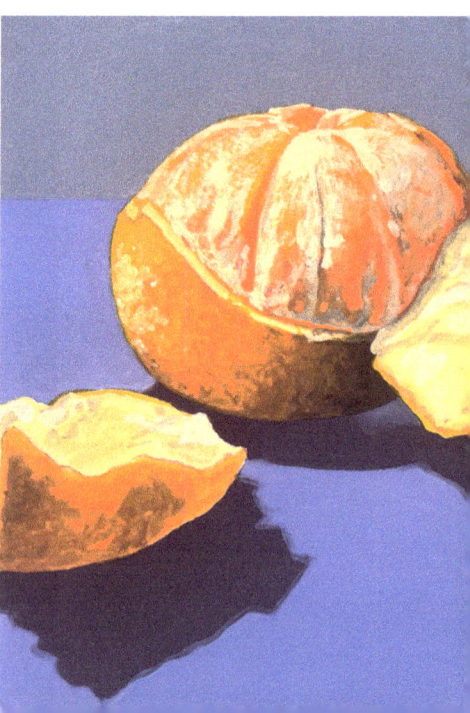

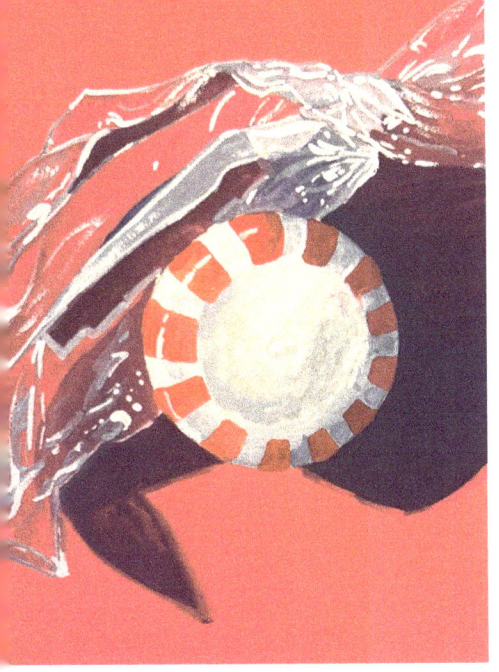

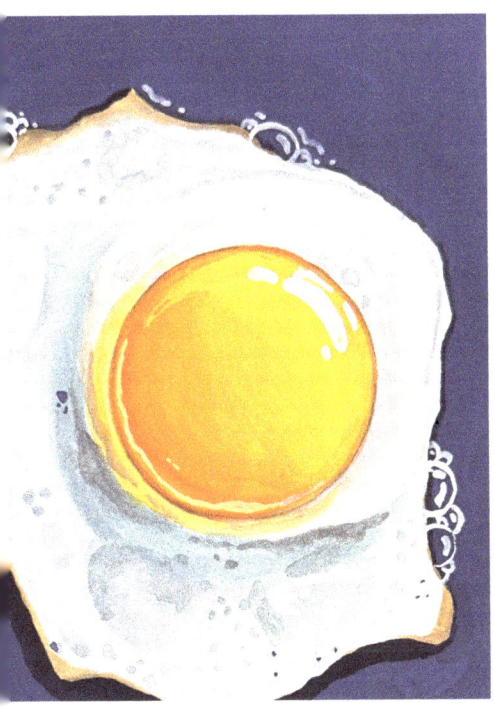

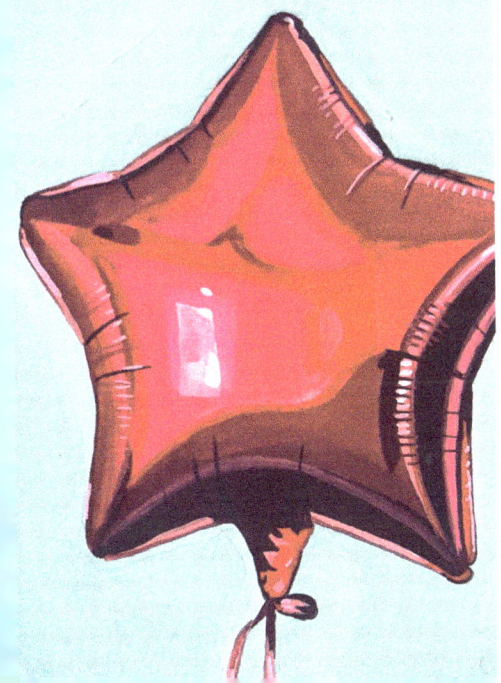

FIVE

THE PROJECTS

You did it! You gathered all your supplies. You set up your paints and pallets. You familiarized yourself with your paints and brushes and you're finally ready to get started painting a finished piece.

I often hear from beginning students that it can be difficult to come up with ideas for things to paint, so for now, you can let go of coming up with your own imagery and try out a wide range of subject matter with step-by-step instructions to guide you through the process.

In the following section, you'll find twelve different projects with instructions to take you from blank page to finished painting. Each of the following projects will also focus on a different technique or material, highlighting some specific subjects for you to learn about while you complete these paintings. After you've finished this book, you should have a solid foundation to help you tackle any imagery you want. So now you can take these ideas forward with you as you begin to create your own creative work.

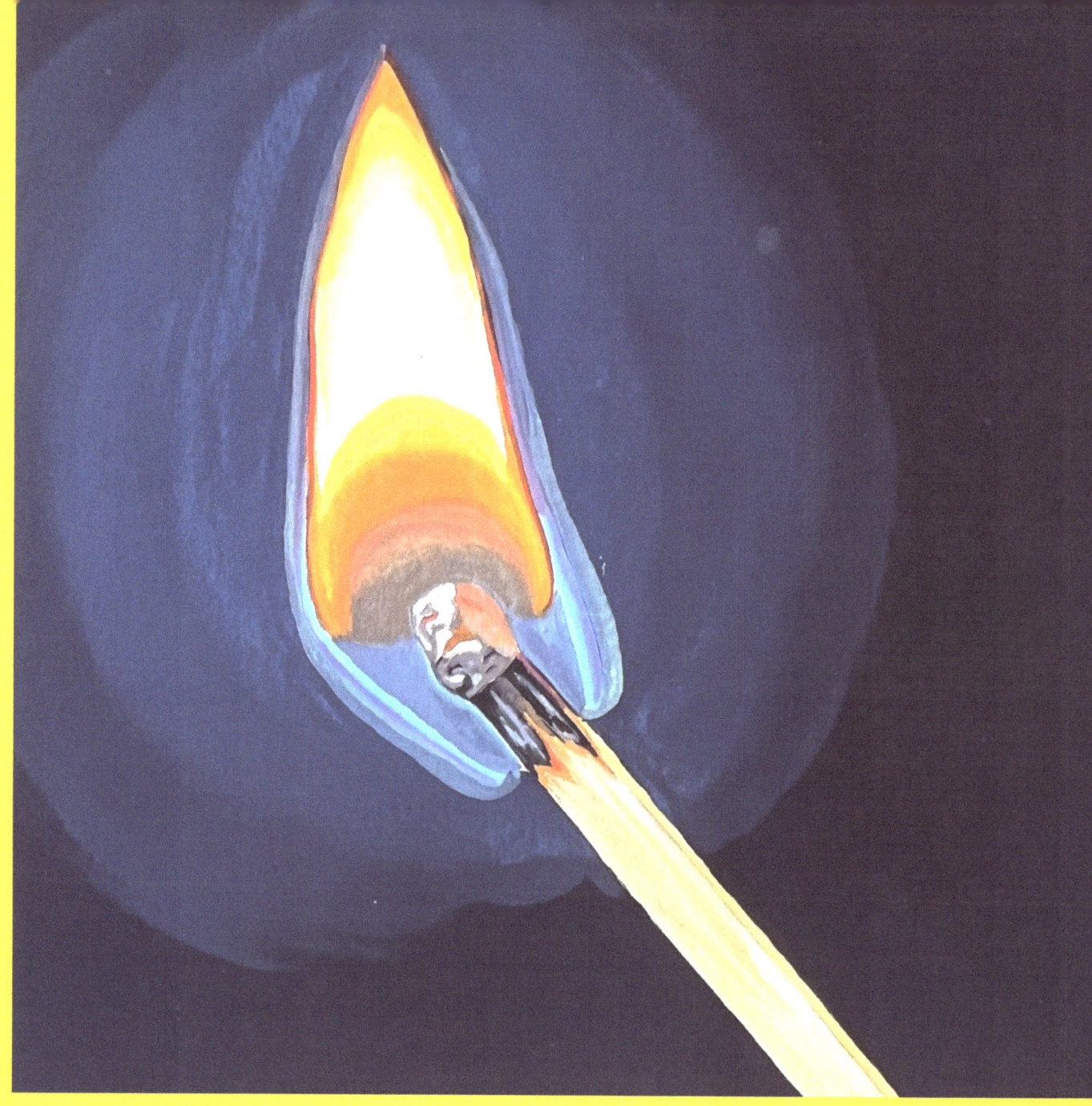

Painting Subtle Colors

MATCH FLAME

Our eyes often gloss over an image, making assumptions about what we're seeing. Because of this, the flame might initially read as having fewer colors inside it than if you actively look at it for a longer amount of time. To train your eyes to see all those colors, take a few minutes before starting your painting to analyze the reference photo. Make note of all the colors you see inside. If you want to go above and beyond, write down all the colors you see. Try to find as many as possible.

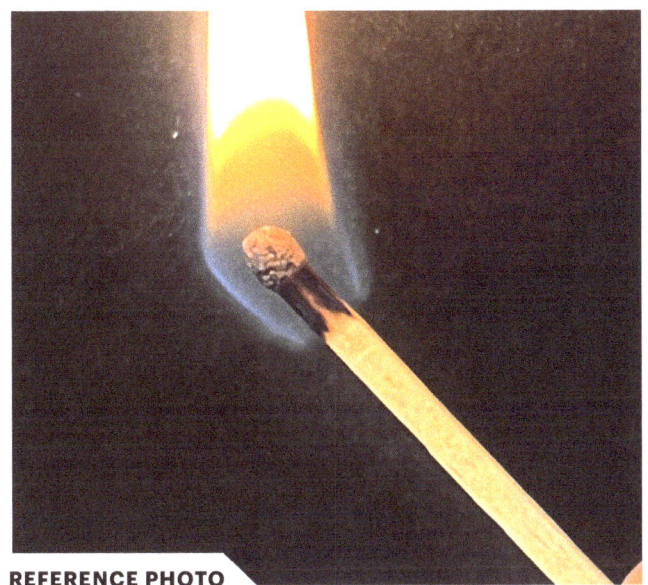

REFERENCE PHOTO

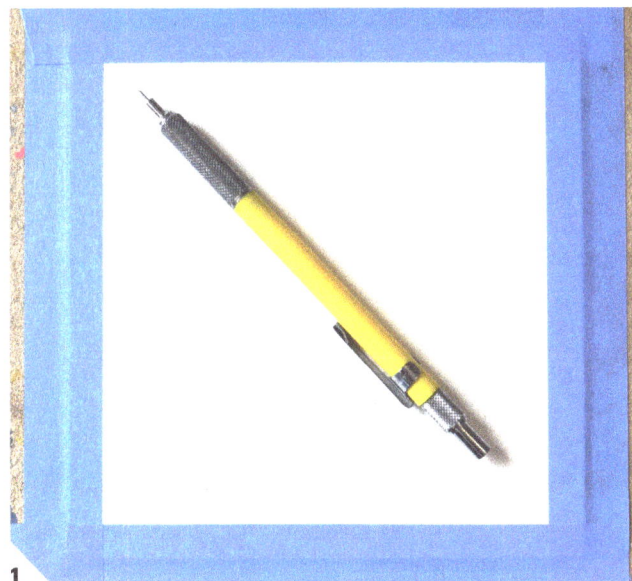

1

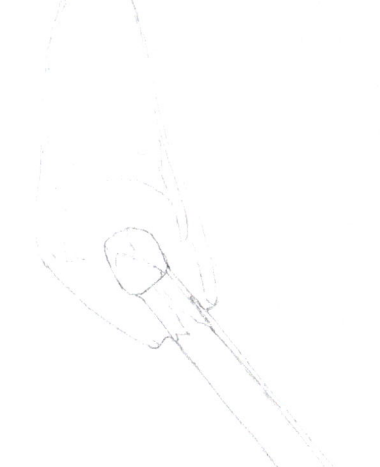

2

1 We're always going to prepare to paint the same way. Make sure the board you're attaching your paper to is small enough to move around your surface to ensure you can access your painting from all angles. It's also important to tape your paper securely to your board to prevent it from buckling during your painting process.

2 Getting the underdrawing correct is one of the most important steps in any painting because it influences all the subsequent steps. If something feels a little off in the underdrawing, it's probably going to feel off in the finished painting too, and because gouache can only be layered a few times before becoming muddy, big changes are difficult to make mid-process.

I don't get overly detailed in this step because there will be the opportunity to come in with detail brushes once I start laying paint down. Right now I want you to think about proportions and placement. Think about the shapes you see in the objects you're drawing. For instance, you'll notice in the match head, I've drawn a diamond shape on the far right and a triangular shape on the left bottom portion. These shapes represent the shift of shadow within the match head and will help give it dimension when it's painted.

In the flame itself, I've tried to keep my lines fairly light so they don't show through the lighter paint colors.

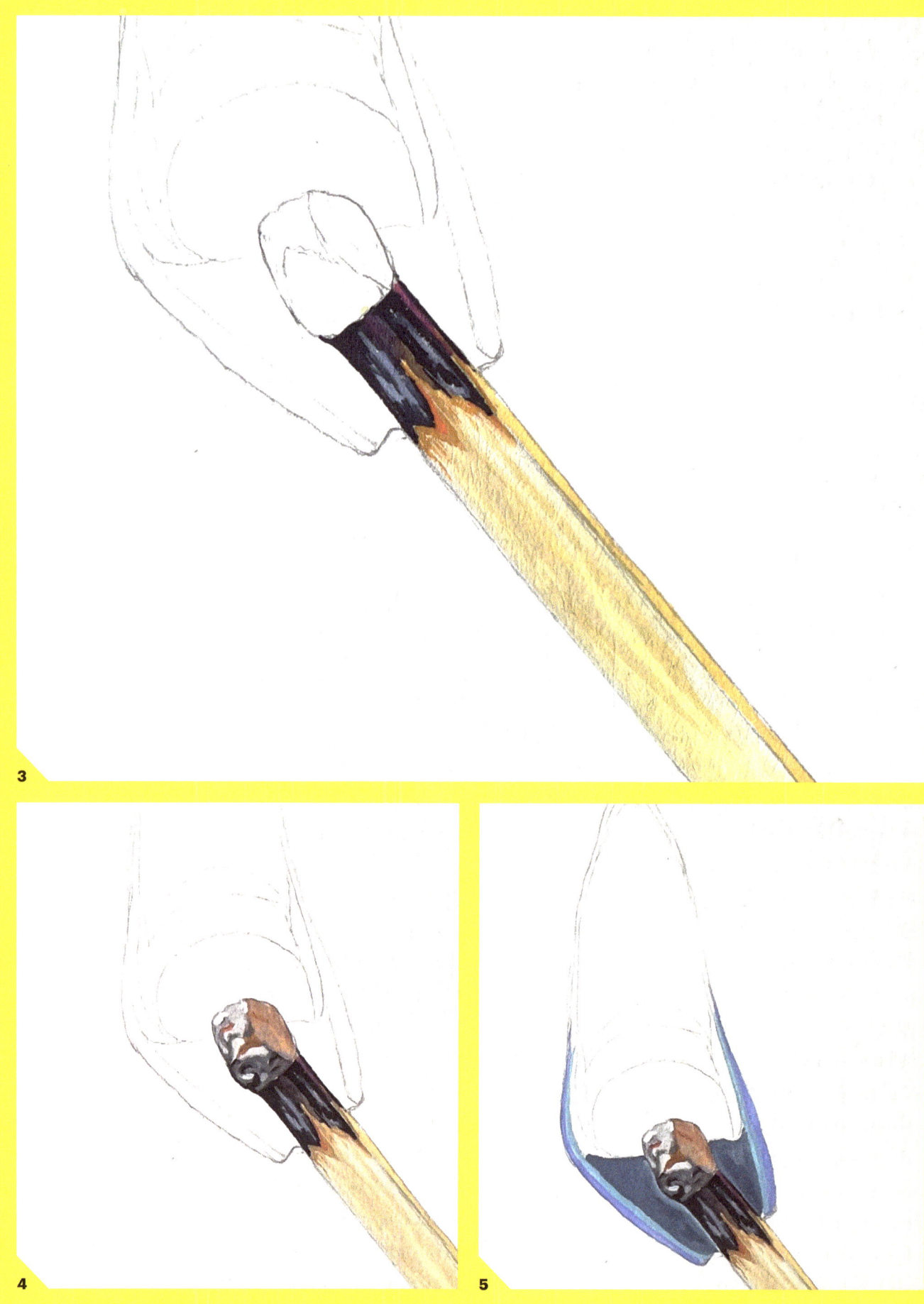

3

4

5

3 And now for the fun part . . . the PAINT!

Because there are some very delicate lines, I moved between using two brushes on this step: my smallest round brush and a No. 4 filbert.

I don't have a set way I begin my paintings. Sometimes I begin on the background, while other times I begin on the object in the foreground. Here we'll paint the entire matchstick and flame before we add the dark background.

To create a light wood color, I blended a bit of tan paint with very small amounts of yellow and white. The right edge of the matchstick has a bit of a darker hue, which I achieved with a bit of ochre mixed with tan. This can also be used on top of the pale part to give it a bit of grain. If you want the left edge of the match to pop a bit, you can add a small amount of white.

You'll notice that the very top of the matchstick, where the unburnt wood transitions into the burnt wood, there's a small section that's darker ochre. You can even add a bit of orange to this if you want to really accentuate it before moving into the black.

As you studied the reference photo before you began painting, did you notice there was actually a bit of grayish-blue in the charred part of the match?

———————————

BRUSHES: *No. 1 round and No. 4 filbert*

4 Remember that sort of diamond-like shape we drew on the right side of the match head? That portion will have the most color. To mix the correct color, try adding a bit of ochre with a small amount of gray, and even a tiny bit of lavender. You can choose to use the filbert or the round brush. Whatever you're most comfortable with.

You can use that same lavender-gray mixture on the lower portion of the match head. For the top, lighten your previous color with a bit of white.

The small crevices will definitely require your smallest brush. Notice that the crevices aren't all the same color. Those in the bottom left are the same black as the charred part of the stick, and they change as they move toward the top.

To finish off the match head, add a few brighter white highlights to the very tip.

———————————

BRUSHES: *No. 1 round and No. 4 filbert*

5 Notice there's quite a lot of blue in the bottom portion of the flame. Because many match heads contain different chemicals, the blue is caused by a chemical reaction at the beginning of the burn. And it definitely makes for a more interesting painting!

Using your brightest blue, paint a thin line with your small round brush, running up from the bottom of the flame and tapering out about halfway to the top. Next to that blue add another blue, this one much more turquoise. Again, taper this color out where the previous color did.

The middle portion of the flame is a bit darker and grayer. Using a mid-toned blue, mix in a very small portion of orange to create a dark gray. To retain more of the blue hue, be sure to not add too much orange.

To make the edge of the matchstick stand out from the dark background, run a very small amount of turquoise along the edge and blend it well into the darker blue you just painted.

———————————

BRUSH: *No. 1 round*

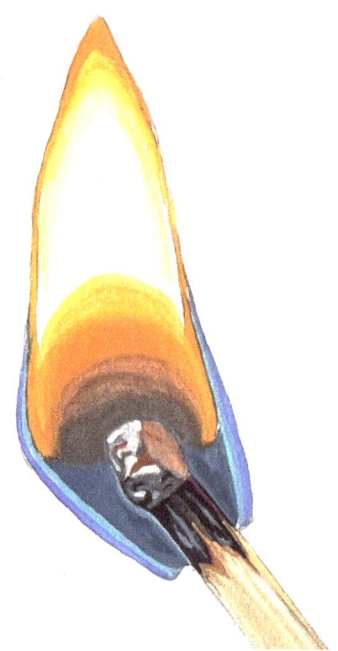

6

You'll remember from the blue-orange we mixed in step 5, these two colors gray each other out. This time we want a more dominant orange color. To achieve this, use your dark orange and mix a small amount of blue into it. You'll fill the rest of the crescent shape with this color, blending the edge of it into the color above.

To make the inside of your flame really glow, load up a clean brush with a good amount of white and fill in the entire center portion of your flame. Before the white has dried, add a small amount of pale yellow to the edge of your clean brush and draw it along the outside edge of the white, right next to the darker yellow. After rinsing your brush, you can finish blending the yellow into the edge of the white, making sure to keep it pure white in the center.

BRUSHES: *No. 1 round and No. 4 filbert*

6 Next up we're going to bring this flame to life! The range of oranges and yellows inside the flame are the most eye-catching part of this image, and if you're anything like me, this is the part I'm always the most excited about painting.

Yellows can easily be contaminated by darker colors in your palette, so before you begin, make sure your brushes are clean. Choose a bright yellow and paint it on the inside of your reference line, running it along the entirety of the inside of the flame. You'll continue the shape of it down along the edge of that blue.

Transitioning to a bright orange, continue the crescent shape of the flame at the bottom, and also paint a bit at the very top of the flame. Along the line of the crescent shape where the yellow and the orange meet, blend the edges of the colors together. Dampen the end of your brush and lightly paint over that edge to soften the colors together.

Start with the darker orange color, filling in the top part of that crescent shape and blending into the orange above it, following the same step you just did.

7 We've predominantly been using small brushes for the majority of this painting, but now it's time to break out a brush that can cover a larger area as we finish up the background.

Because you'll use so much of the same color on this background, you'll want a whole bunch mixed up to the consistency of whole milk or half-and-half. The color I'm using in the background is a mix between black and violet. I want a very dark color, but I rarely use pure black because I find it much more exciting to use a more vibrant dark.

With your No. 8 filbert, begin filling in the back of your image. Start along the edges, making sure to follow the tape so the edges will be cleanly filled. Next, carefully follow the edge of your matchstick up about two-thirds of the way. Then, branching out in a circular shape, make an arch around the flame, like a halo. With your brush partially dried, drag it slightly into the white part of the circle so the edge isn't as sharp.

BRUSH: *No. 8 filbert*

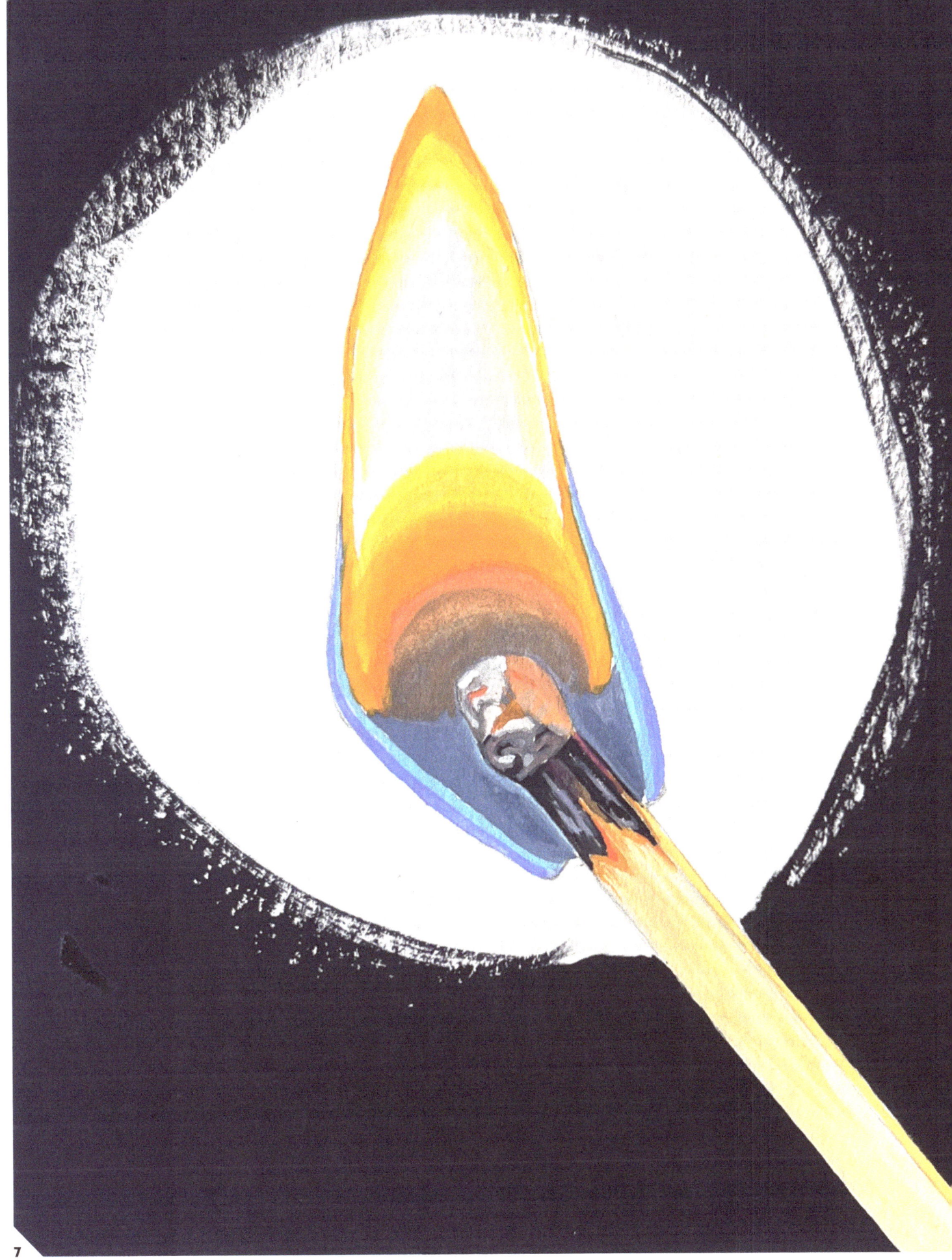

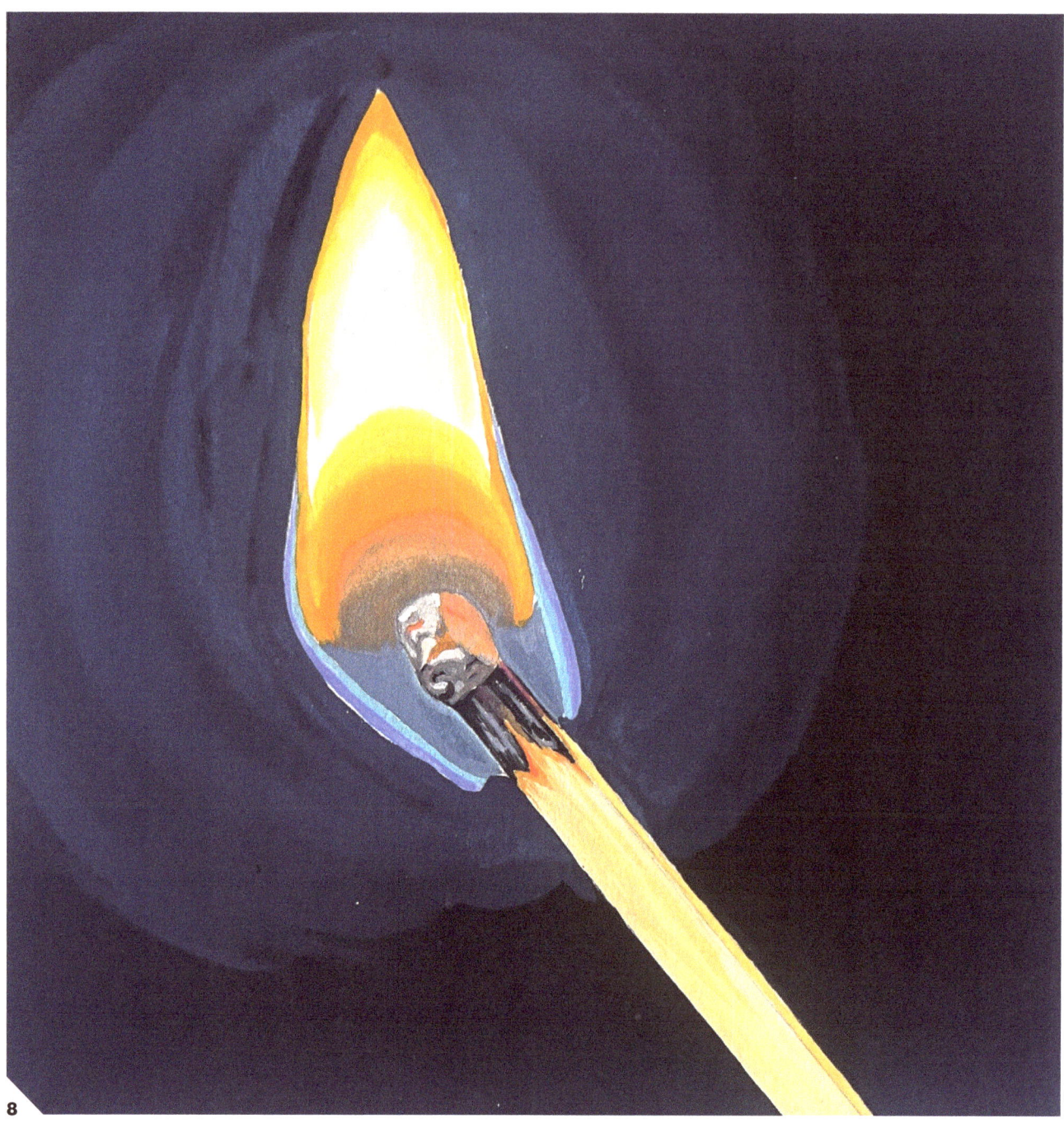

8

8 To create a glowing effect, blend a slightly lighter blue-black in the center part of the halo you just painted around the flame.

In the same way you applied the paint in the previous step, continue filling in the paper, following arched strokes. You'll blend the background colors together with a damp brush, brushing the paint in the arched shape to amplify the halo effect.

When you get to the edge of the flame, you may want to switch to a smaller brush so you have a bit more control over the edges.

_____

BRUSHES: *Nos. 8 round and 4 filbert*

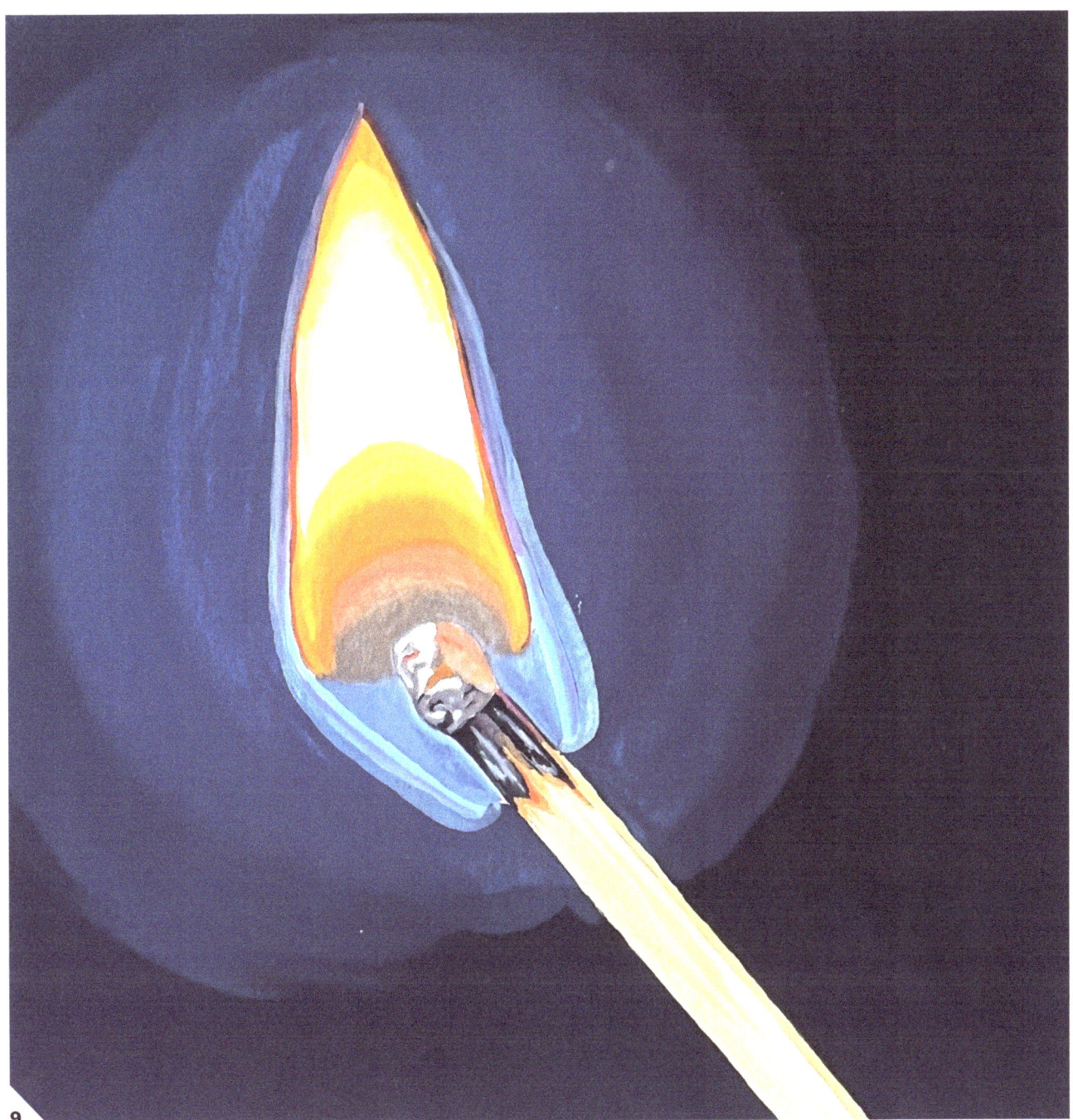

9

9 At this point we're just putting the finishing touches on this painting. To begin, pick up a small amount of red on the tip of your brush, drawing a fine line around the outside of the orange flame. The edge of this brushstroke can stay pretty sharp—just make sure it's a delicate stroke.

Next, mix a bit of turquoise and light green to create a minty color. Using your small brush, blend this minty color along the outside edge of the flame, adding a bit more of the color at the bottom near the blue part of the flame, and tapering off at the very top.

If there are any small changes you'd like to make, or places where you want to touch up any paint, now is the time.

Congratulations on completing your first project!

_____

BRUSH: *No. 1 round*

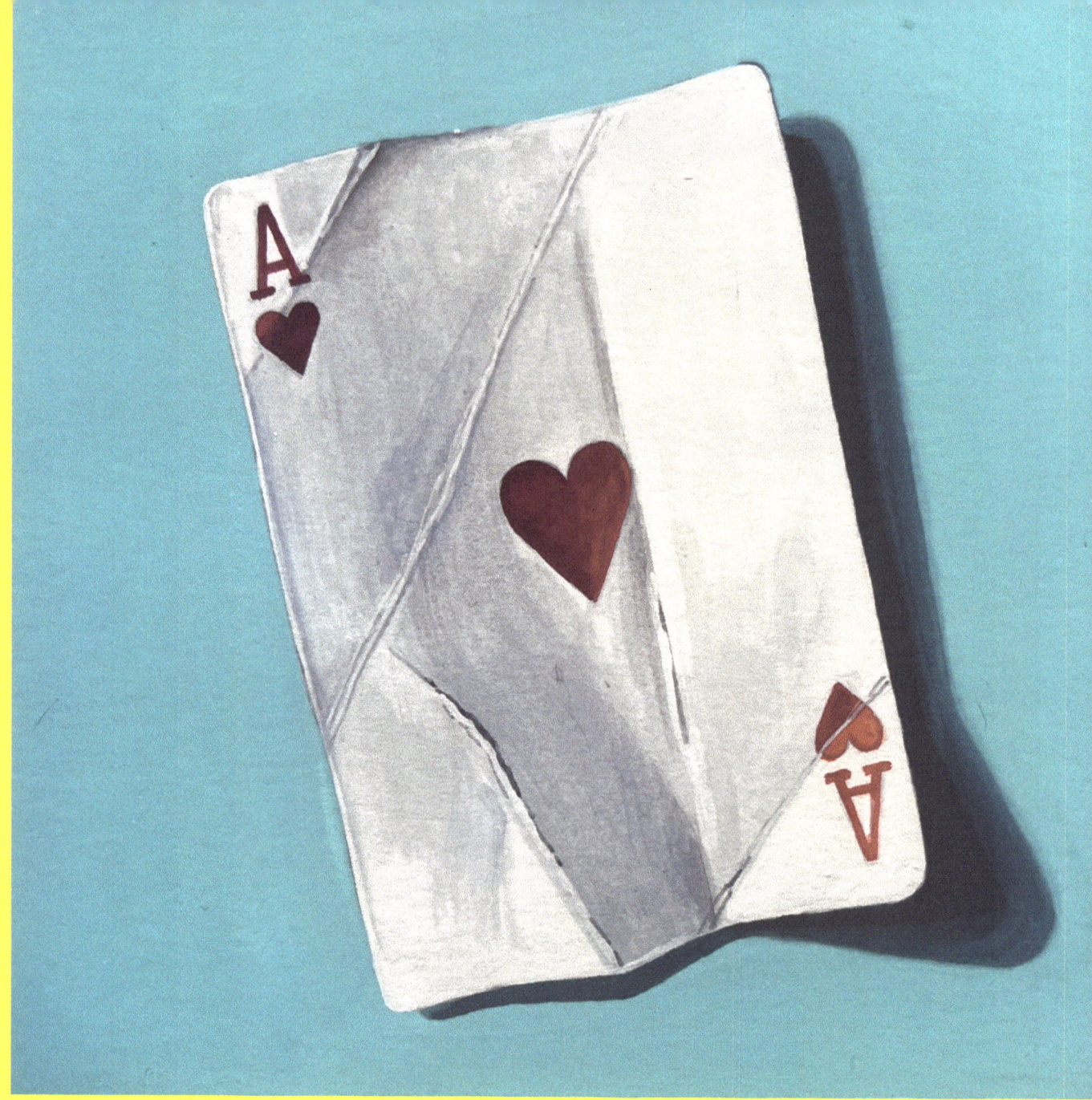

Painting Lettering

ACE OF HEARTS

One of my favorite things to paint is lettering. It's a fun and unique way to add something special to your art, whether it's in a sign on a building or on a candy bar wrapper.

Lettering can often be intimidating, but if you think of it as shapes that can be broken down and viewed in a more structural and abstract way, you'll find it's far less difficult than you might have assumed.

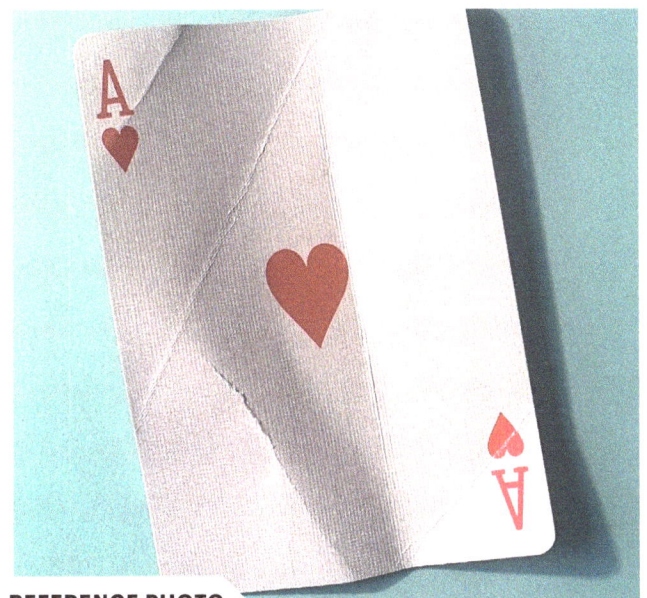

REFERENCE PHOTO

1 The underdrawing is important in every painting, but when dealing with lettering, it's especially important. You'll be using fairly thick paint (either the texture of thick cream or butter) to paint your letters. Because of this, it's difficult to go back over them to make many changes.

I've kept my lines fairly light inside the card, especially on the letters, so the pencil lines don't show through the paint. You'll also notice I only lightly sketched in the shape of the A without thinking about the width of the line. This is because I'm using my underdrawing as a guide, not as a shape to fill in.

2 You'll be doing both big swaths of color and some smaller details, so I recommend using a large flat or filbert (No. 6 or 8) as well as a smaller filbert (No. 4).

The background and shadow are helpful to lay in first in this painting because they add a basis for comparing the lighter tones of the card once we start adding the subtle shadows. When mixing the colors for your shadows, keep your paint the consistency of heavy cream. I applied two coats of turquoise, making sure the first layer was fully dried before applying the second layer.

The shadow is darker next to the card and blends into a lighter shadow toward the edge. I recommend starting with the darker shadow and working your way outward. To soften the edge of your shadow, run a thin, damp brush lightly along the shadow's edge to blend it lightly.

BRUSHES: *Nos. 4, 6, and 8 filbert*

1

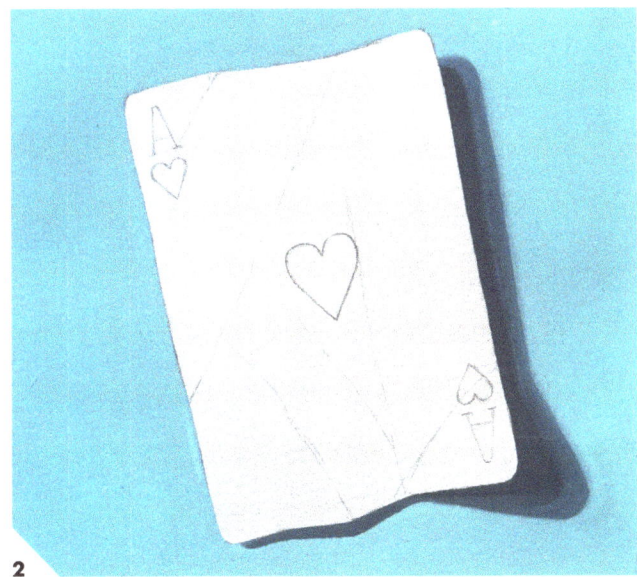

2

Tip

One of the things I want you to notice is how your brain treats the letter differently when it's flipped upside down. You can remember this as a useful technique. When it's upside down, you can more easily focus on the angle of the lines, the distance between edges, and the width of the marks.

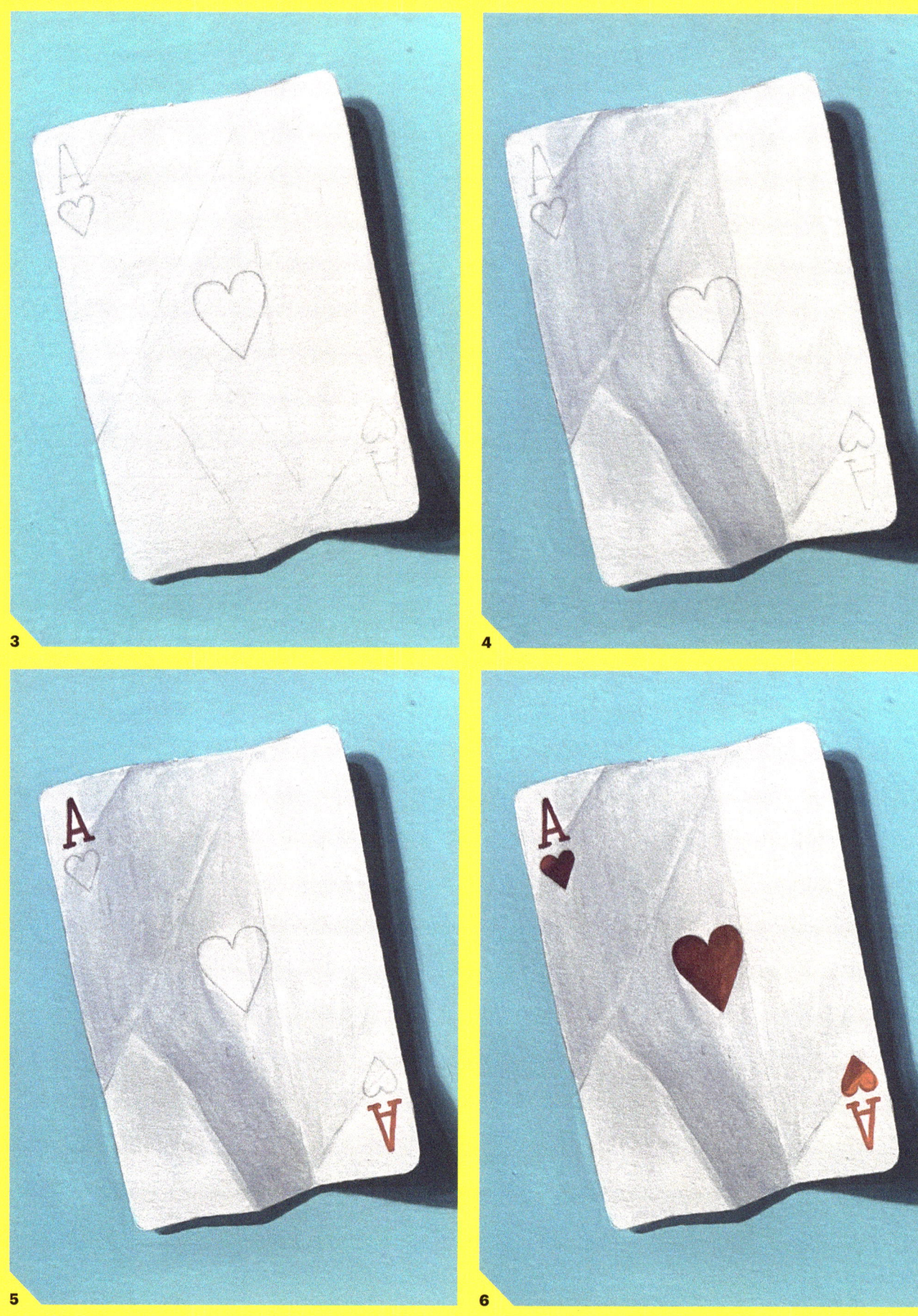

3 To get a nice white base to work off of for the card, you're going to water down a small amount of white to a thin consistency, between milk and water. Carefully cover the entire card, being sure to keep a nice crisp edge along the sides. Don't worry about covering your underdrawing. Because the paint is thinned down, your drawing will show through just fine when it has dried.

_____

BRUSH: *No. 6 filbert*

4 During this step you'll add the shadows to the card to accentuate the folds in the paper. Take a moment to study the reference photo to get a good sense of the subtle differences in the shadows. The gray tones you'll want to mix for these shadows are quite blue. Experiment with mixing a few different grays and painting them on an extra piece of paper before you begin painting on your card. You will probably want to paint these shadows with a few layers, so remember to keep your paint fairly thin (milk).

_____

BRUSHES: *No. 1 round and Nos. 4 and 6 filbert*

5 You've made it to the fun part: lettering! Before you jump right in, take a moment to notice that the As are not the same color red because of the way the card is folded. When mixing your colors, you want to have a lot of pigment in your paint, meaning the paint will be pretty thick. When loading your brush, make sure to only get paint on the top half to quarter of the brush to avoid paint drips or globs, giving you an uneven line.

Lettering can be delicate work so take your time. You've already spent time getting the shape of your letter down, so move slowly and precisely. This is a good place to think about negative as well as positive space. For example, the white triangle inside the A is quite long and narrow, which will help you fill the tall shape of the A and will help with the placement of the lines.

_____

BRUSH: *No. 1 round*

6 As you move on to the red hearts, notice that the colors of the red change, depending on how much light they receive. In the places where the heart is in full light, the red is very bright. You can achieve this by using an orange/red.

As the red moves into shadow, you'll use a darker crimson color. If the red you have still doesn't appear dark enough, try adding some dark violet to it to deepen the value. If you add black to your red to darken it, it will dull the color quite a bit.

_____

BRUSHES: *No. 1 round and No. 4 filbert*

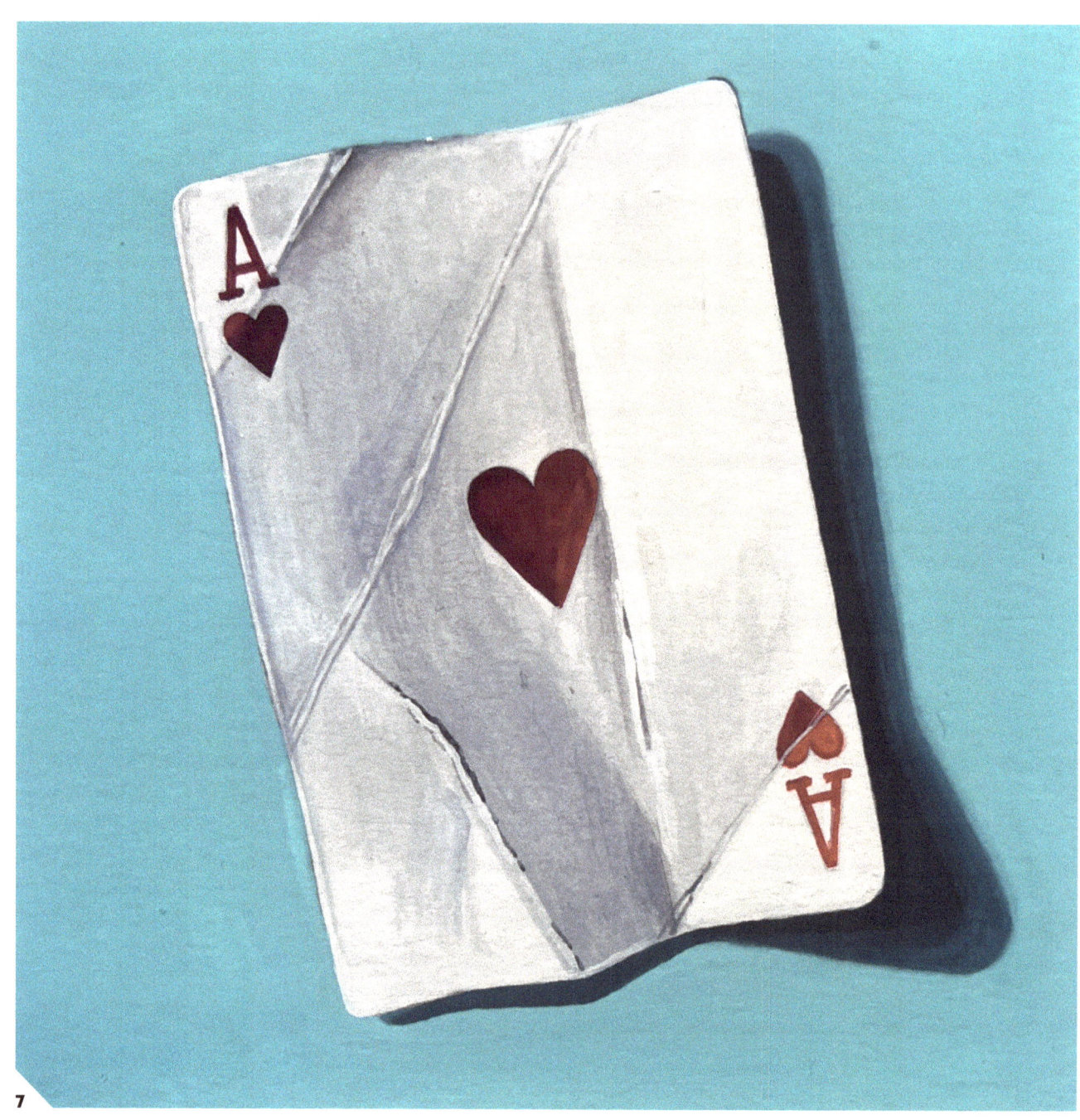

7

7 The next two steps focus on refining your shadows and adding to the details of the folds in the paper. As you've added some darker values to your card, you may notice the shadows you added earlier might not look as dark in comparison. This is totally normal. You can adjust those shadows by adding thin layers of gray with one of your filberts.

As you look at the reference photo, notice that the folds of the card create their own small shadow along the creased edge. You can use your No. 1 round to darken this shadowed edge. Use the smallest amount of paint on the very tip of your brush to keep these lines really delicate.

_____

BRUSHES: *No. 1 round and Nos. 4 and 6 filbert*

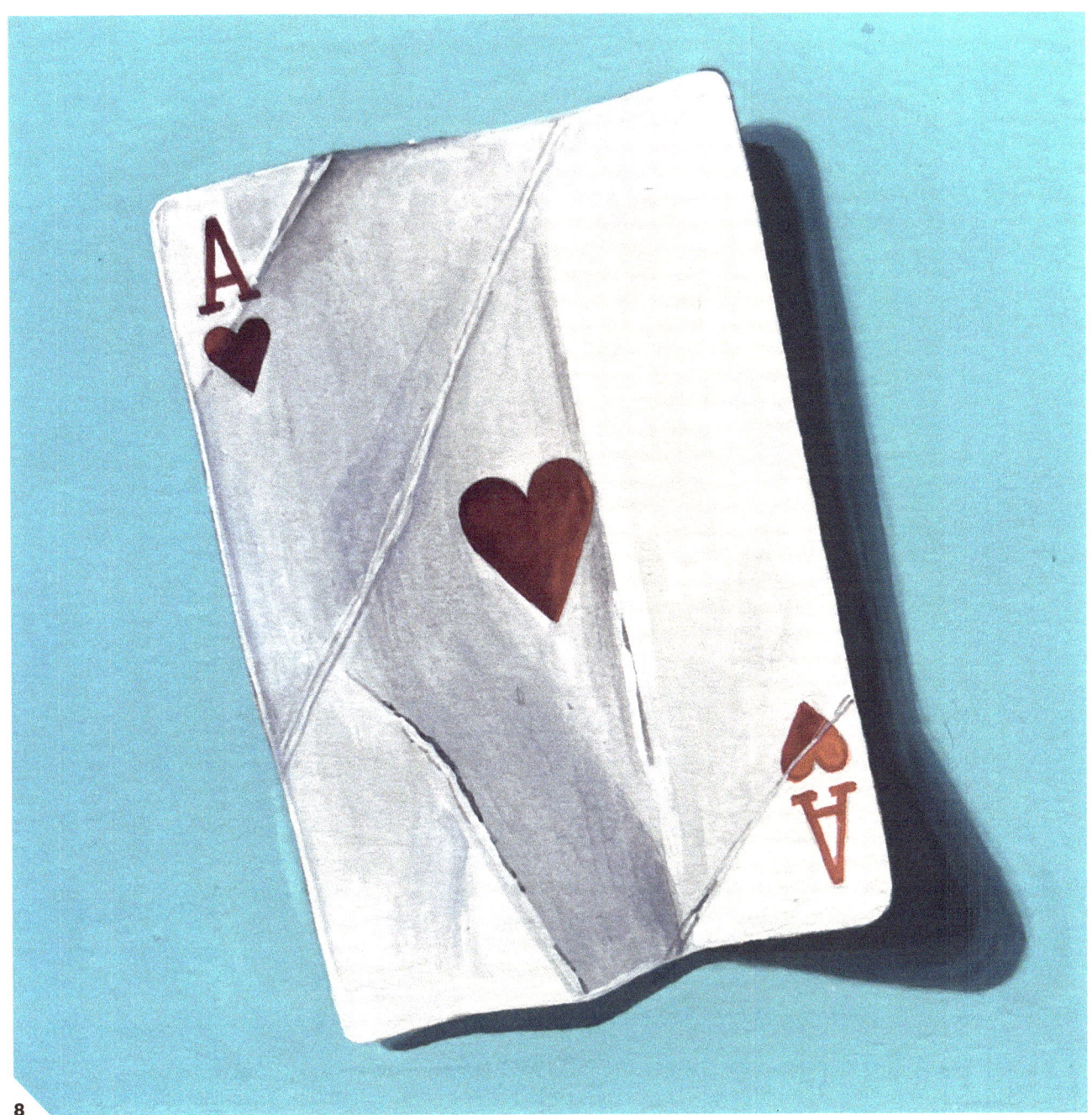

8

8 For the final step, you'll focus on the areas of white in your painting that you really want to POP. Pay close attention to the edges of your card so you can create a nice, crisp edge. Again, be careful when using your No. 1 round. Try not to add too much paint to your brush. These final touches can be quite small, but a little bit can go a long way.

BRUSH: *No. 1 round*

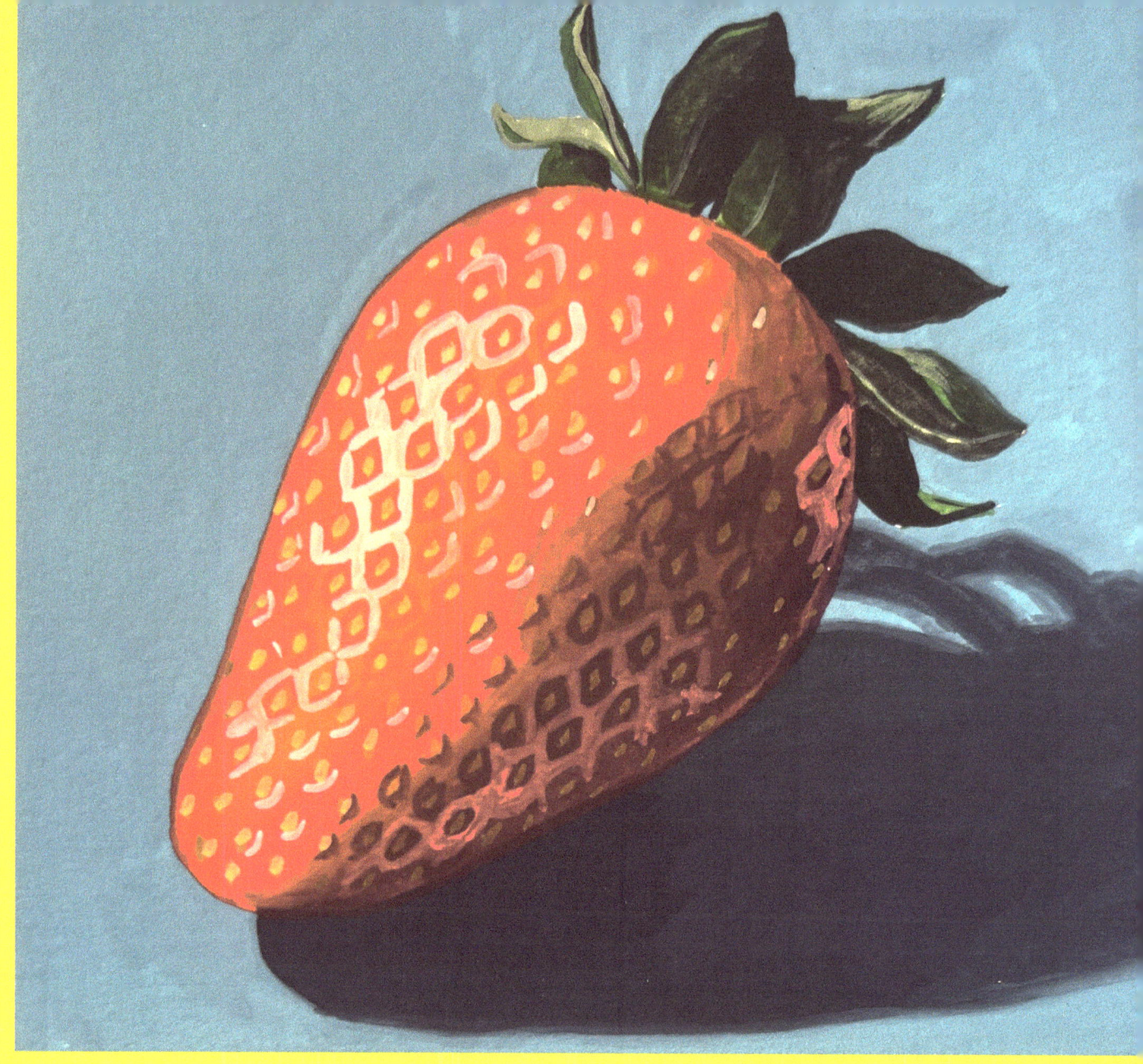

Painting Texture with Highlights

STRAWBERRY

During this project you'll encounter a number of different textures all contained in one object (the strawberry). You'll see the way light reacts differently on the fleshy surface of the berry as opposed to the small seeds and the less shiny leaves. Because the surface of the berry is pocked with those tiny seeds, the light reflects differently off the areas with direct lighting, as opposed to the places receiving only a small amount of reflected light. The strong highlights you'll be able to achieve are a great example of how highlights can give so much dimension to a subject.

1 As you begin drawing your berry, don't worry about adding any details within the berry itself. All the seeds and shifts in shadow will be addressed with the paint, so there's no need to spend time on an overly complicated underdrawing.

2 Lay down the flat color in the background, as well as a slightly graded color in the shadow. To avoid streaks, make sure you have an ample amount of creamy paint mixed for at least one coat, possibly two.

When moving on to the shadow use a slightly darker color the closer you are to the underside of the strawberry. A very deep blue works well here. While the paint is still wet, you can add a bit of turquoise to your shadow color, blending it out to the edges of the shadow.

_____

BRUSHES: *No. 6 or No. 8 filbert or flat*

Tip

You can soften the edges of your shadow by wetting a smaller brush (a No. 1 round works well for this) and running it along the edge of the shadow and the background, which will slightly blend the colors.

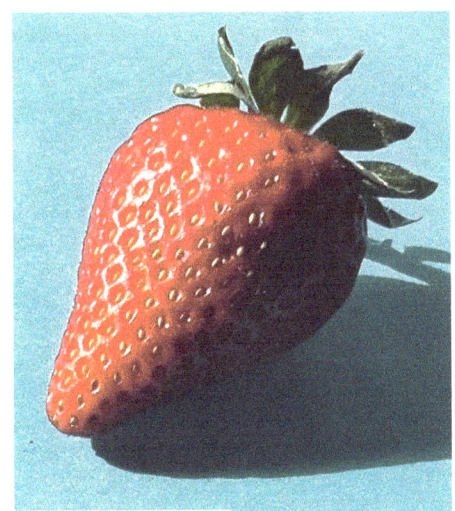

REFERENCE PHOTO

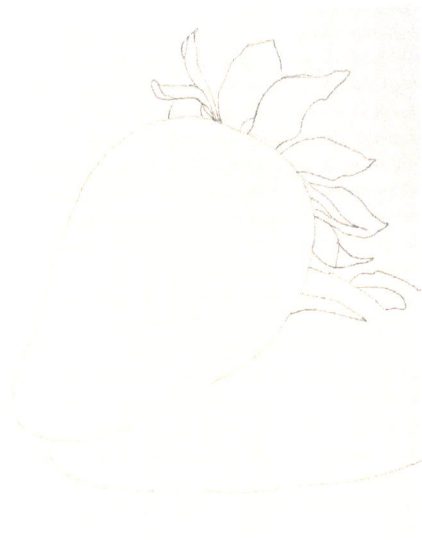

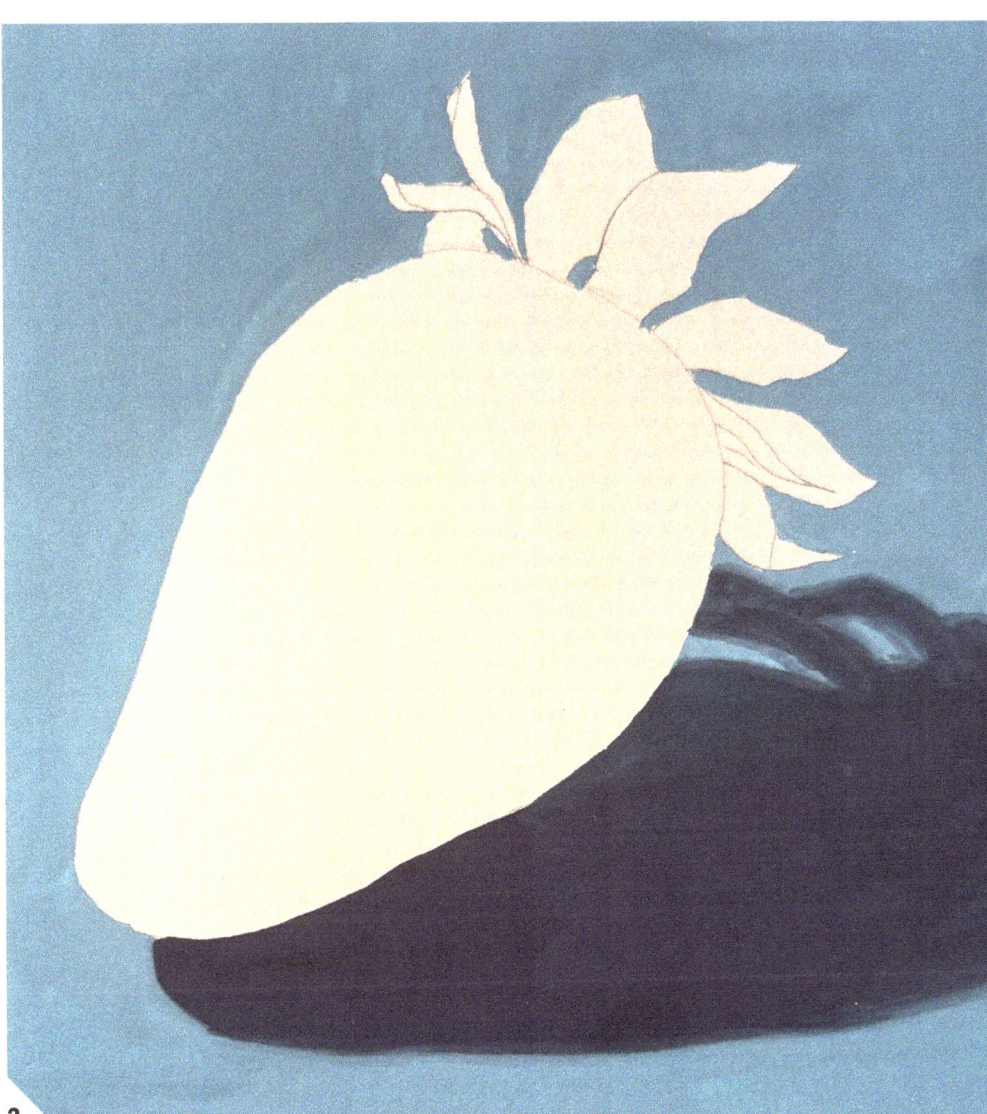

1

2

3 With a clean, wet brush, add a stripe of yellow-orange to the section of the berry with the most direct light in the reference photo. (You will blend this with red, so it won't end up this yellow.) Around that stripe of yellow add some bright red, bringing it all the way to the left-hand edge of the berry. After rinsing your brush, soften the edges of your red, blending it into the yellow.

BRUSHES: *No. 4 or 6 filbert*

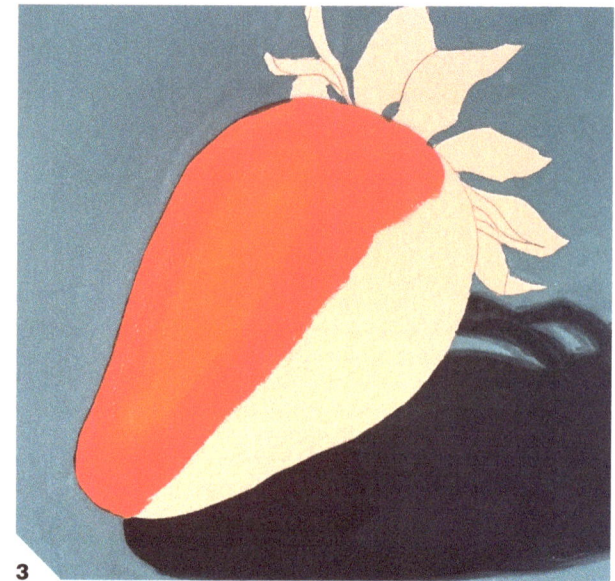

4 Using a deeper crimson, paint along the entire edge of the part you just painted, extending the right edge slightly. Next, with a very dark crimson mixed with deep violet (and a small amount of black), fill in the remainder of the right-hand side of the berry.

BRUSHES: *No. 4 or 6 filbert*

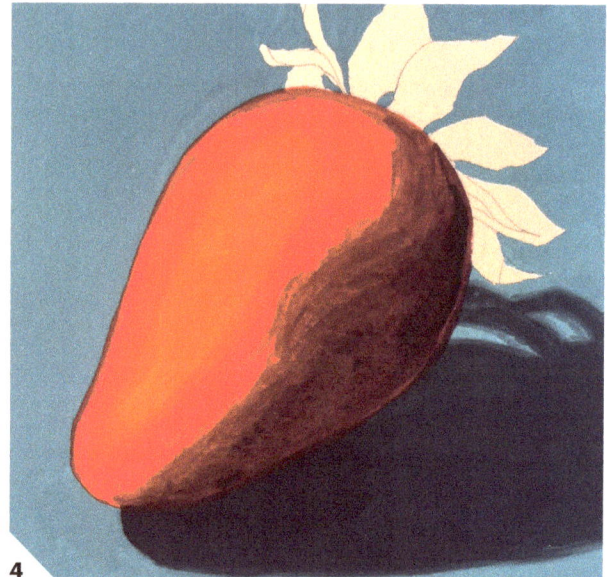

5 The addition of the seeds will really start bringing your berry to life. Pay attention to how the yellow of the seeds in the direct light is so much brighter than the seeds in the shadow, which are closer to a greenish/ochre than a traditional yellow.

I like to pick a line of seeds toward the center of the berry to start painting first, because the rest of the rows will be easier to base off this one. The line of seeds moves diagonally up the berry from left to right. Finish one row completely, even though you'll need to switch between light and dark coloring for the seeds. When moving on to the next rows, stagger the seeds so they're placed between each of the seeds on the next line. Continue until the berry is covered.

BRUSH: *No. 1 round*

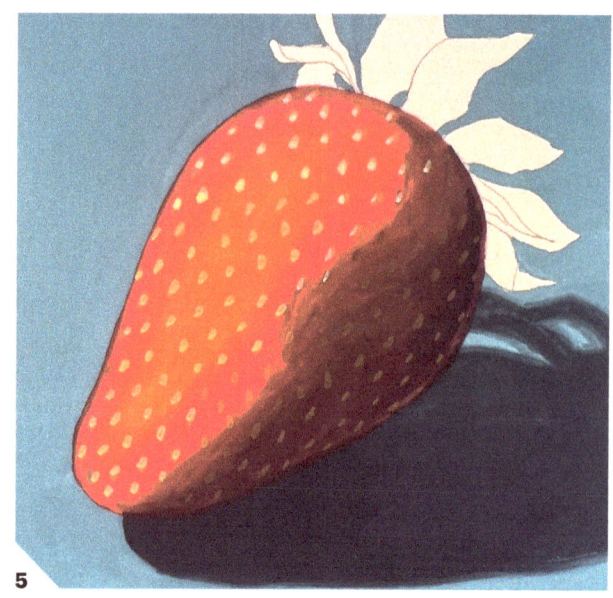

6 With a slightly darker color than the bright red on the lit part of the berry, outline the seeds. It's not necessary to do ALL of them, but outline the majority. In the shadowed part of the berry you'll need to mix an even darker shade of crimson, including more violet and/or black.

BRUSH: *No. 1 round*

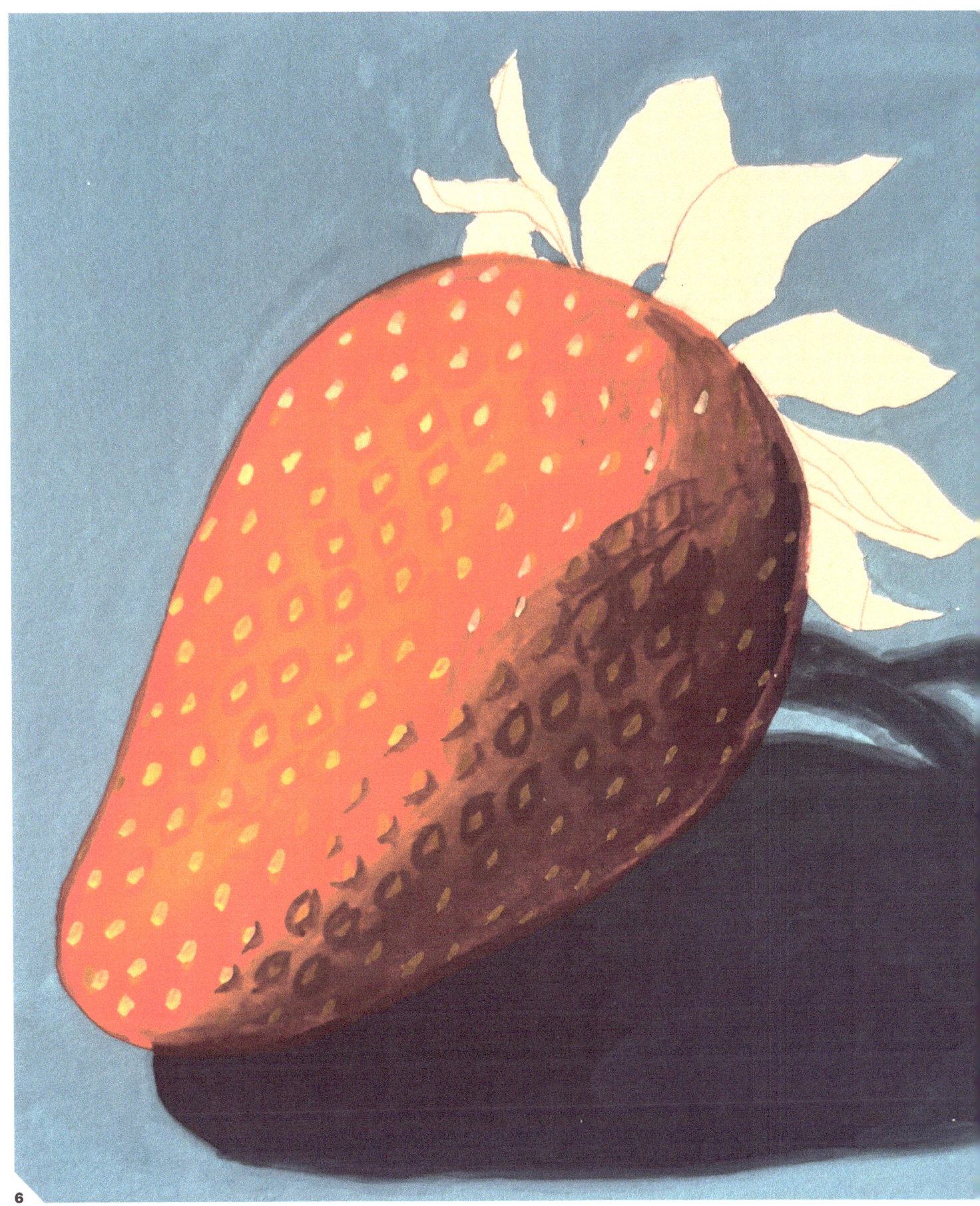

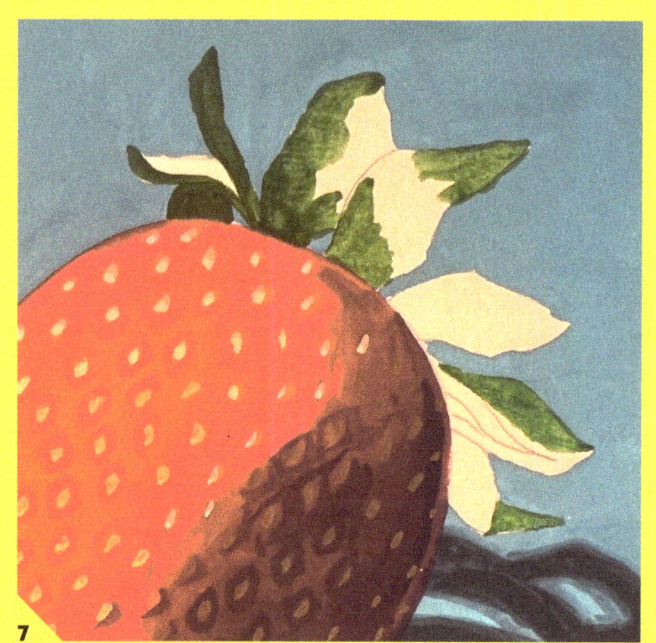

7

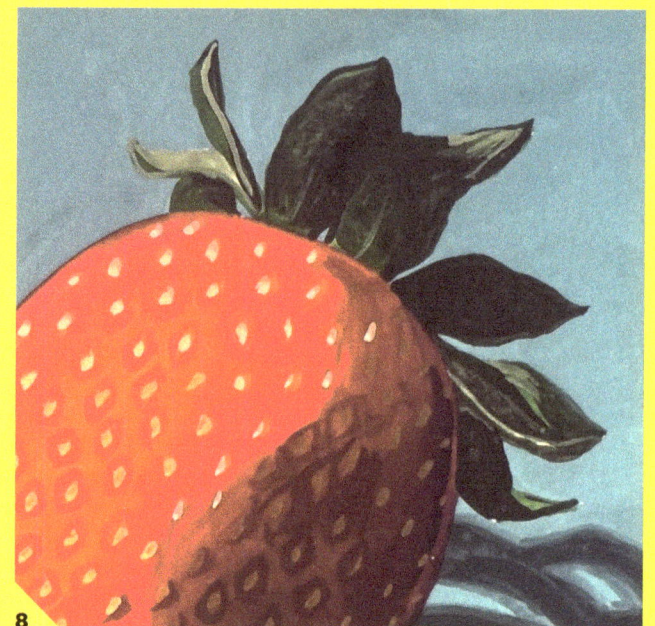

8

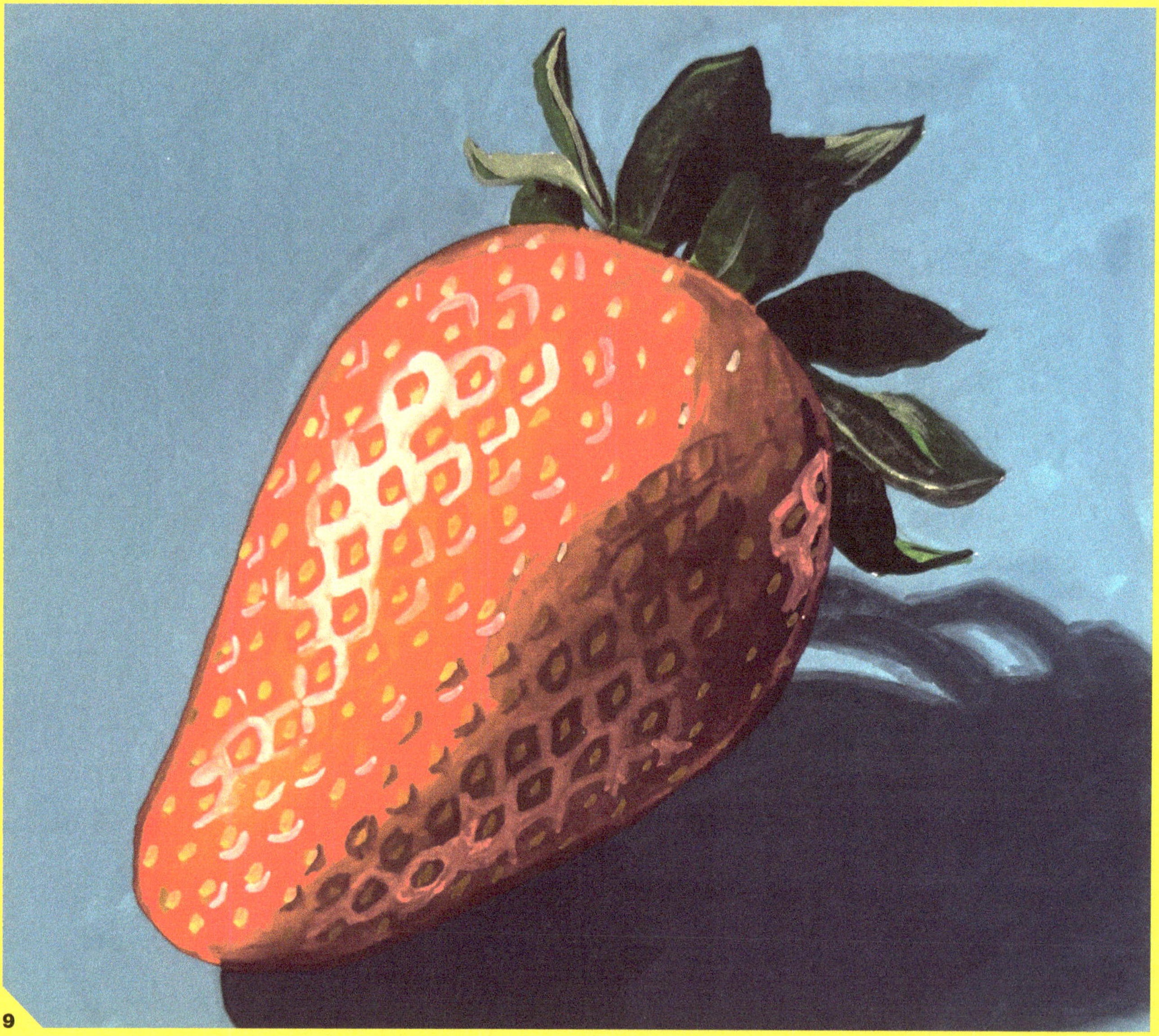

9

7 You'll be working on the leaves for the next two steps. I find it helpful to block in the lighter greens before I move on to the darker ones so I don't go too dark too fast. It's easier to make greens darker than to make them lighter. This is because greens tend to be a bit more transparent than other colors, so if you want a bright green it's best to get those down directly on the white of your paper.

_____

BRUSHES: *No. 1 round and No. 4 filbert*

8 Working from lighter to darker green, continue filling in the leaves, blending the darks into the lights. When you're satisfied with the look of your leaves, you can add a bit of white to your light green to add the highlights. Notice how much more minty this color of green is.

_____

BRUSHES: *No. 1 round and No. 4 filbert*

9 You've made it to the most fun step: highlights and reflected light. If you've ever wanted to feel like a magician, invite someone to watch you complete this step, because they'll definitely "oooo" and "ahhh" over how magical it seems.

Starting with the reflected light, mix a dark pink color for your highlight on the underside of the berry. Observe the reference photo to see the areas most affected by the reflected light. Being careful to not paint up to the very edge of the seeds, make a diamond shape around the seeds, following the lines of the rows you created in step 5.

Now that you've achieved the reflected light, finish off with the bright white in the hot direct light on top of the berry. Again, make those diamond shapes follow the lines of the rows of seeds. Notice that the farther away you move from that spot of direct light, the less fully the highlight surrounds the seed in that diamond shape. In fact, it will begin to make only half of a diamond. This tiny highlight on the side of the seeds will still add a lot of dimension to your painting, so be sure not to overlook it.

Congrats! You've painted a dimensional strawberry!

_____

BRUSH: *No. 1 round*

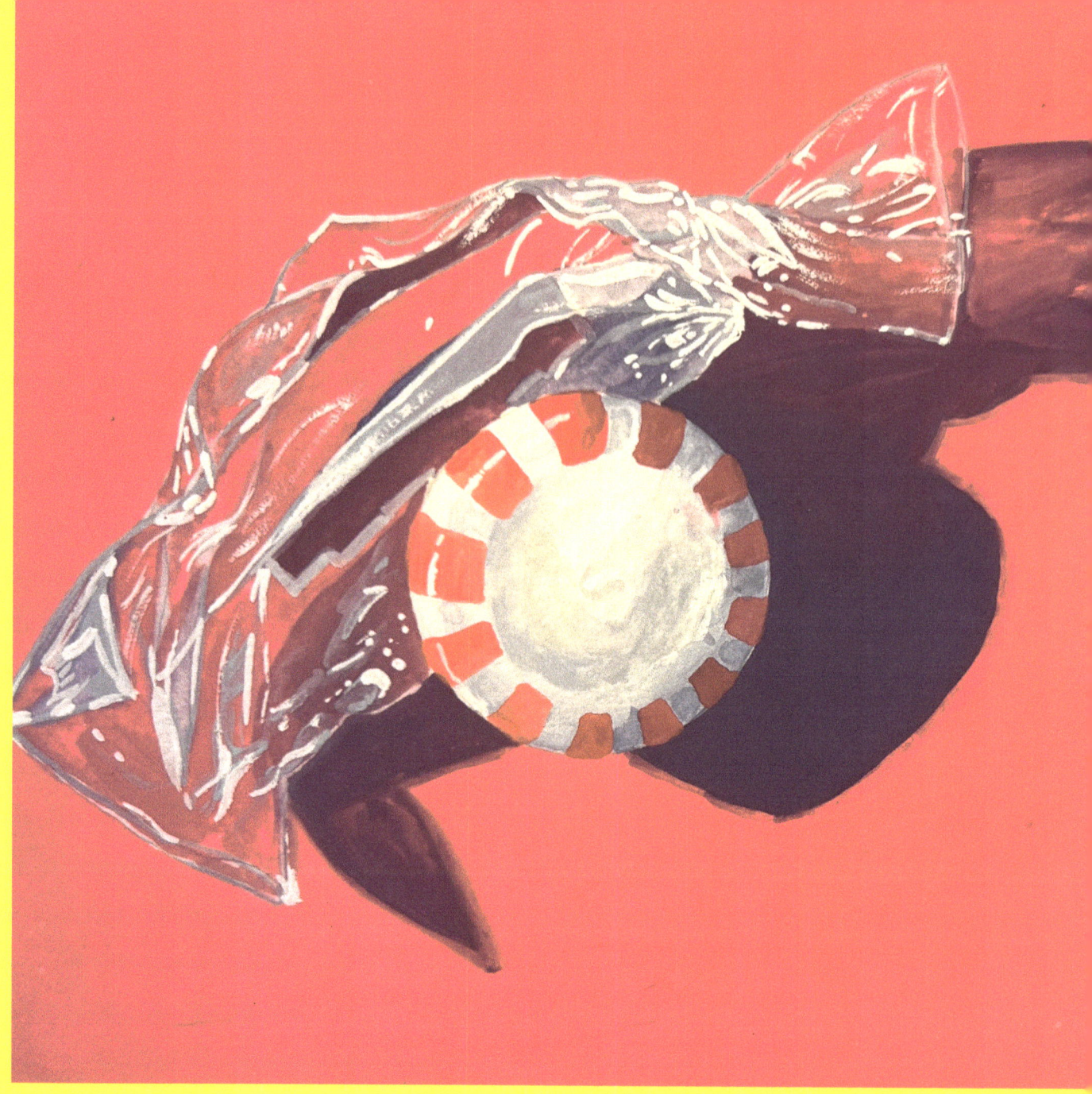

Painting Transparency

CANDY WITH CELLOPHANE WRAPPER

During this lesson, you're going to learn about painting items that read as see-through. For some reason, the thought of painting transparency often feels more intimidating than the actual act of painting it. The fact is, you've already been training yourself how to observe a reference photo and break it down into its more simple forms. You've been learning to pay attention to shadow and highlight. In essence, you've got the skills for this—you just need to put them into practice.

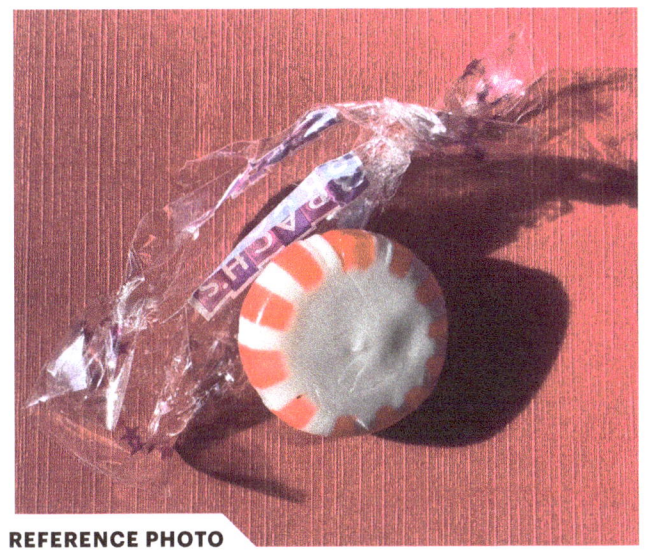

REFERENCE PHOTO

Tip

Unless you're painting perfect realism, you don't need to include every wrinkle and tiny shift in tone. A few well-placed marks actually go a long way.

1 With this drawing, start off by lightly blocking in the placement of the wrapper, the candy, and the shadow. Drawing lightly here will make it so much easier to adjust your drawing. Keep the shape of the wrapper quite simple, trying to include what feels like the most general shapes. When drawing the candy, pay attention to the way the red stripes bend to fit the round contour of the candy.

2 Be sure to mix an ample amount of paint for the background and shadow. Remember, you want enough color mixed to a creamy consistency to be able to cover at least two coats.

When you paint the shadowed area, notice that the shadow directly below the candy is the darkest. As you move to the shadow created by the wrapper, mix some of that colored background in with the gray of the shadow to give the appearance of light traveling through the object.

BRUSHES: *No. 4 and No. 6 filbert or flat*

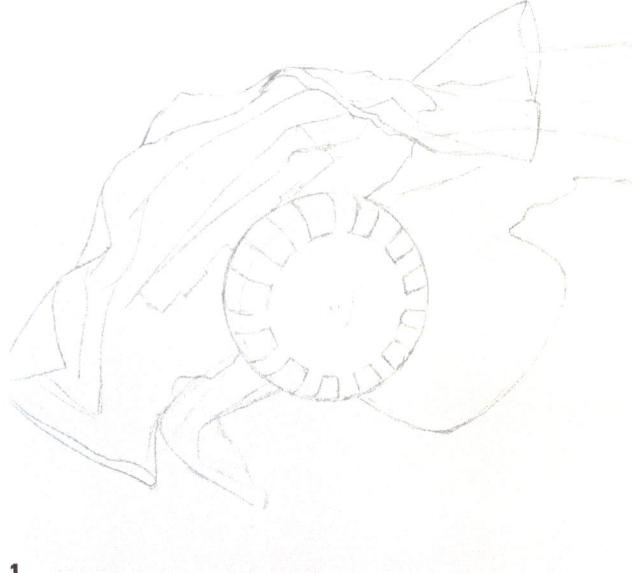

1

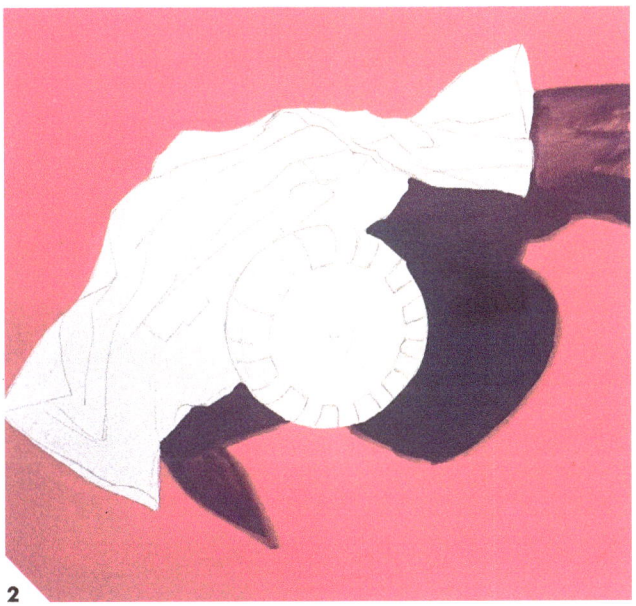

2

3 Using your drawing as your guide, paint just inside the lines using a slightly darker color than the background. Leave the tiniest bit of white to indicate the edge of the wrapper. You may choose to keep a few of the more complicated areas blank for now, but block in the majority. In the place where the shadow of the wrapper shows underneath the cellophane, use a darker gray.

———————

BRUSHES: *No. 1 round and No. 4 filbert or flat*

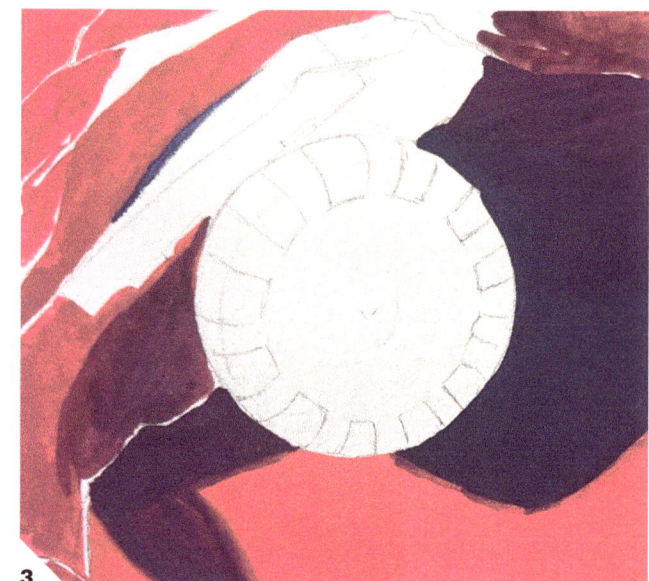

3

4 During this step, you'll add dimension to the candy. I suggest starting by painting the entire candy a pale white before going in with the darker shadows along the right edge. Also, notice there's a small area of shadow on the inner circle along the left side of the candy near the bottom of the stripes. Pay close attention to the subtle changes in the white. I added quite a bit of blue to my shadow color, which I find much more interesting than just mixing white and black to create the gray.

———————

BRUSH: *No. 4 filbert or flat*

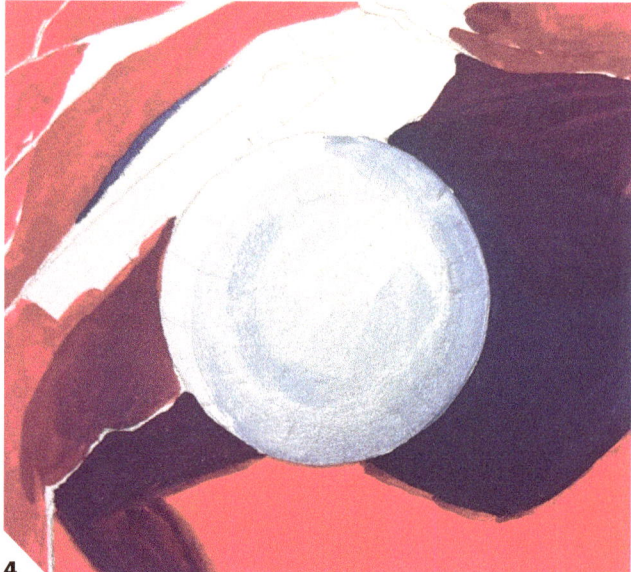

4

5 During this step, you'll finish off the peppermint candy by adding the red stripes. As you begin, start with the brightest red in the areas where direct light hits the candy. You might be tempted to use pure red in these sections, but I suggest adding some orange to your red. Surprisingly, this makes it appear brighter and doesn't end up reading as orange to your eye. As the red moves more into shadow, you can use pure red. For the full shadows, add a bit of violet to your red to achieve the right value.

To finish off the candy, add a small bright white highlight along the edge where the light hits.

———————

BRUSH: *No. 1 round*

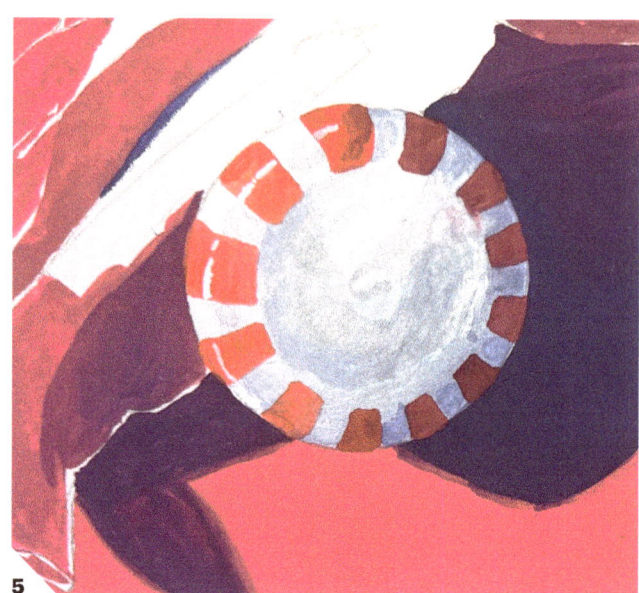

5

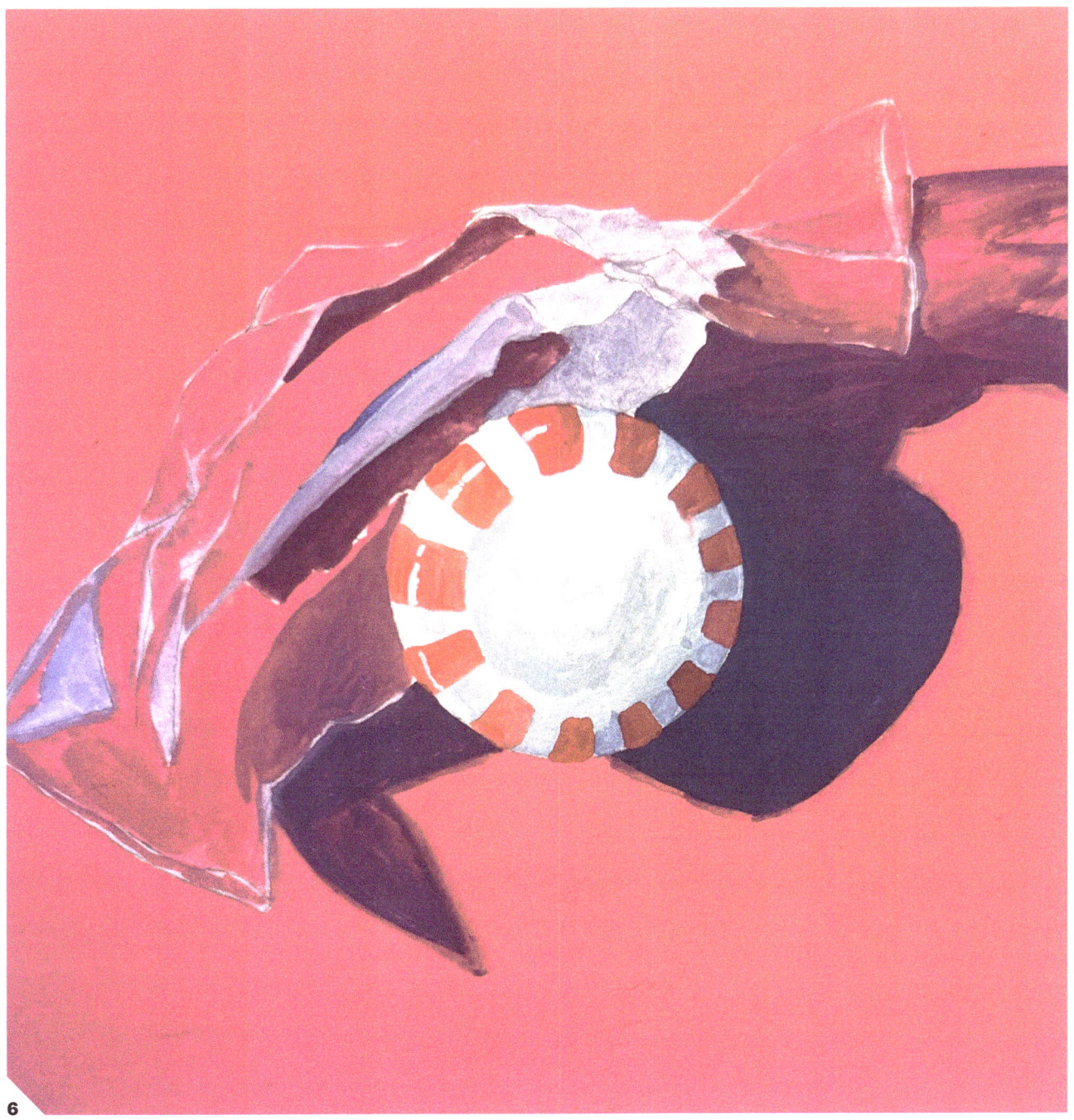

6

6 In the remaining white areas on your candy wrapper, mix a range of grayish blues. You'll use a fairly watery mixture to fill in the whites, with the exception of the places on the wrapper where there's a darker image. For those sections, you can mix a nice cranberry color.

When painting the lighter grayish blues onto the thin, unpainted areas, be sure not to apply too much paint to your brush. You want to make these lines as thin as possible, which will help suggest the illusion of plastic.

———————

BRUSHES: *No. 1 round and No. 4 filbert or flat*

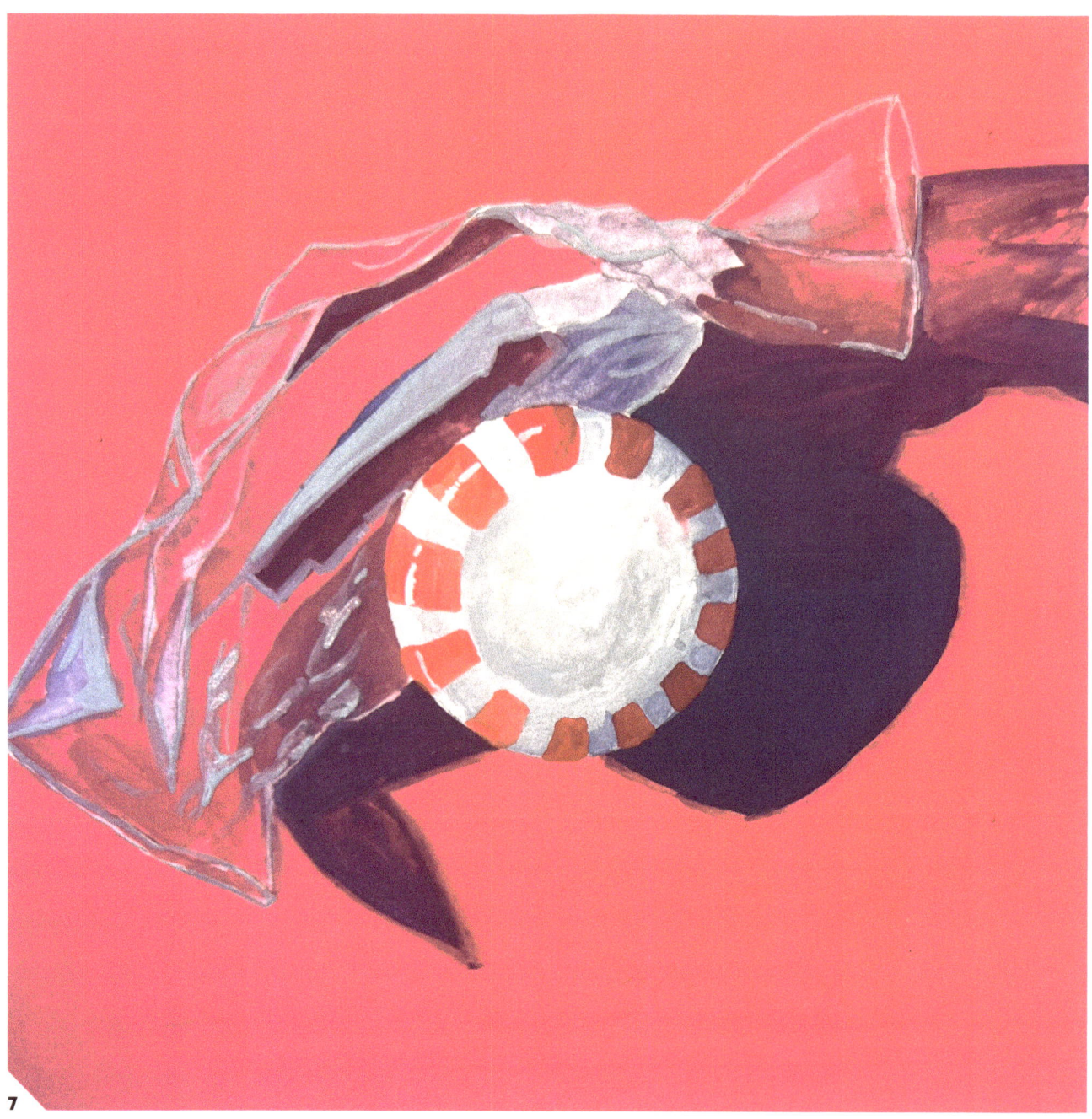

7

For this step, you'll again use a range of bluish grays, but you'll want them to be a bit thicker than in the last step. You can achieve this by mixing more or by allowing the colors you've mixed to evaporate a bit.

Take a good look at the wrapper and pick out the areas where the light seems to reflect the most off the plastic. Often, the small folds create triangular shapes. Without getting too caught up in including every single highlight, pick a half dozen or so to place across the wrapper. One of the important parts of creating a successful painting is being able to edit. Deciding what *not* to include can, at times, be as important as deciding what to include.

BRUSH: *No. 1 round*

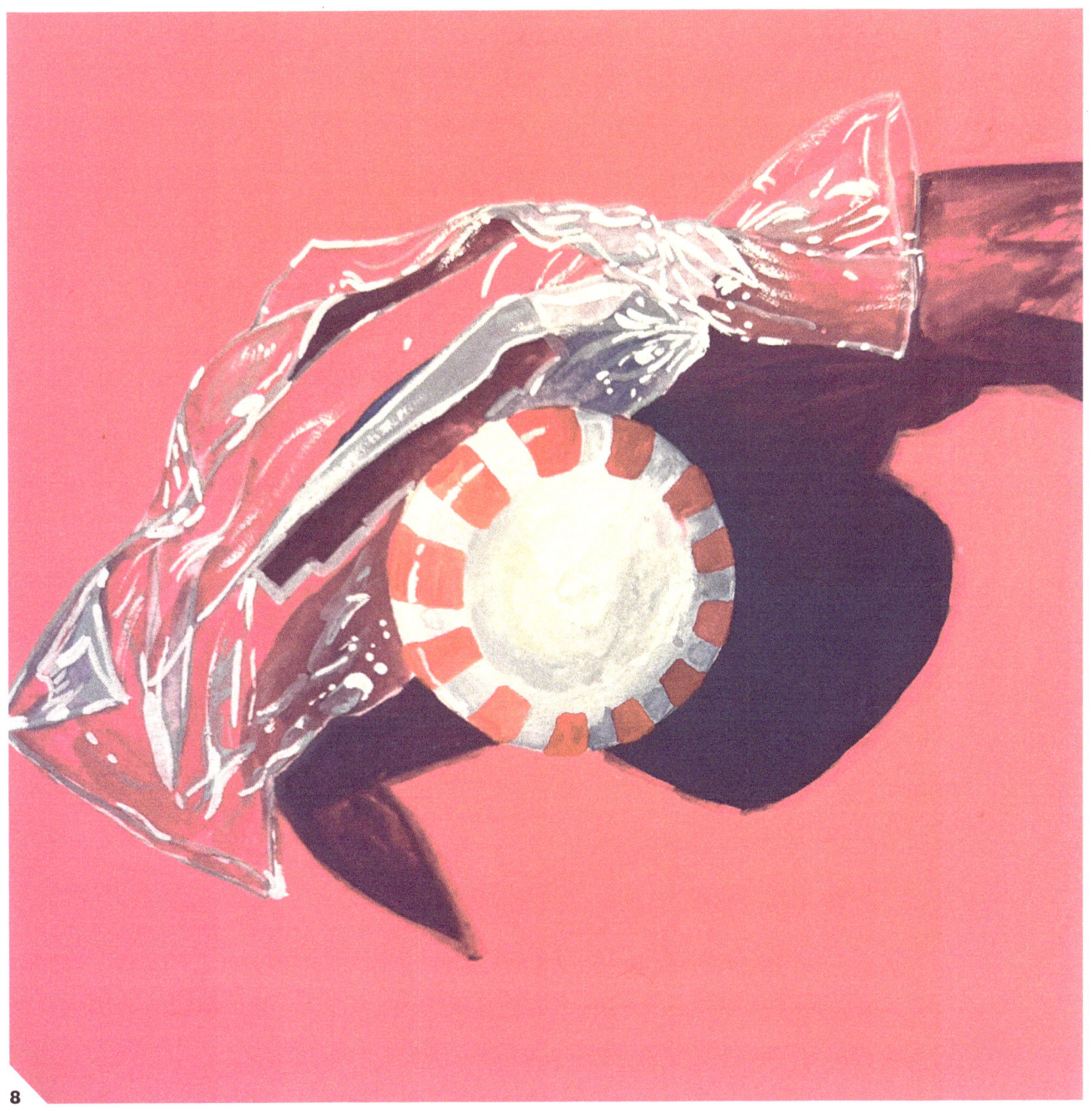

8

8 We've gotten to the most rewarding part of painting plastic: adding the highlights. Using a pure white mixed to a creamy consistency, carefully load the very tip of your brush, making sure there's not too much paint. Without just tracing the outline of the wrapper, look for the places where you can add a pop of bright white, accentuating the folds, while still allowing the bluish gray from the layer below to show as well.

Notice on the right side of the wrapper that these white lines follow the contour of the twisted wrapper. It's these white lines that give it shape. The white lines are most prominent where the wrapper is scrunched together the most.

BRUSH: *No. 1 round*

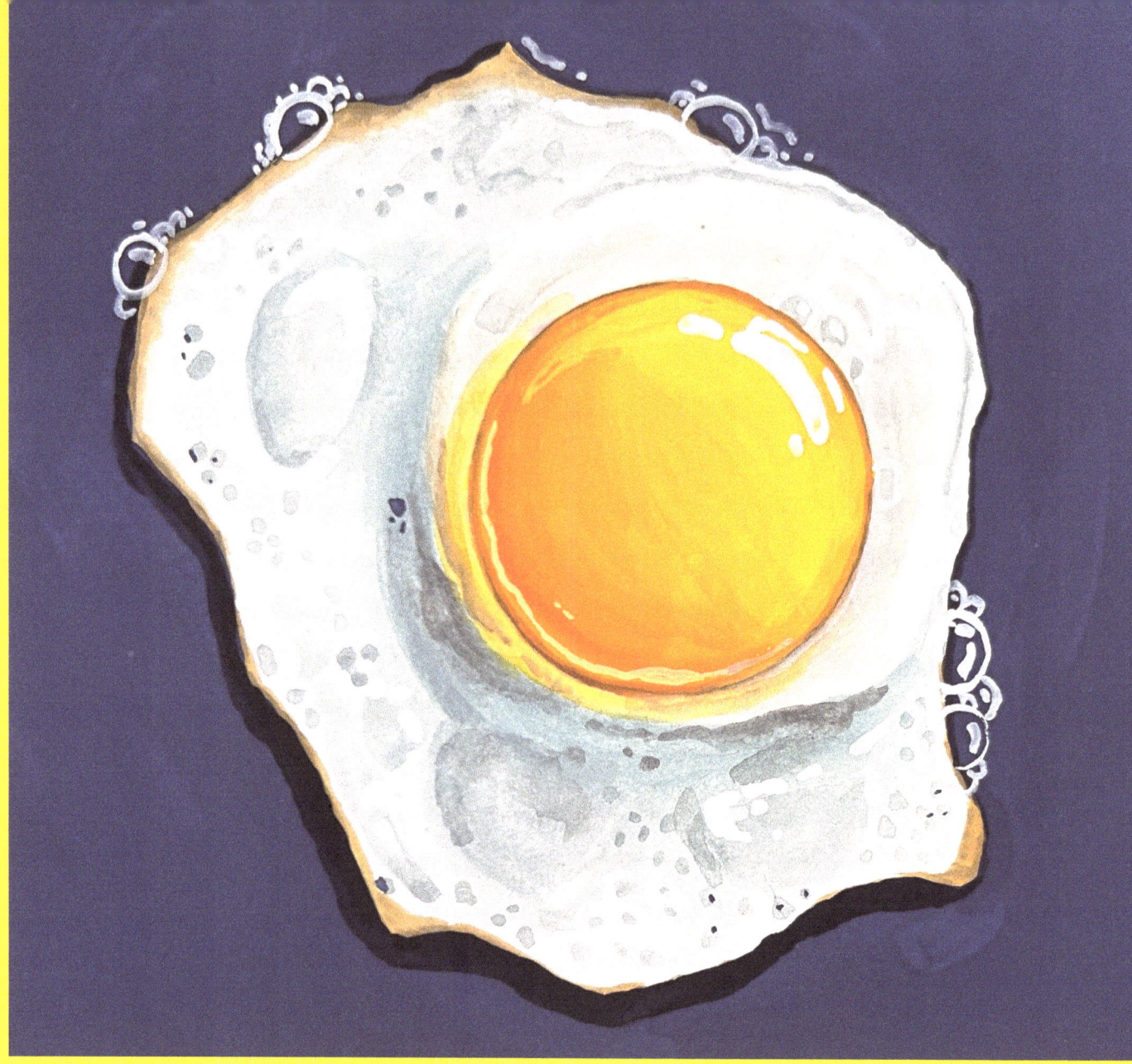

Painting Convex & Concave Shapes

FRIED EGG

At first glance, a fried egg is a blob of white with a circle of yellow in the center, but there is so much that even small changes in tone, tint, value, and hue can do to bring a flat, two-dimensional piece to life with three-dimensional effect.

In this project, the yolk appears convex by placing the shadow on the far edge of the light source and the highlight on the section nearest to the light. Had we wanted the egg yolk to appear as if dipping down into the egg white, we'd place the shadow on the other side of the yolk, closest to the light source, with the highlight falling on the far edge.

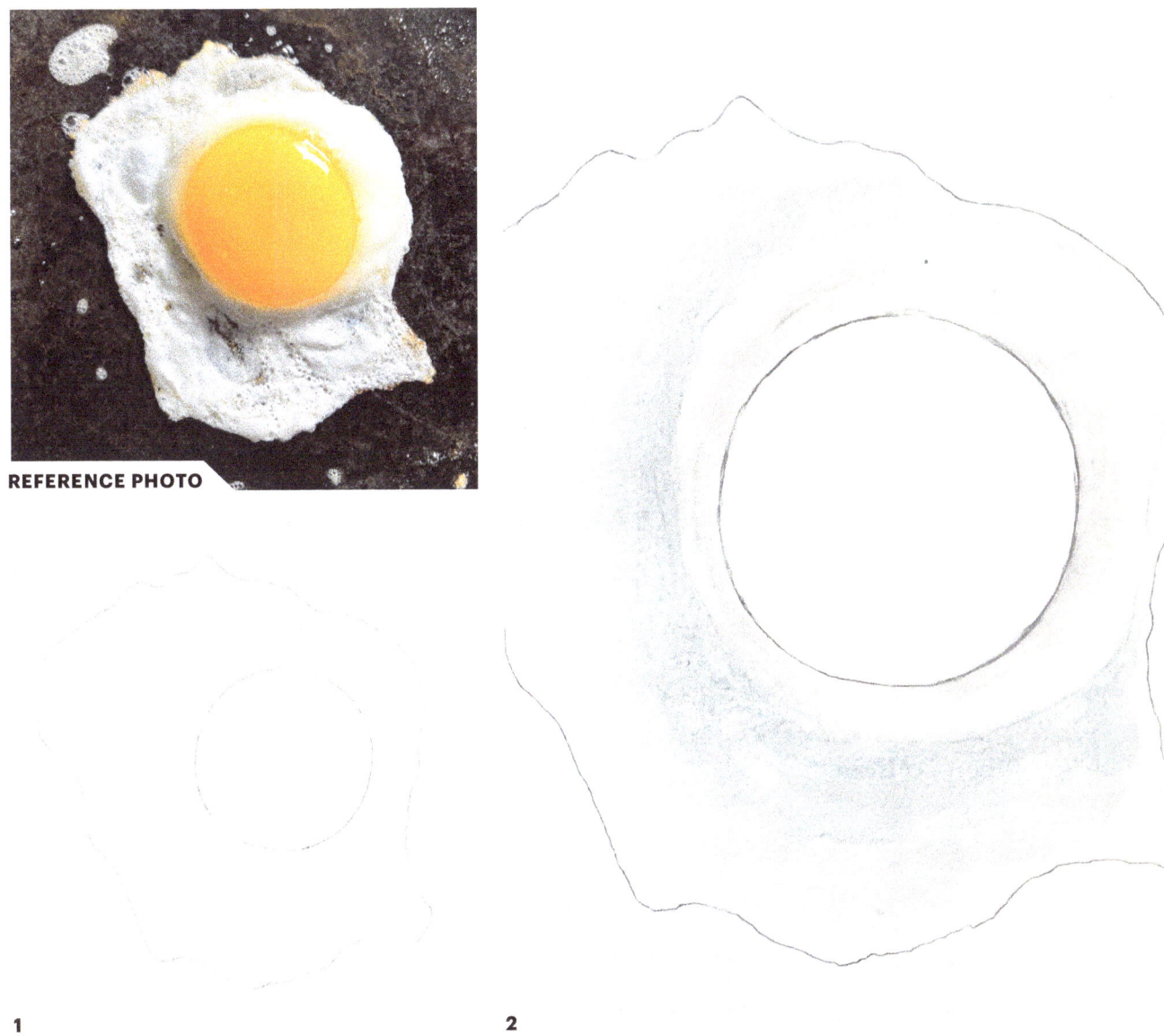

REFERENCE PHOTO

1

2

1 Drawing a good circle for the yolk can feel a bit daunting, so feel free to use a tool like a compass if you like. Or, if you want to try drawing it freehand, remember to keep your linework light when you're first getting the shape and placement down. After you're happy with the shape, you can come back in with a slightly darker line.

2 You'll focus on the subtle shifts in value within the egg white, so be sure to start with clean brushes and water.

For this first step, cover the entire egg white with a thin layer of almost pure white; this way,

when you add the subtle whites and grays, they'll have a bit of a common base to mix with.

Notice that the shadow in the white is closest to the raised edge near the yolk and fades out the closer to the edge of the egg it gets. Also pay attention to the subtle differences between the raised part of the white versus the flat part. Is there a small difference in the temperature? Make the top part of the egg white a bit warmer. In this area, the yellow from the yolk casts some warm reflections on the white.

———————————

BRUSHES: *No. 4 and No. 6 filbert or flat*

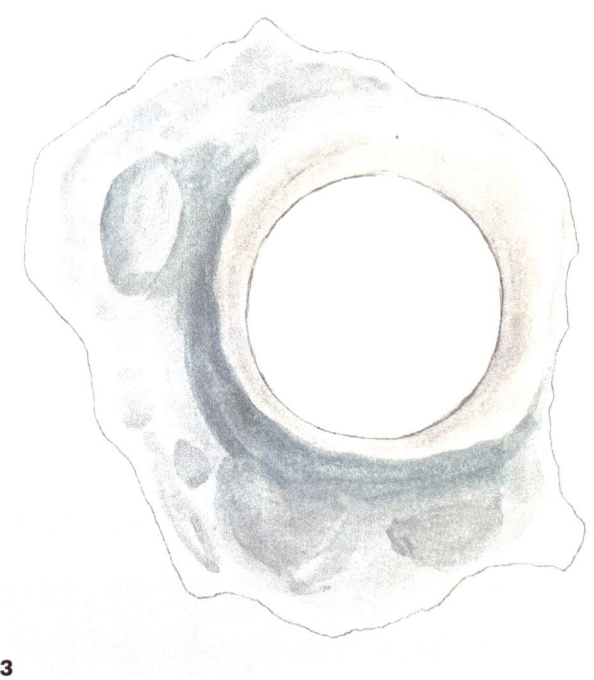

3

egg white. You can make parts of this crispy edge thinner in some parts and thicker in others. Darken the very outer edge, keeping your line very thin.

BRUSH: *No. 1 round*

5 If you're anything like me, adding the yellow to the yolk is the step you've been itching to complete. The vibrant yellows and oranges within the yolk are definitely what make a fried egg exciting to paint (for me anyway!). Starting with a bright, pure yellow, mixed to a nice milky consistency, fill in the entirety of the yolk. Add a bit of this same yellow to the outer left edge of the egg white.

Before this layer dries, mix a slightly darker yellow, adding a bit more orange to your mixture. This layer will run along the entire outer edge of the yolk and cover the whole left-hand side where the shadow begins to darken the yolk. You can rinse and dampen your brush to blend this layer into the lighter layer beneath, along the edge. Continue darkening your yellow by adding orange, moving farther left with each layer. Close to the edge of the yolk you can even add a bit of red here.

Using your small round, mix a reddish-copper color to line the entire base of the yolk. This will really make the yolk pop.

BRUSHES: *No. 1 round and Nos. 4 and 6 filbert*

3 It can feel a bit overwhelming looking at all those tiny bubbles and bumps, shadows and highlights within the egg white, but you only have to include as much detail as you want. If you thrive off all those little details, by all means focus on them, but it's not necessary. The suggestion of these parts of the egg will be enough to give you a beautiful (and even realistic) egg.

Squint at the reference photo and notice the shadows within the white that jump out to you. Squinting can be a very helpful tool when the part of your brain that wants to focus on details takes over.

BRUSHES: *Nos. 4 and 6 filbert*

4 To give the outside of your egg that toasty brown look, mix yellow ochre and brown to create a nice warm brown. Trace along the edges of the flat part of the

6 Using a cool gray, amplify some of the shadows you added in step 3. During this step you can also add some of the indentations in the egg white. Try not to go too dark. It's always better to start light and get darker than to go too dark too fast.

BRUSH: *No. 1 round*

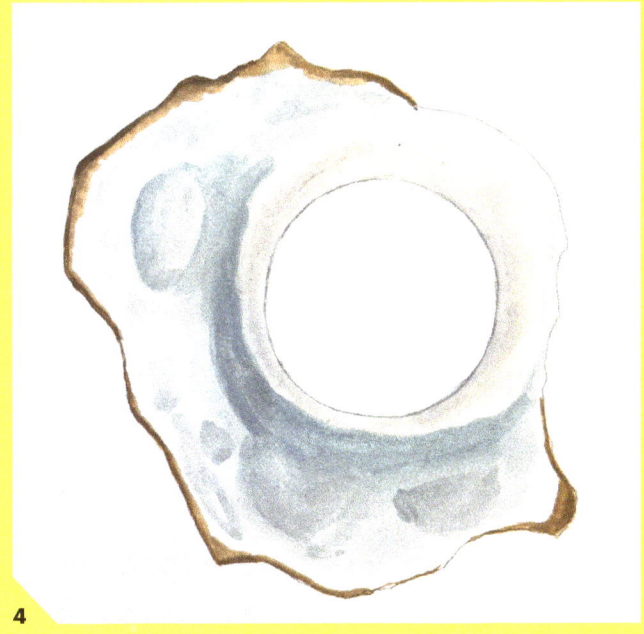

4

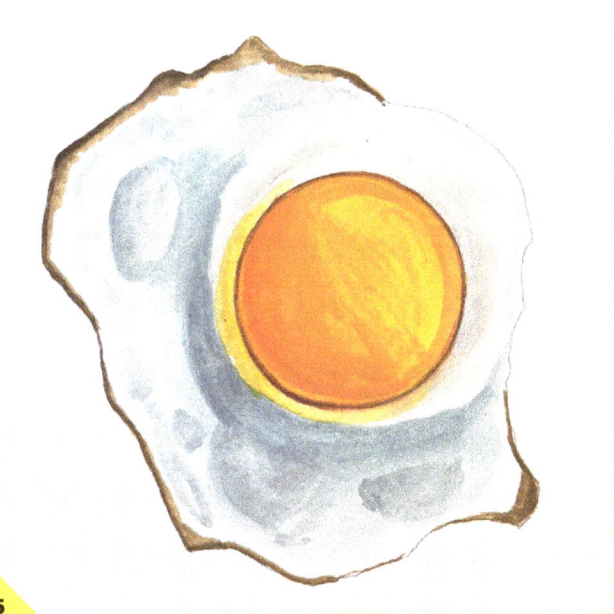

5

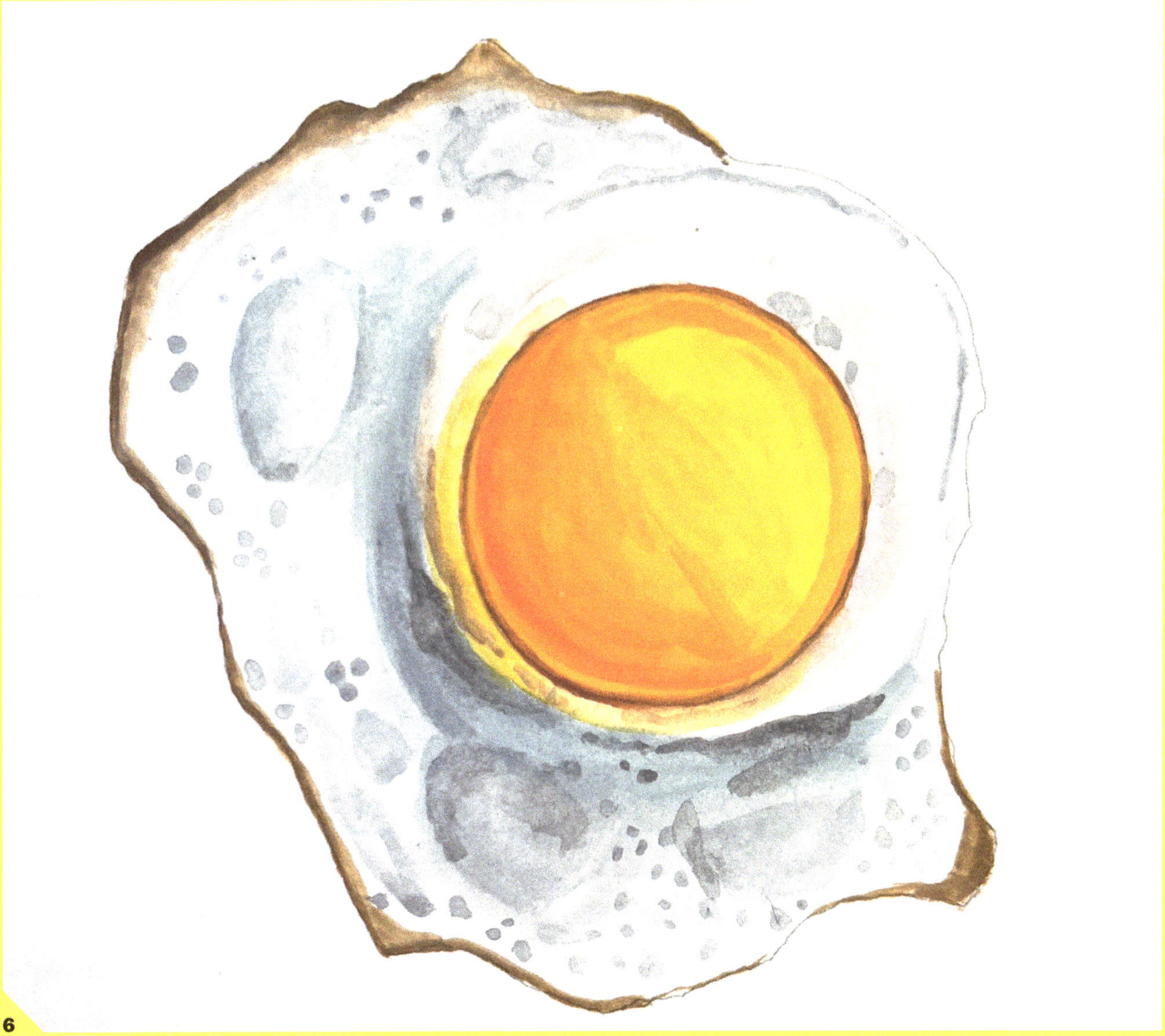

6

7 We're finally to the step that's going to make your egg jump off the page. You've been so patient about adding that background color. You can choose whatever color you want here, but the darker the value, the more the egg will stand out.

Mix plenty of creamy paint for your background color. Starting with your filbert or flat, cover the entire background, cutting a nice clean edge around the egg. Be careful not to cover the brown edge.

After the background has dried completely, add a shadow along the left-hand edge of the egg white.

BRUSHES: *No. 1 round and No. 6 or 8 filbert or flat*

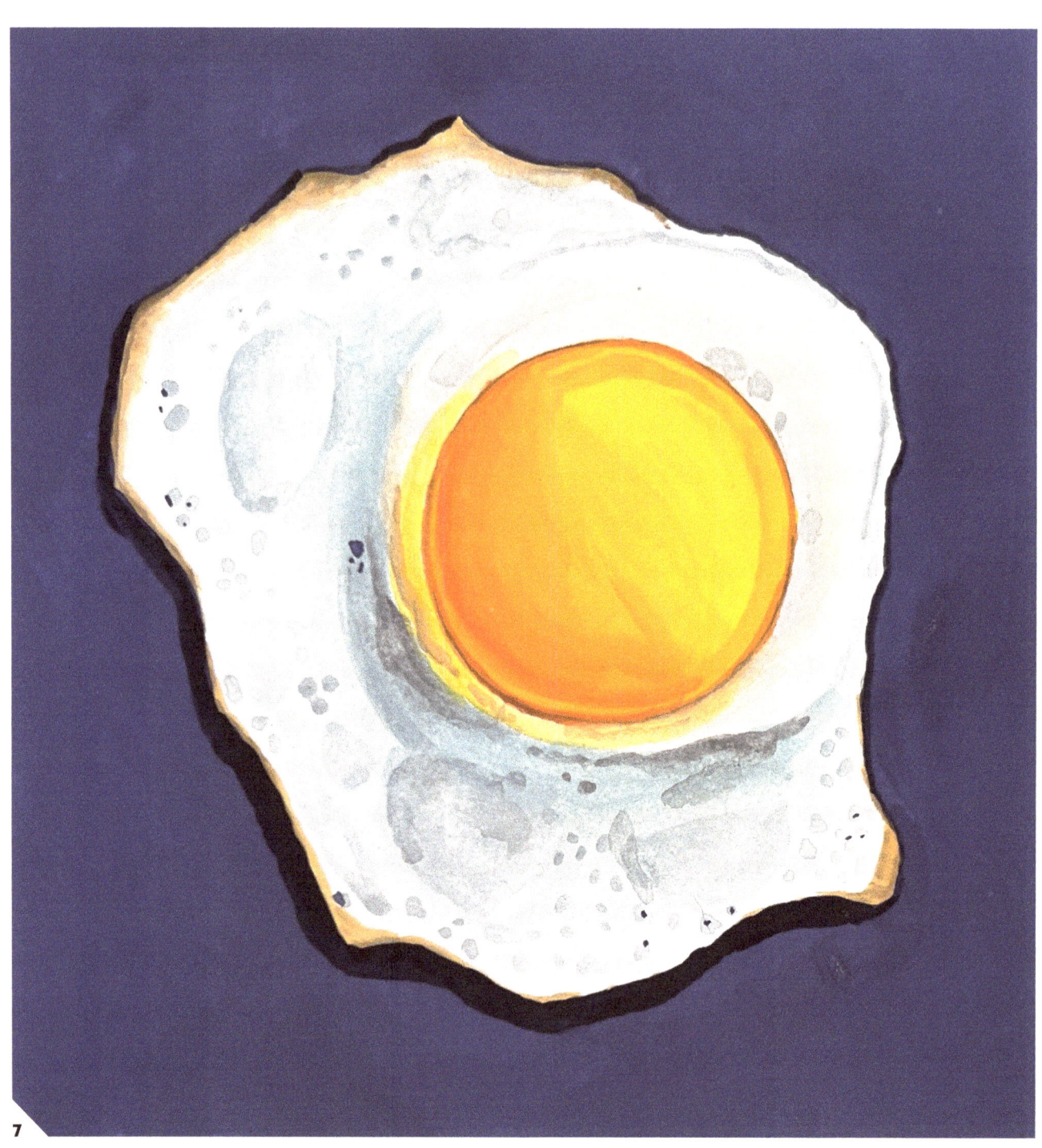

8 Break out your pure white, because it's time for high-lights! Keep your paint really thick and don't add too much to your brush at once. You want the paint to sit on the very tip of your brush.

The most obvious highlight is on the yolk. To make this highlight really pop, add a couple layers of white. You can also add a bit of pale yellow along the left edge of the yolk for the reflected light.

Travel around the egg white, adding highlights where you notice them in the reference photo. Although the reference only has a couple of bubbles, you can add more if you like (as I've done).

———————————

BRUSH: *No. 1 round*

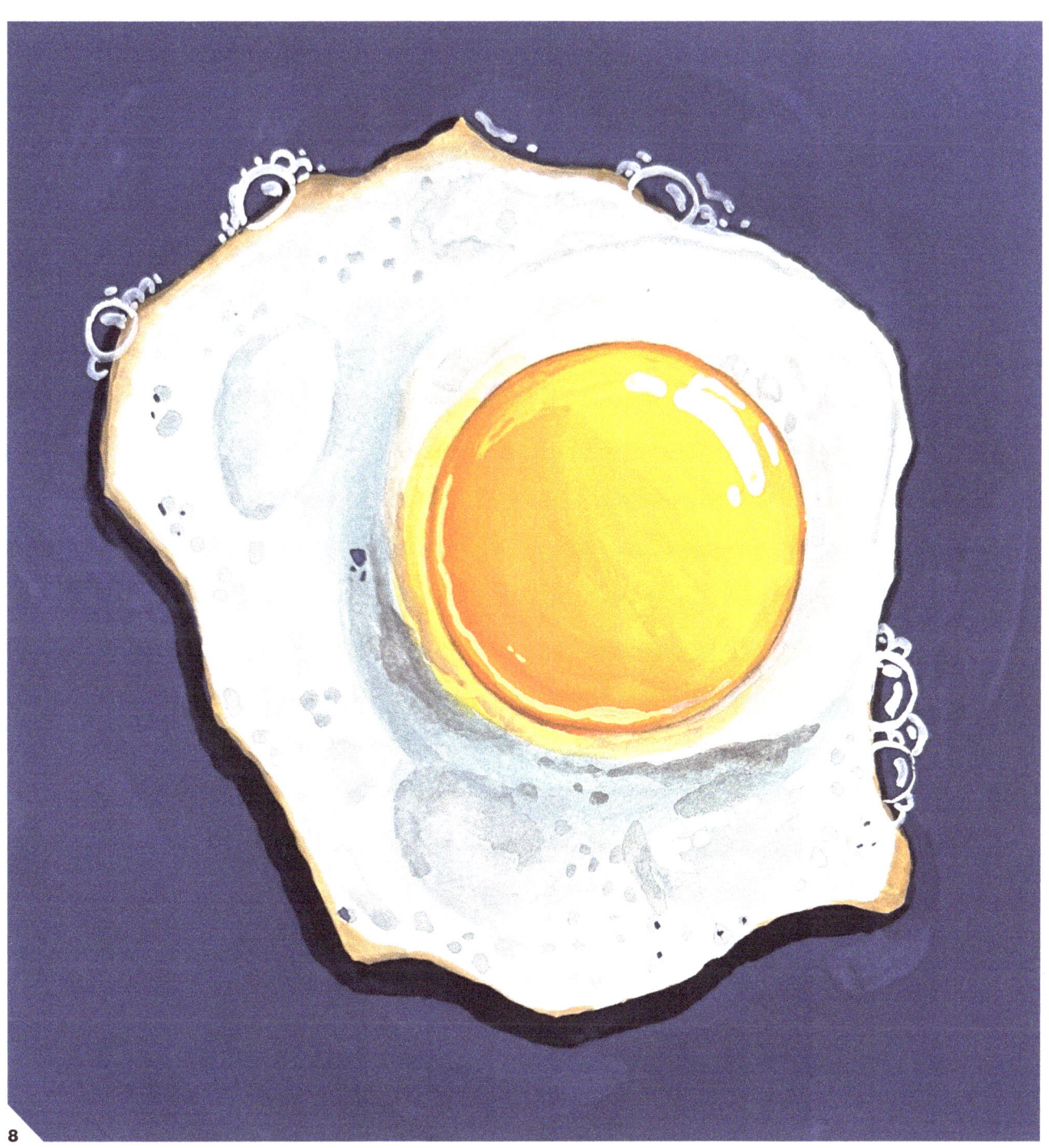

8

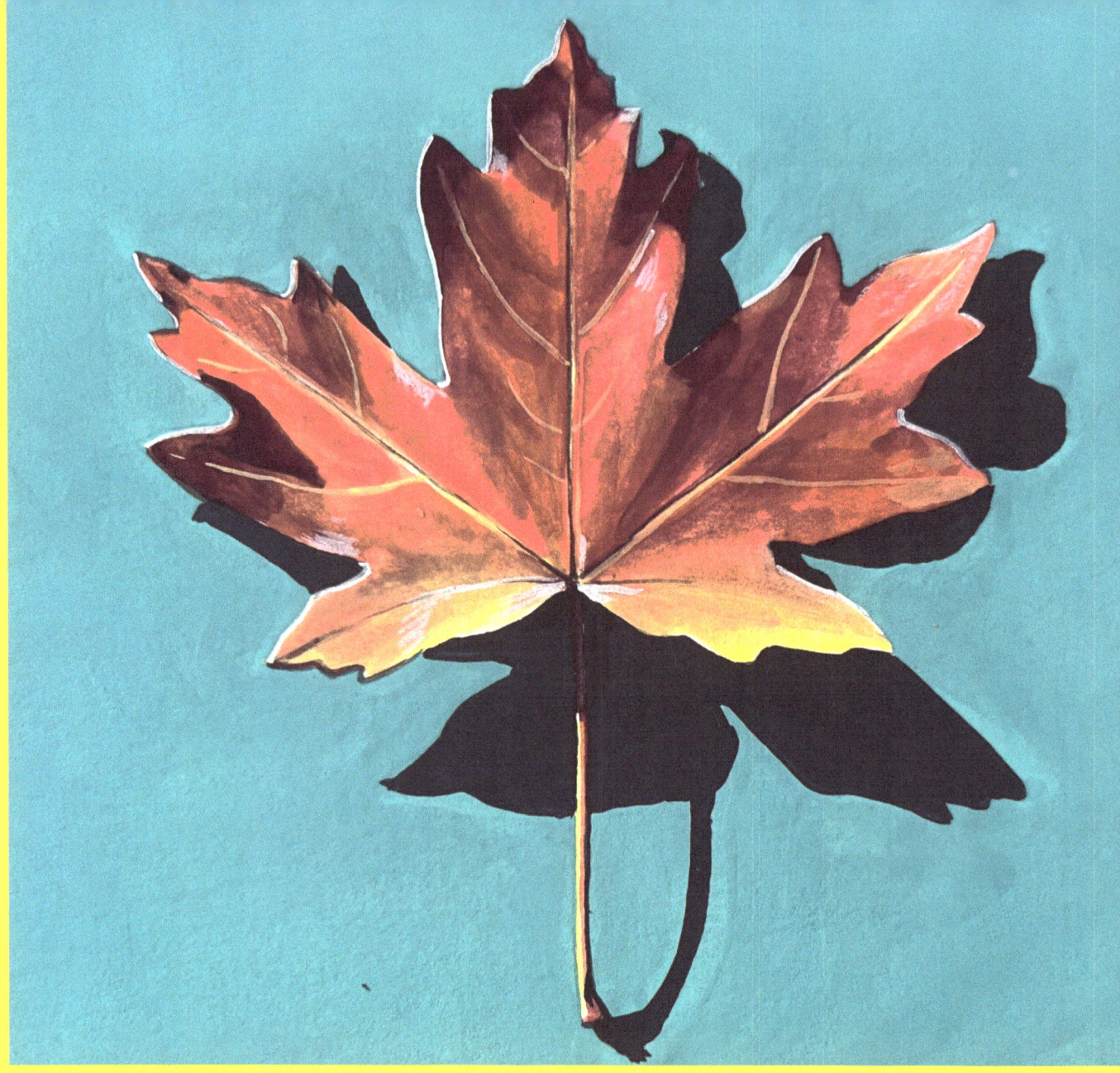

Painting Color Gradation

FALL LEAF

There will be countless times when you come across subjects that require a smooth transition from one color to another. To be able to paint this gradation without the appearance of strong lines separating the colors may take a bit of practice. This project allows you to practice the transition of a full range of warm colors, from bright yellow to orange to red.

Successfully transitioning between colors can be achieved a few different ways. You can blend by painting wet paint into wet paint or by using a damp brush to blend two dry colors together. You can also use a combination of drybrushing and damp brushing to create a good blend.

1 The leaf outline is very simple, but the shape of the cast shadow does a lot to help define the curves of the leaf and stem. Pay attention to where the shadow falls in comparison to the leaf.

brush to keep your edge sharp and precise, you can switch to a smaller brush here.

_____

BRUSHES: *Nos. 4 and 6 filbert or flat*

2 Mix plenty of your background color to the consistency of cream, making sure that the paint is fully incorporated into the water. This step is particularly important when you're mixing your own color. Make sure each of the colors you've used have fully blended into one another to prevent streaking.

With your large flat or filbert, cover the background, keeping a crisp clean line along the outline of both the leaf and the shadow. If you're uncertain whether you'll have enough control with your large

3 After mixing your shadow color to a nice creamy consistency, fill in the shadow shape in your underdrawing. Depending on your preference you can choose to soften the edge of your shadow using a clean, damp brush. In this piece, I chose to keep the edge of the shadow quite crisp to accentuate the harshness of the light source.

_____

BRUSHES: *No. 1 round and No. 4 filbert*

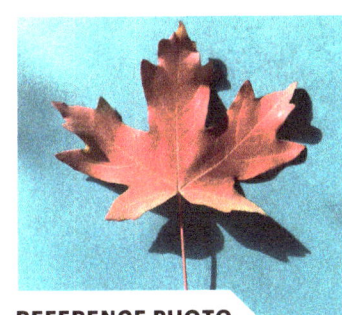

REFERENCE PHOTO

1

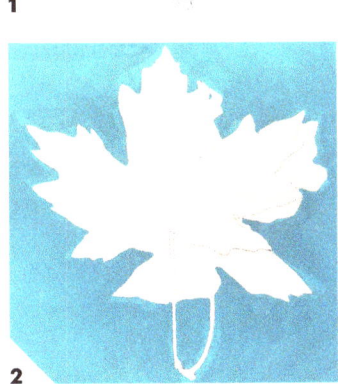

2

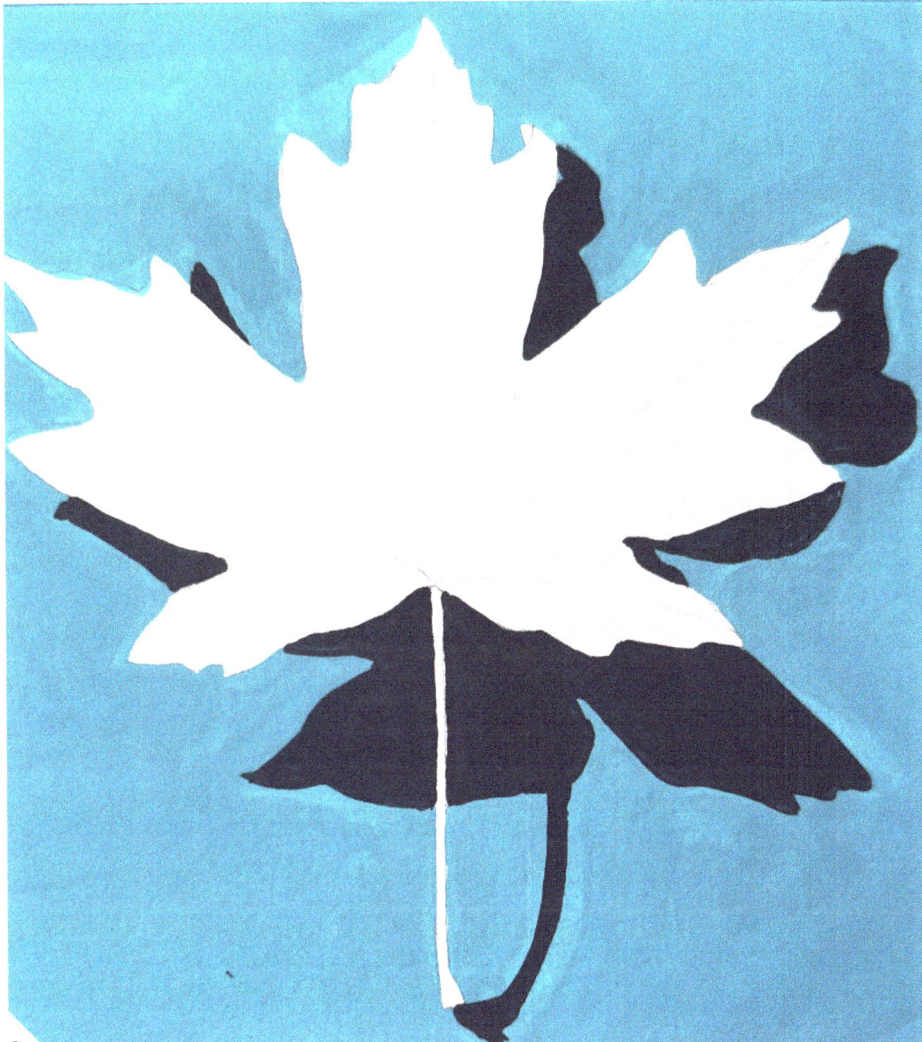

3

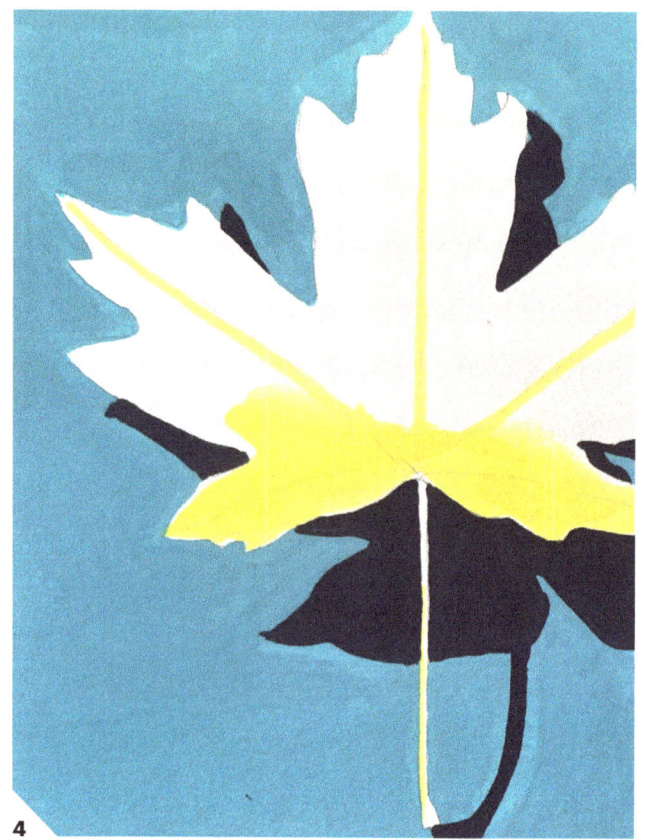

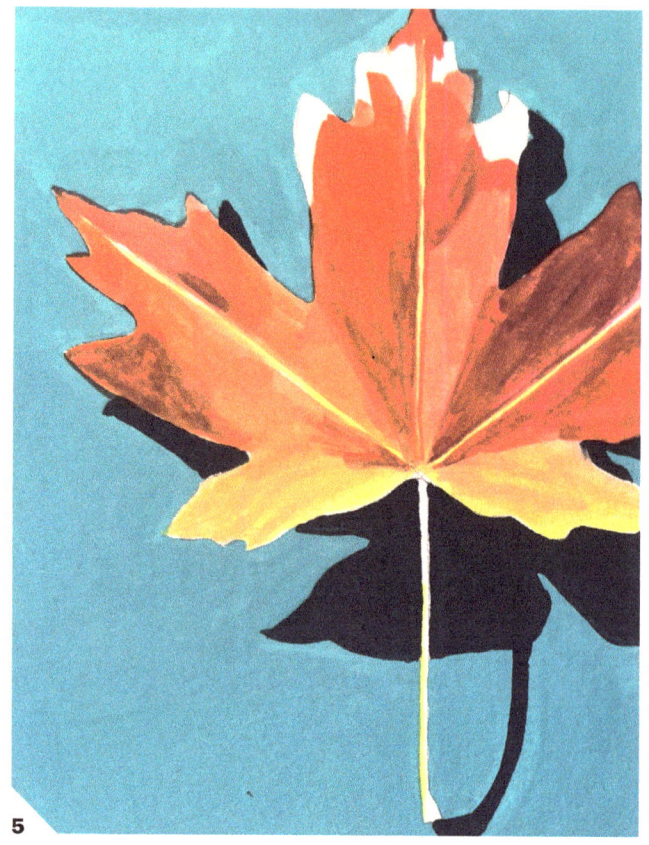

4 After mixing a pale yellow, fill in the bottom lobe of the leaf, stopping about a quarter of the way up the leaf. Using the edge of the filbert or switching to your round, draw three veins up the middle of the remaining portions of the leaf.

BRUSHES: *No. 1 round and No. 4 filbert*

5 During this next step, you'll do some subtle mixing of colors as you begin to blend and gradate from yellow to orange on the parts of the leaf in the brightest light. Using the light yellow you just mixed, blend it with a very small amount of orange. Starting at the bottom, near the edge of the yellow you just painted, lay down a layer of pale orange. After rinsing your brush, softly blend these colors into one another.

Moving up the left lobe of the leaf and partway up the middle, continue adding a bit more orange to your color, rinsing your brush and blending as you go.

Notice there are a few other places on the leaf that catch some of the strong light and need to be painted with this brighter orange.

BRUSHES: *Nos. 4 and 6 filbert*

6 Mix a new color of burnt orange. If you don't already have this color, I recommend mixing orange, red, and a bit of brown.

There are a couple places on the left lobe that need to be darkened before you move up the center of the leaf and to the right-hand side. Notice that the burnt orange color gets a little bit deeper on the right-hand side. You can achieve this by adding more dark red to your mixture.

Where the darker burnt orange meets the lighter orange, use a clean, damp brush to softly blend the colors together.

BRUSHES: *Nos. 4 and 6 filbert*

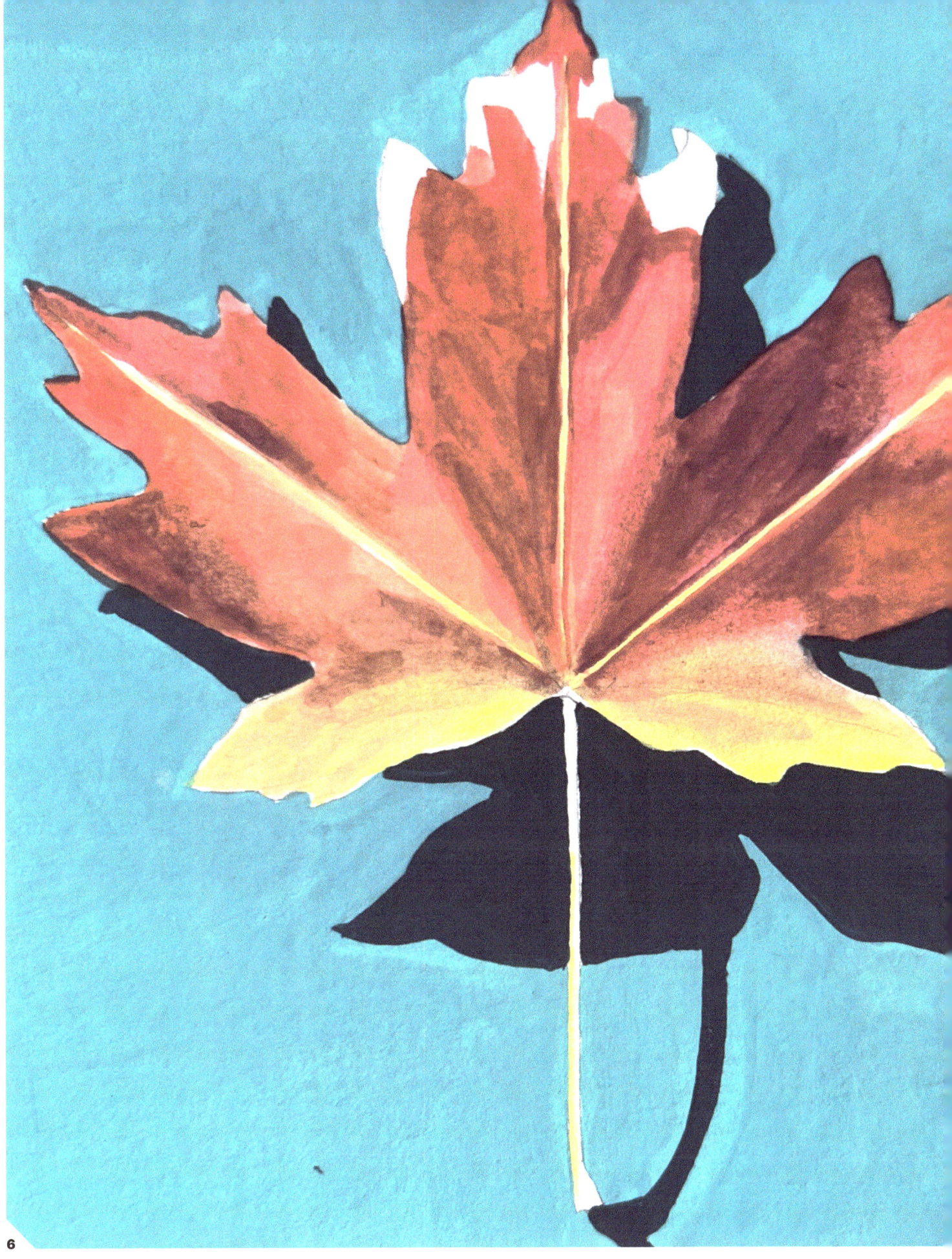

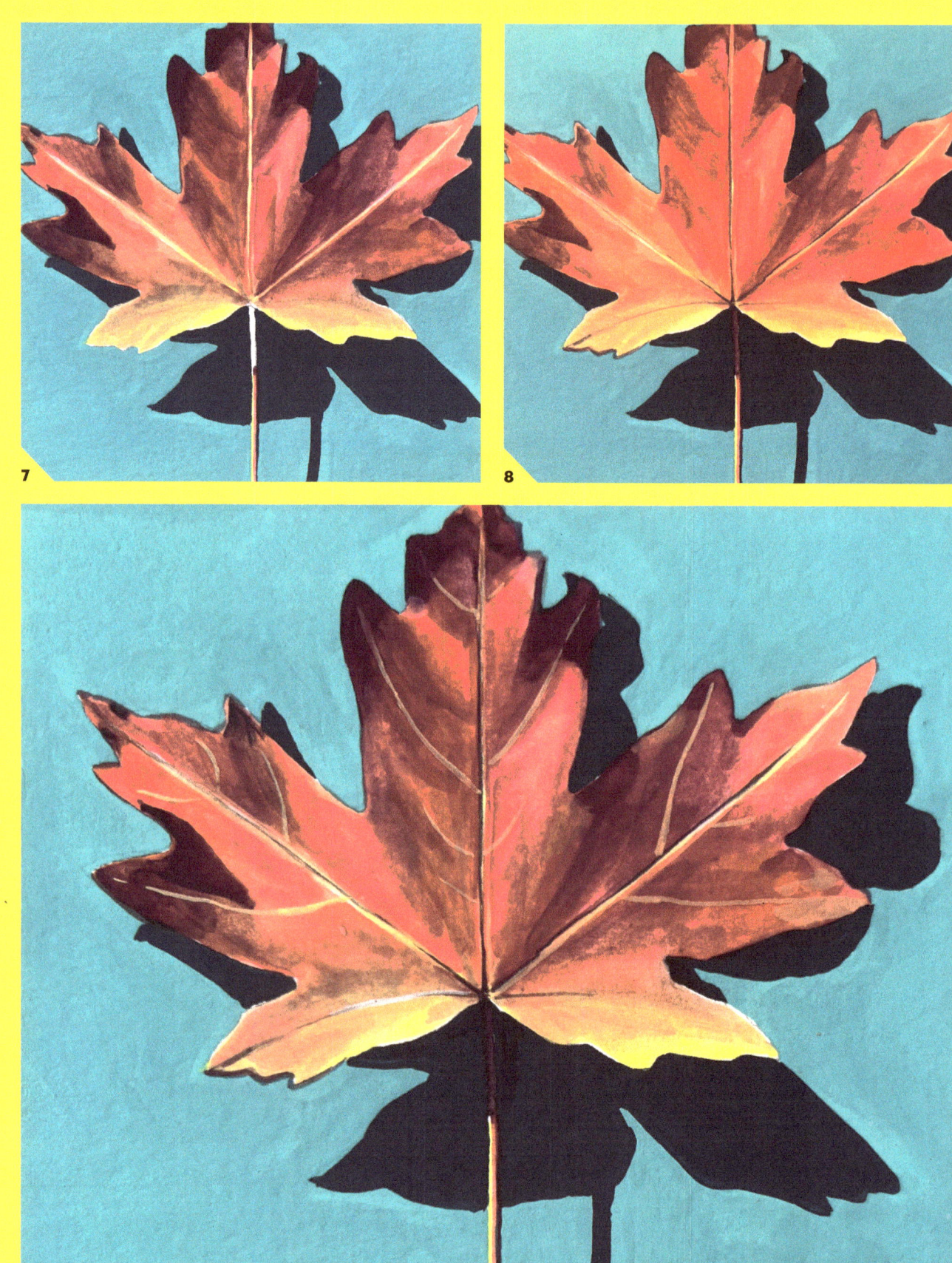

7

8

9

7 It's time to mix the deepest red. Using crimson and a bit of violet and dark brown, paint in the remaining portions of the leaf. You can also darken the shadowed portions. As you paint, continue to clean your brush and blend. Clean and blend, until you're happy with the transitions.

Using the round, you can also paint in the bottom portion of your leaf's stem. Notice that the left edge is bright yellow, while the shadowed edge is the same deep red as the last color you just mixed.

_____

BRUSHES: *No. 1 round and No. 4 filbert*

8 Mix a warm gray dark enough to add a shadow to the top of the stem without blending in completely with the rest of the shadow. Add a few small shadows to the yellow veins within the leaf. These shadows will be darkest on the middle and right veins and at the base of the veins where they meet the stem.

Before you move on to the final step, use a clean No. 1 round to add a few extra-thin yellow veins to your leaf. To make sure these veins stand out against the dark burnt-orange color, be sure to mix your yellow with an ample amount of white to make sure your paint is opaque.

_____

BRUSH: *No. 1 round*

9 For this final step, you'll add a few small shadows and highlights along the edges of the leaf. This tiny step will add a bit of depth. Although it's almost flat, even a leaf has a tiny bit of dimension. You can also add a few small highlights to portions of the leaf where the direct light hits.

_____

BRUSH: *No. 1 round*

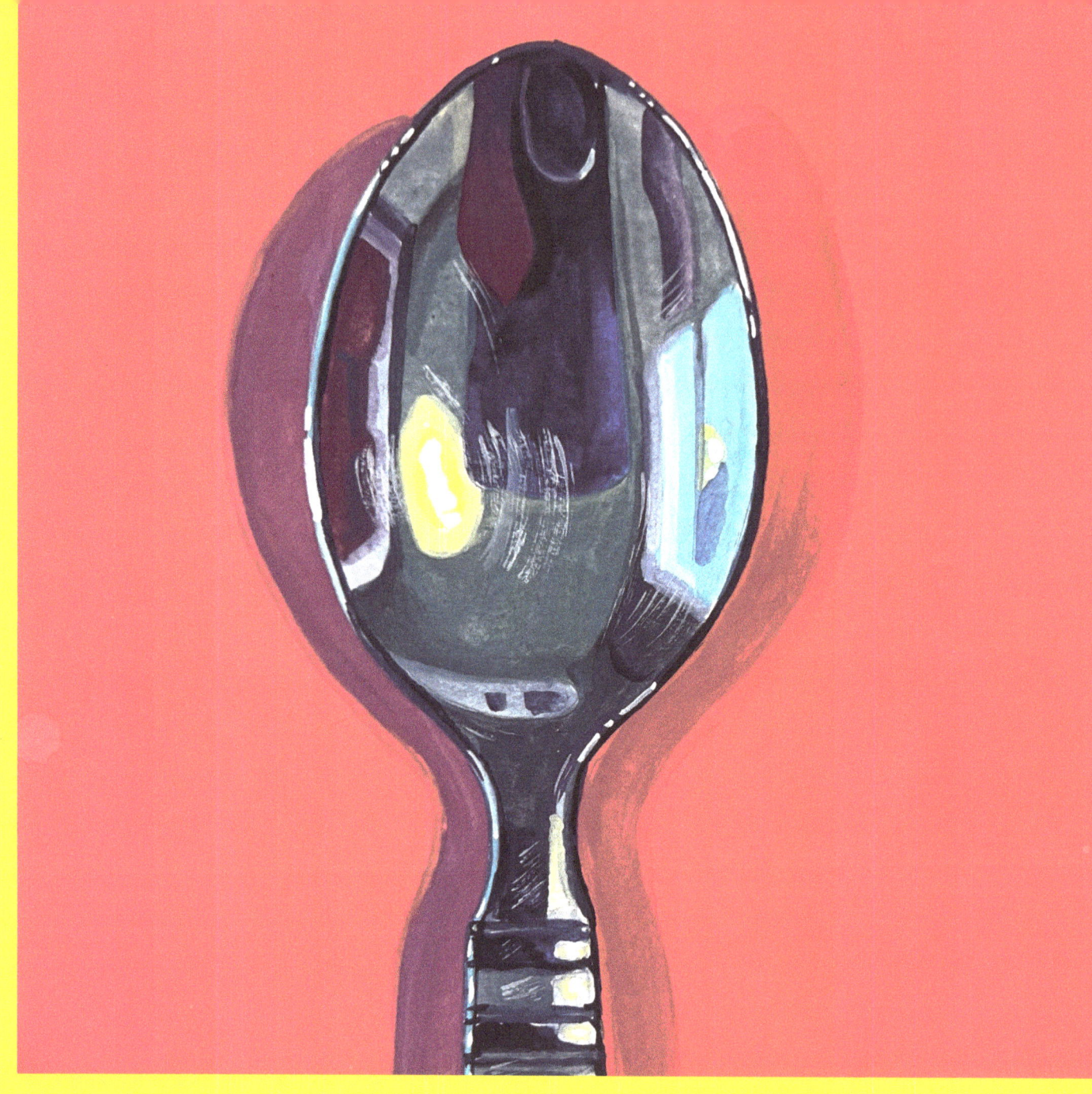

Painting Metallic Surfaces

SPOON

The lines of the objects reflected in the surface of a metallic object follow the contour of the object, making the shape much easier to render three-dimensionally. I'm sure you've noticed the way your own reflection changes when you stare at yourself in a spoon, bending to fit its oval shape. Perhaps you've also noticed it appears upside down when the spoon is concave versus appearing right side up when the spoon is convex. This is one more piece of information your viewer has to determine the shape of the object.

1 Because the reflection does have quite a few details, the more time you can spend getting the placement correct in the underdrawing, the less you'll have to fuss over fixing things while you're painting.

2 By now, you're probably used to laying down your background color. Remember to keep your paint a nice creamy consistency and to let it dry completely before adding a second layer if you need to cover any streaks. Notice that instead of one cast shadow, there are two. This is because there are two sources of light shining on the subject. When rendering the shadows, notice that they aren't identical. The one on the left is slightly darker and a bit cooler in temperature.

After you've completed the shadows, mix a rich black, including a bit of purple or blue. Begin by painting in the darkest shapes. These dark spots will provide the appearance of depth to the spoon, as well as give shape to the ornamental decorations on the spoon's handle. Remember to add the dark edge that runs along the entire edge of the spoon's outer rim.

BRUSHES: *No. 1 round, No. 4 filbert, and No. 6 filbert or flat*

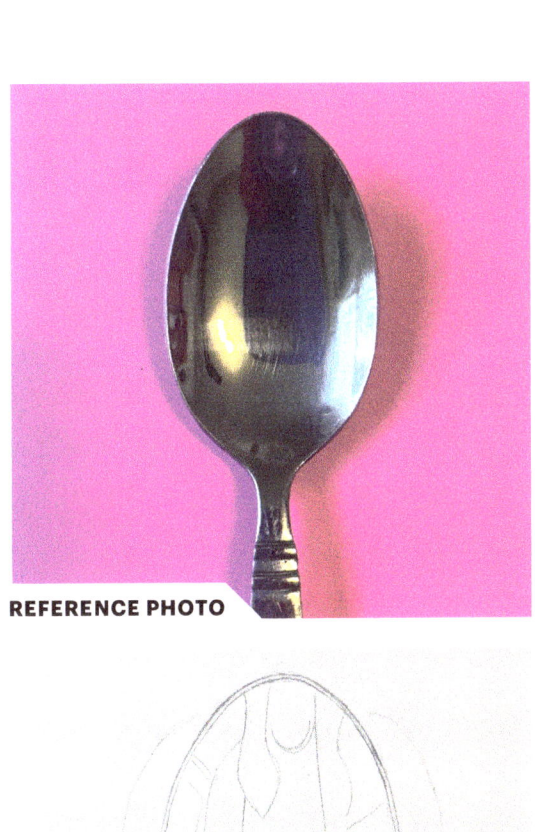

REFERENCE PHOTO

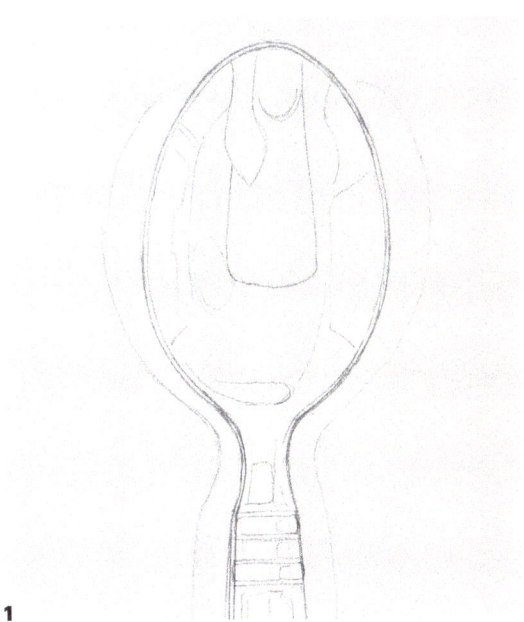

1

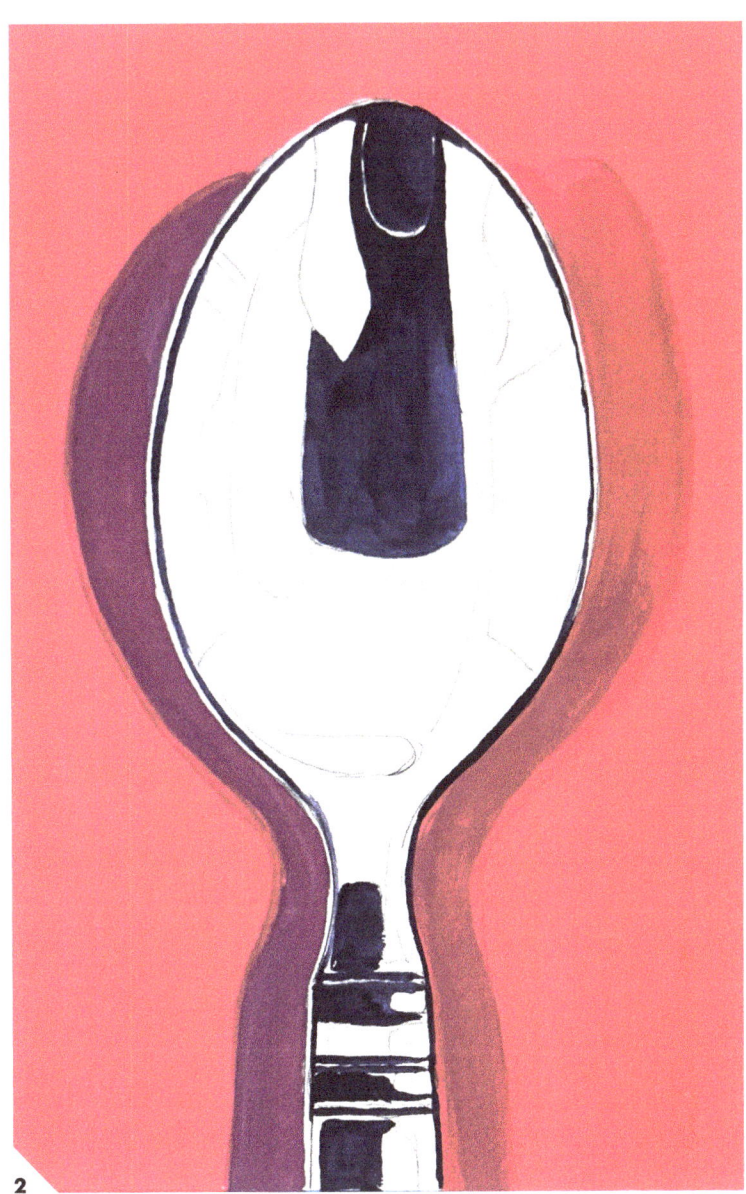

2

3 During this next step you'll focus on the middle-range values, although your colors will fall into the gray category. Notice that the grays I've used range from cool bluish gray to a warmer brown-based gray. Because the background is so warm, I chose to lean into the cool colors of the majority of the gray I used. This is a great place for you to deliberately put some thought into your color choice.

————————

BRUSHES: *No. 1 round and No. 4 filbert*

4 Again, in this step, you'll mix gray—this time quite a bit lighter in value. Looking back at the value exercise you did in the beginning of the book, remember the grays ranged from 0 to 100 in 10-percent increments. An easy way to create the grays is to mix black and white to create the value you want (in this case, something between 30 and 40 percent). You can then add a bit of any color to that mixture. In this case, I used a light sky blue, which made an icy gray. You can see the effect it has of making the spoon appear more silver.

————————

BRUSH: *No. 1 round*

5 Now that you've established the temperature of your metal, there are a few remaining places in the spoon that are reflecting color. First, notice the area on the right, which is reflecting the turquoise blue of the sky in the window. The other places (the hand shape at the top of the spoon, the wall decorations on the left-hand side, and the last shape above the window) are similar enough in color that I chose to simplify them and use maroon/purple in those spots to make them feel cohesive.

Add a bit of that turquoise sky color on the left side of the spoon's edge.

————————

BRUSHES: *No. 1 round and No. 4 filbert*

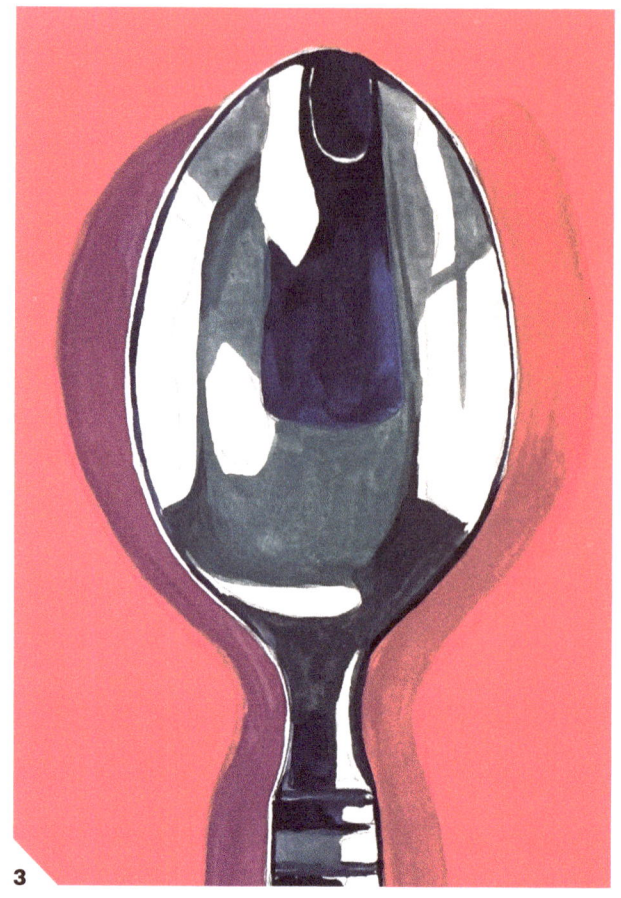

3

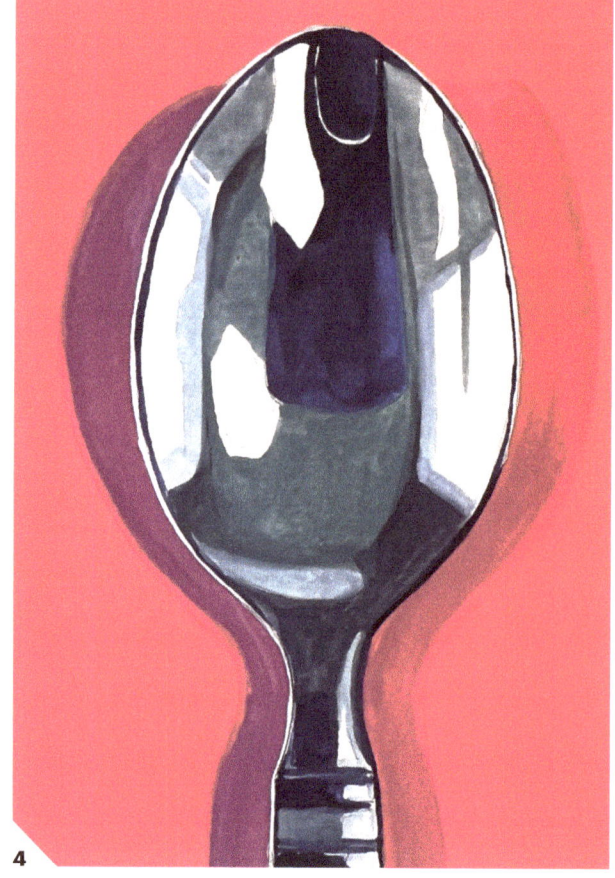

4

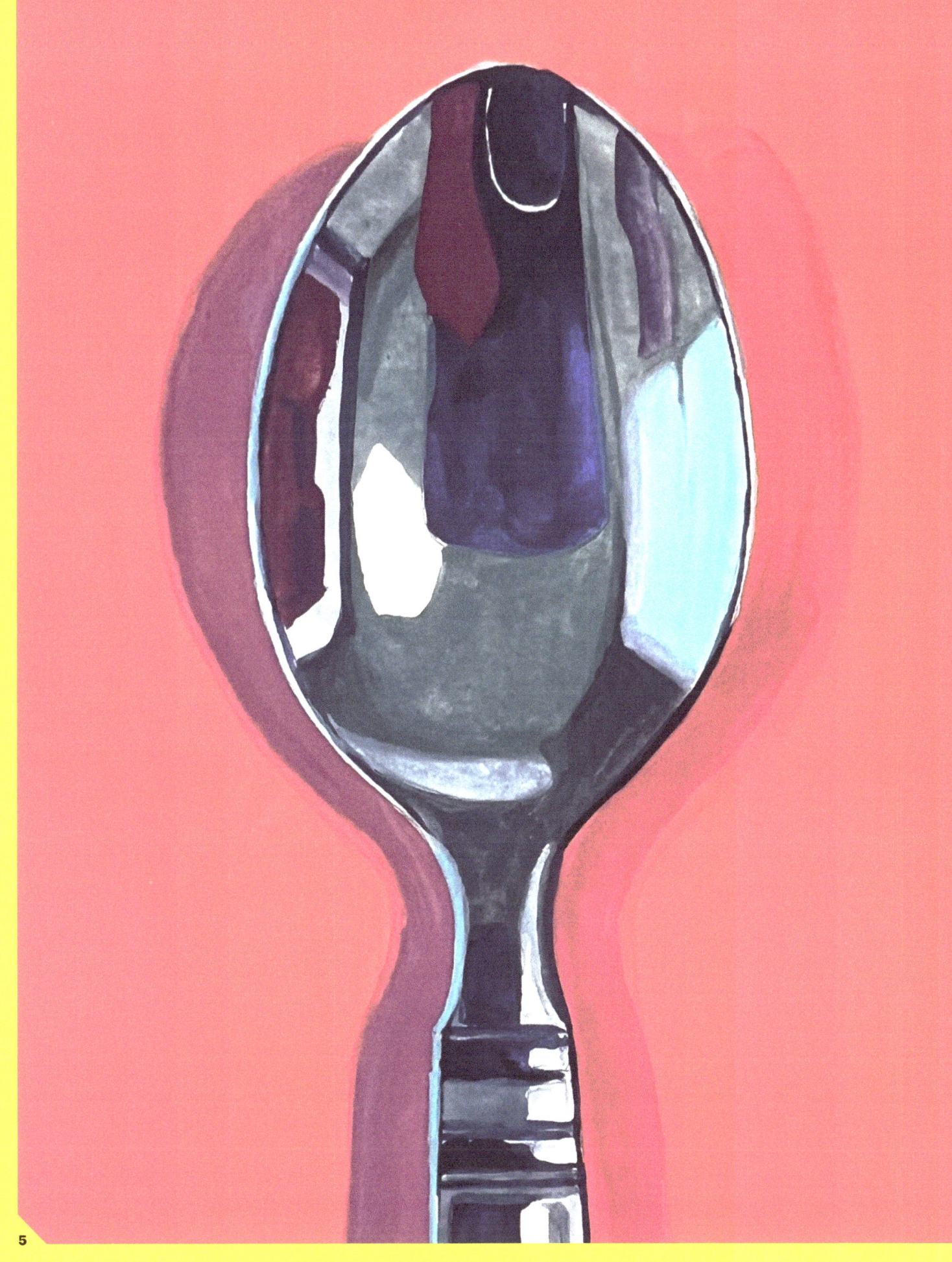

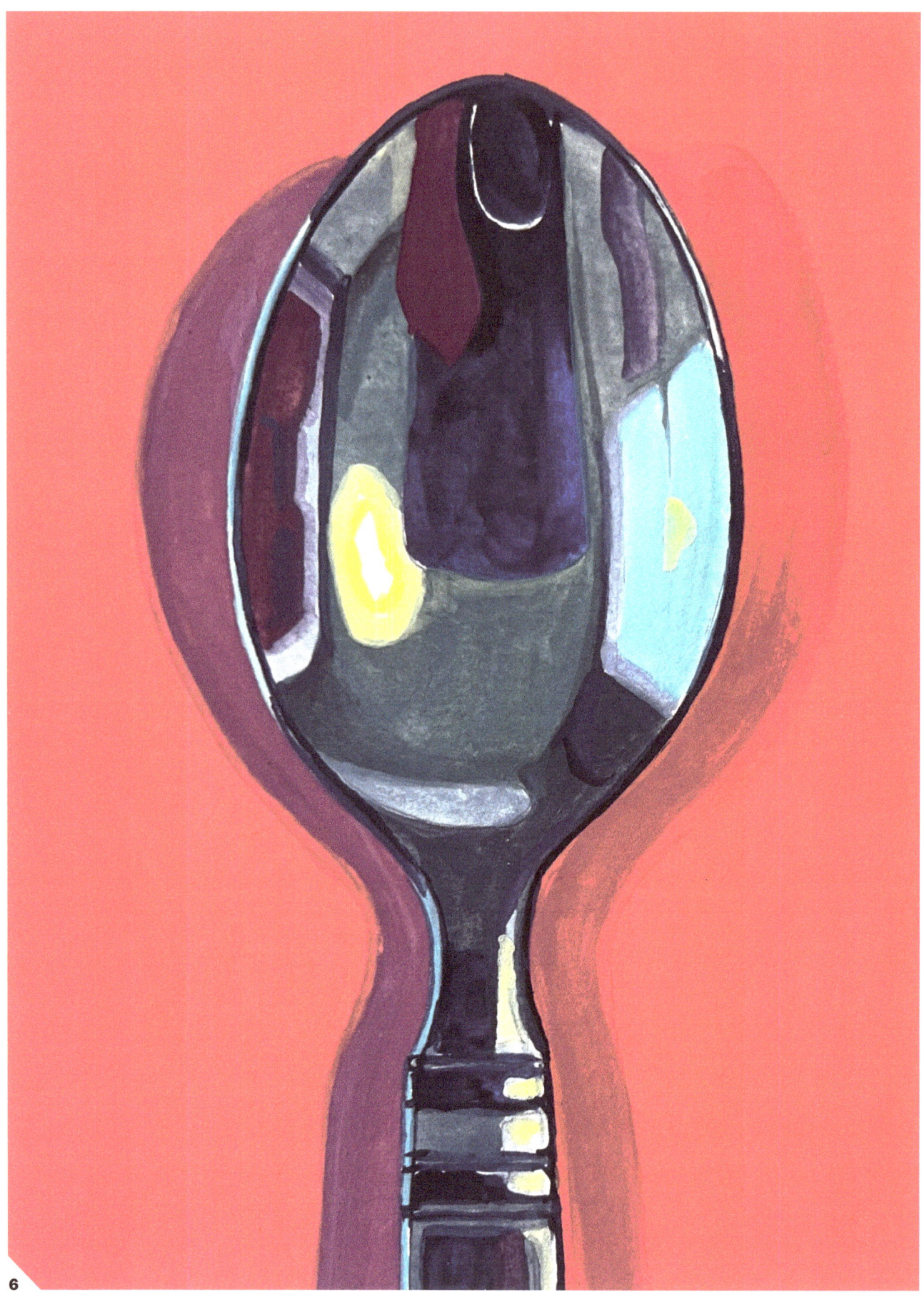

6

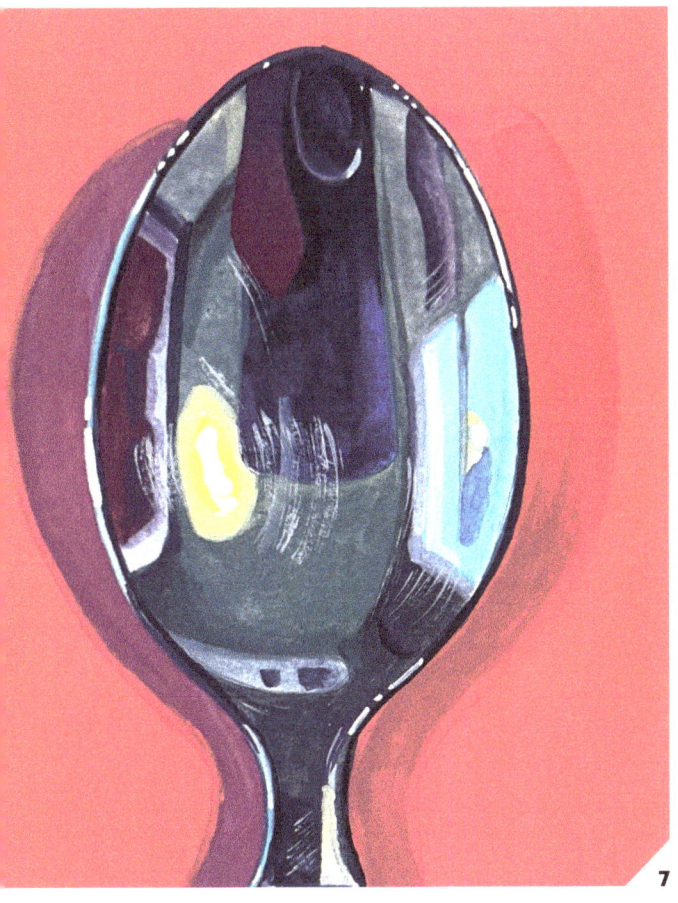

6 Mix a small amount of light yellow for this step. To begin with, work on the glowing light in the center of the spoon. Instead of filling this in entirely, you can add a bit of white to the very center where the brightest point of light is.

You can also add a bit of yellow to the window area, as well as in the highlighted portions at the bottom of the spoon.

———————

BRUSH: *No. 1 round*

7 There are only subtle marks left in this painting, but these tiny brushstrokes can have a big impact, especially when it comes to making the spoon seem reflective. Using a lightly dampened brush and a very creamy consistency of white paint, coat the very tip of your brush with white. Delicately drag the brush along the rim of the spoon. Instead of filling in the entire edge, use small dots of white mixed with longer strokes.

Study your reference photo and see if there are any other places where you might want to add detail.

———————

BRUSH: *No. 1 round*

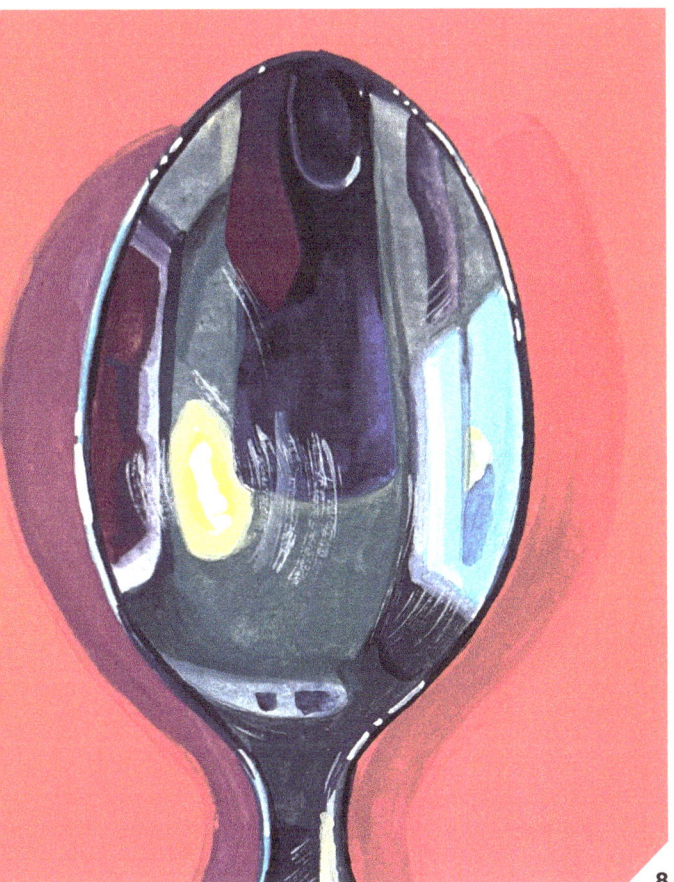

8 A trait you'll often notice with metal, especially if it's not a brand-new piece, is tiny little scratches on the surface that catch the light. Drybrushing is a perfect way to depict these tiny marks.

Using a nearly dry brush, add a tiny bit of white to the tip. Before making any marks on your paper, run the brush along the side of your board or lightly on your paper towel. Very lightly drag your brush across the points in your painting where you want these tiny highlights. If you can, move the brush in a direction that matches the contour of the spoon. This is particularly effective in the center to enhance the concave shape.

———————

BRUSH: *No. 1 round*

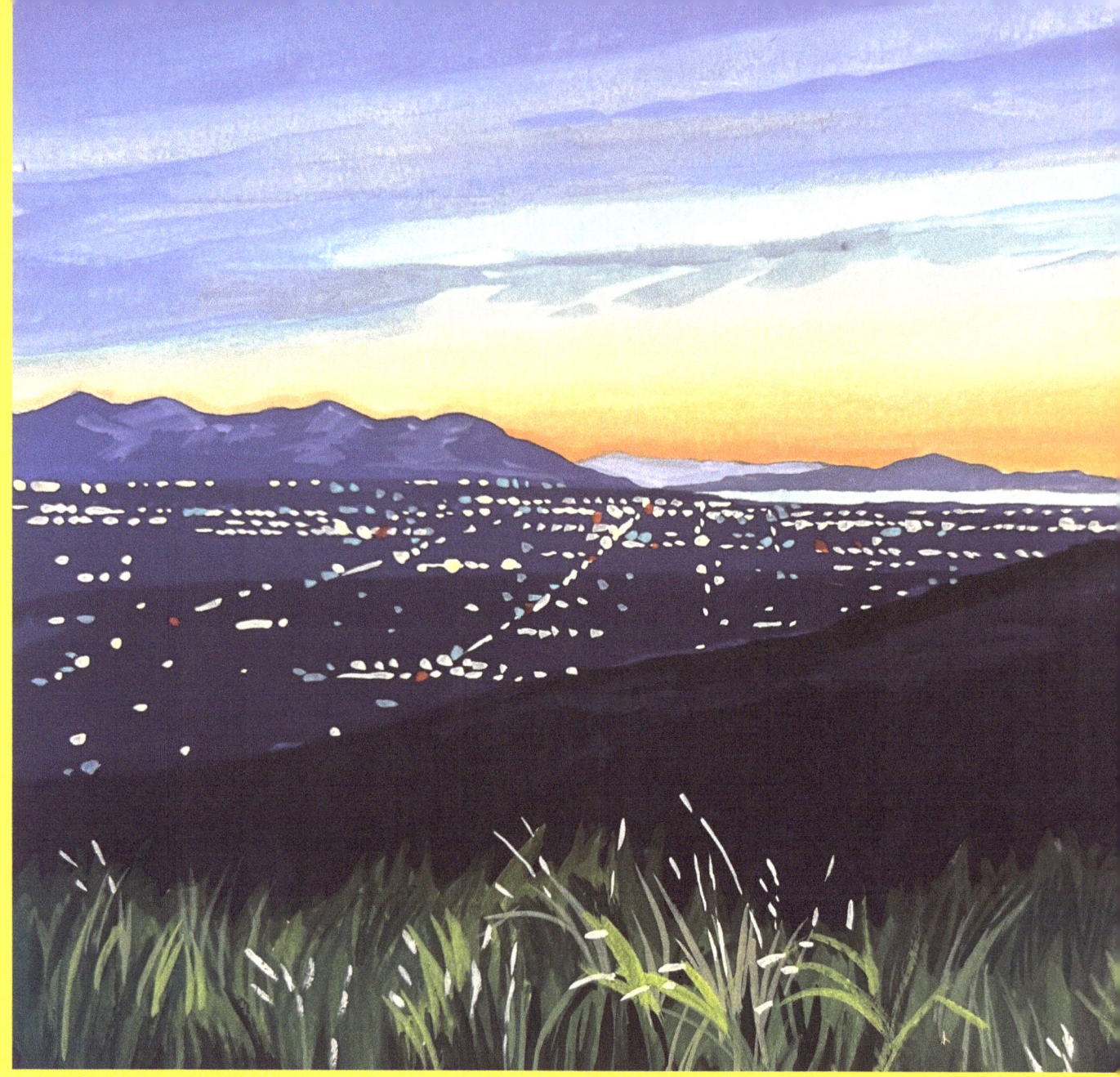

Painting Atmospheric Perspective

LANDSCAPE

One of the most powerful things about painting a successful landscape is creating a sense of depth, as well as conveying a sense of place. There are a few tricks you can use to create this sense of depth. Both scale and value contribute to informing the viewer about how they can interpret your two-dimensional painting as a three-dimensional space. Simply put, the closer an object is to the viewer, the larger it will appear on the page. Similarly, the farther away an object gets from the viewer, the lighter and blurrier it will appear on the page. This is because of the atmospheric particles between the viewer and the object.

1

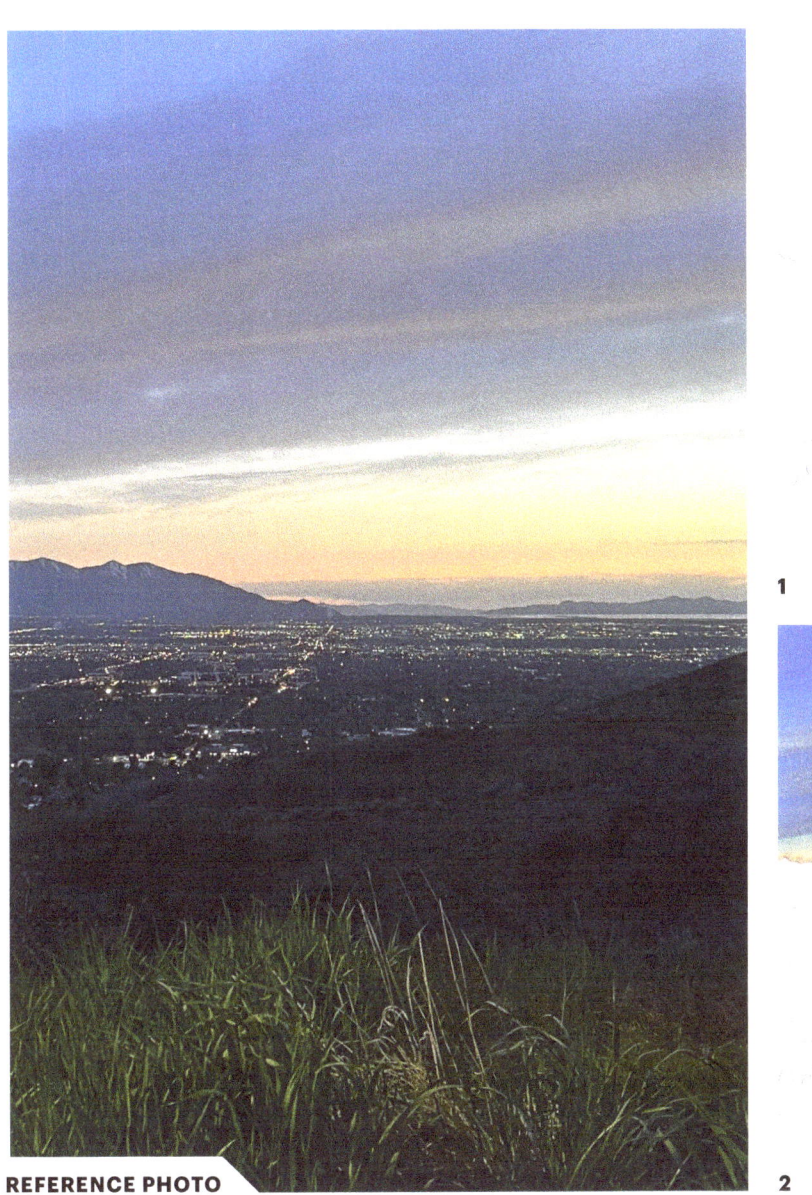

2

REFERENCE PHOTO

1 For your underdrawing on this painting, you only
need to block in the major shapes. Think about
the different layers of perspective in the reference
photo: clouds, mountains (at varying distances),
valley, hill, and grasses in the foreground.

2 Starting with the sky, work your way down this
painting from the most distant part of the landscape to the closest (finishing off with the city
lights). For my painting, I chose to keep the sky
fairly simple and soft.

Beginning with the golden-yellow color, I
moved quickly, so my paint was fairly wet with
each step, allowing the colors to blend more easily
and keeping the edges soft. For the bottom part
of the sky, transition from golden yellow, to pale
yellow to soft turquoise.

BRUSHES: *Nos. 4 and 6 filbert or flat*

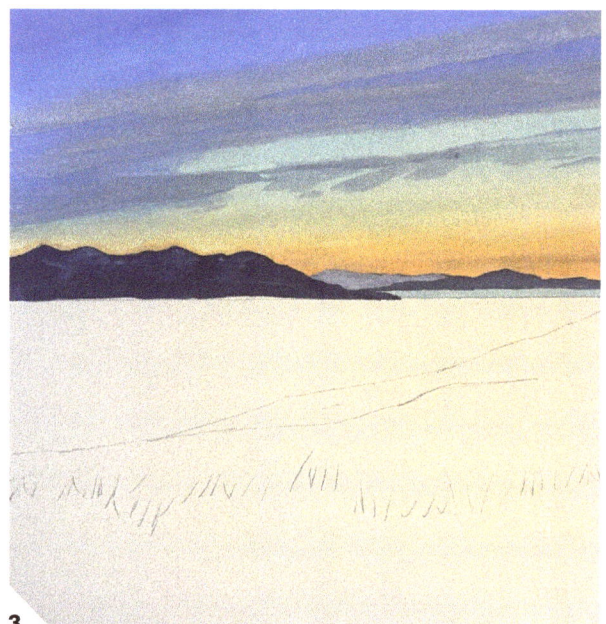

3

edge of your brush to suggest the blades of grass that protrude up in front of the dark background.

BRUSHES: *Nos. 4 and 6 filbert or flat*

5 Because it can be a little confusing to paint the gradations in the grass, I've broken it up into two different steps. For this step use three values of green: a mid-value olive green, a slightly darker value, and a very dark, almost-black, green. Use the two lighter colors to paint in the top quarter of the grass, with the lightest color centered in the middle.

When painting in the dark green along the bottom, continue to paint in the shapes of the grass blades.

BRUSHES: *No. 1 round and No. 4 filbert, flat, or angle brush*

3 In the introduction to this section, I spoke about how objects appear lighter and softer the farther away from the viewer that they are. The mountains in this painting are a perfect example of this concept.

Make sure that the sky area you just painted is completely dry. Start with the lighter (more distant) mountains and move forward. Not only do things in the distance appear lighter, but they also often appear bluer as well. Taking gradual steps up in value, paint in your three mountains, as well as the small strip of lake that runs along the right side of the horizon. The lake can mirror the turquoise color of the sky.

BRUSHES: *No. 1 round and No. 4 filbert or round*

6 For this step, use a selection of midrange to light greens. To begin, use a green slightly lighter than the upper part of the grass from the previous step. Using one of your No. 4 brushes, fill in the remainder of the white, focusing a bit of time on blending the dark bottom portion into the middle portion. Allow this section to dry before moving on.

Mix a couple lighter greens. You want these greens to be light enough to stand out against the base of grasses you've achieved so far. Make sure these greens are quite creamy and slightly tinted with white to add more opacity. You'll want your brush to be damp but not overly wet, so as to keep these strokes nice and crisp. Be conservative with the placement of your blades of grass (too many pieces will actually lessen the impact).

BRUSHES: *No. 1 round and No. 4 filbert or angle brush*

4 Taking the same concept from the previous step, incrementally move down your paper, segmenting the sections into darker shades of paint. Having a few choices of violet and purple to choose from can be helpful for mixing these darker colors.

When you reach the bottom of the darkest section before the grass in the foreground, use the sharpened

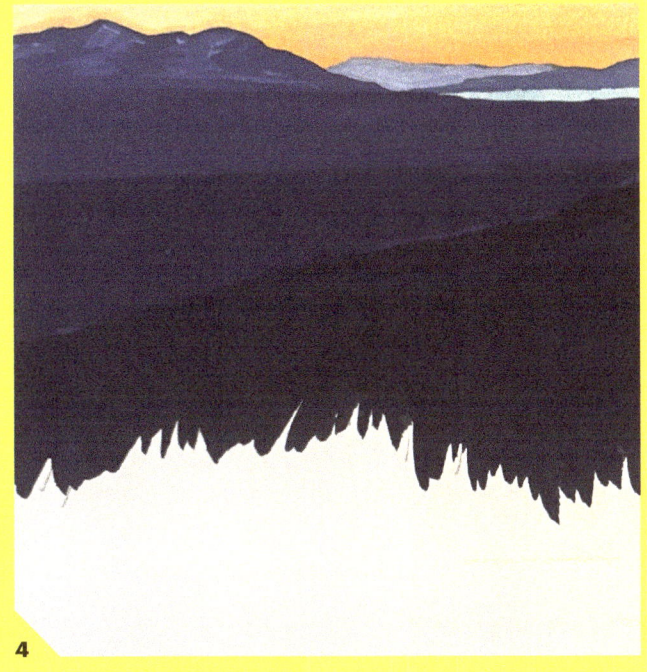

4

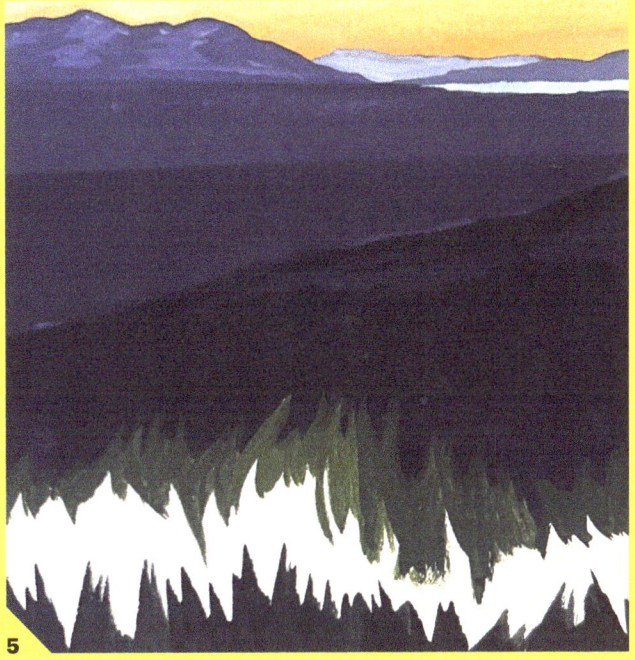

5

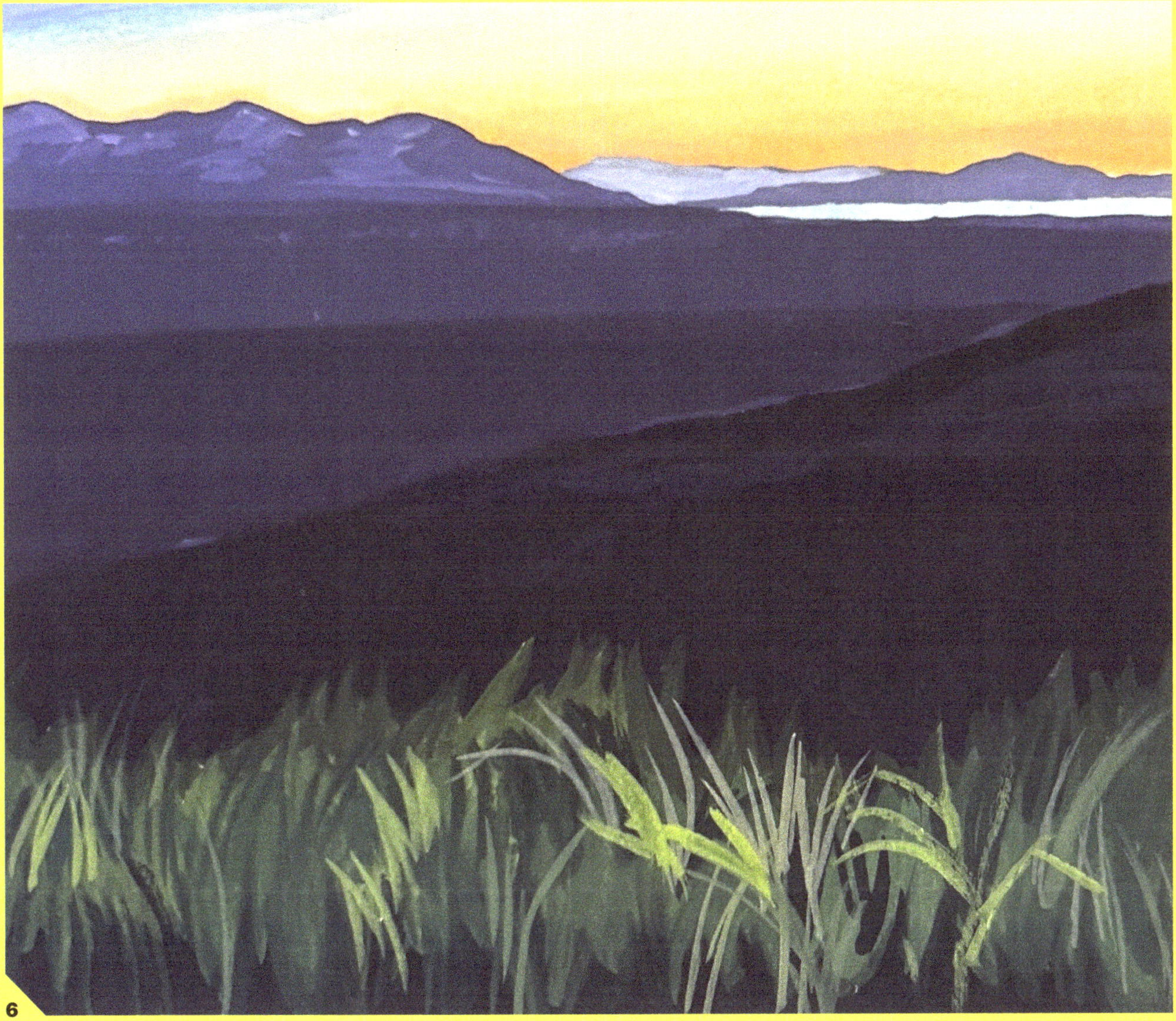

6

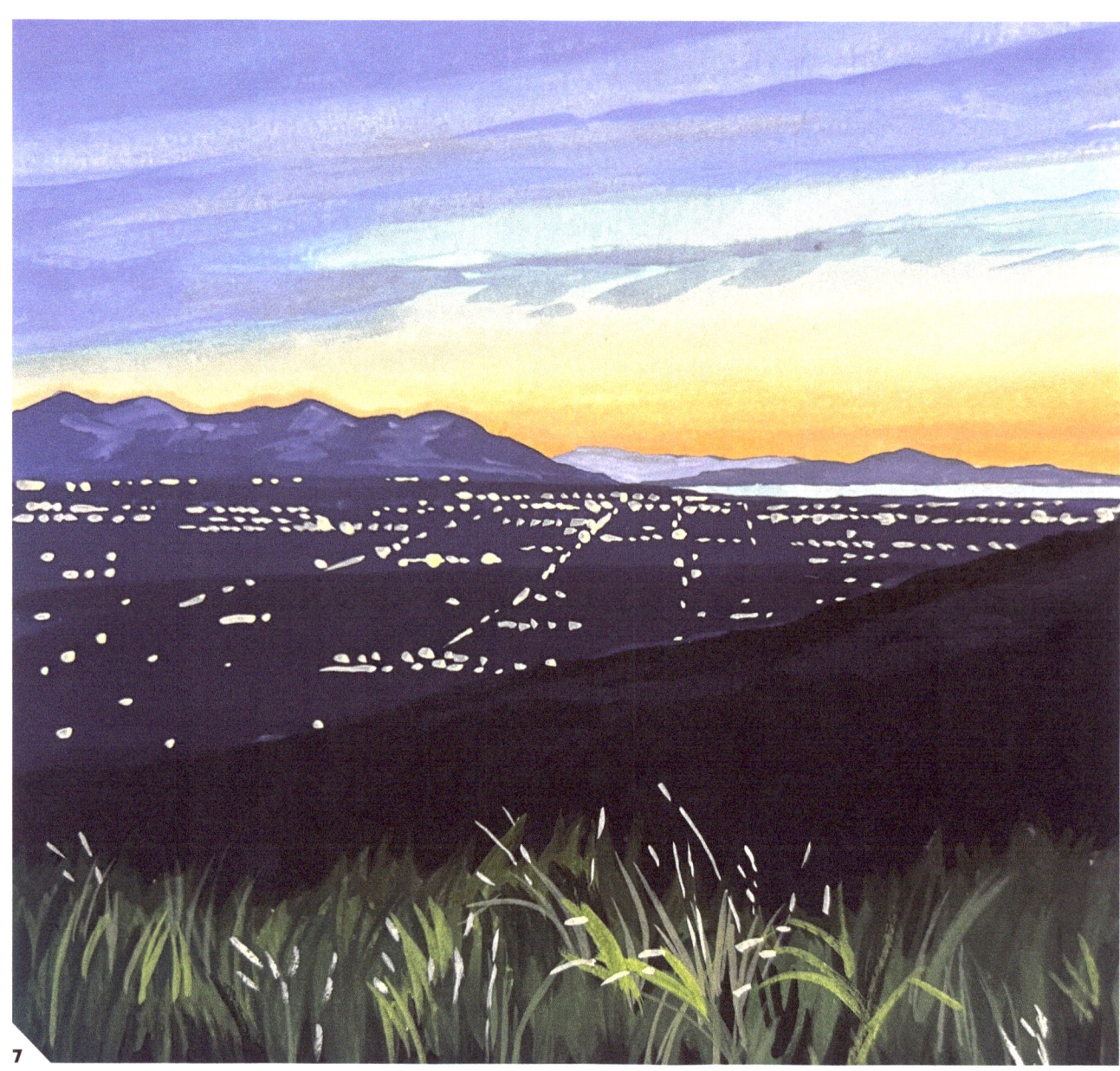

7

7 You've reached the final steps, when this painting really comes to life. For this step, you're only going to use a pale yellow, both for the remaining blades of grass and the first layer of valley lights.

One of the most important parts of this step is getting the perspective correct when placing the valley lights. As you can see in the reference photo, the lights from the roads move into the distance near the mountains, following one-point perspective. You can basically imagine there's a point on the horizon in the very center of the farthest mountain, known as the vanishing point, where all the dots of light are heading.

As you paint these dots of light, vary the size and include small dashes as well as dots. This will help the lights feel more distinct and less uniform.

For the final highlights on the grasses, you can also vary the length and width of the brushstrokes.

BRUSH: *No. 1 round*

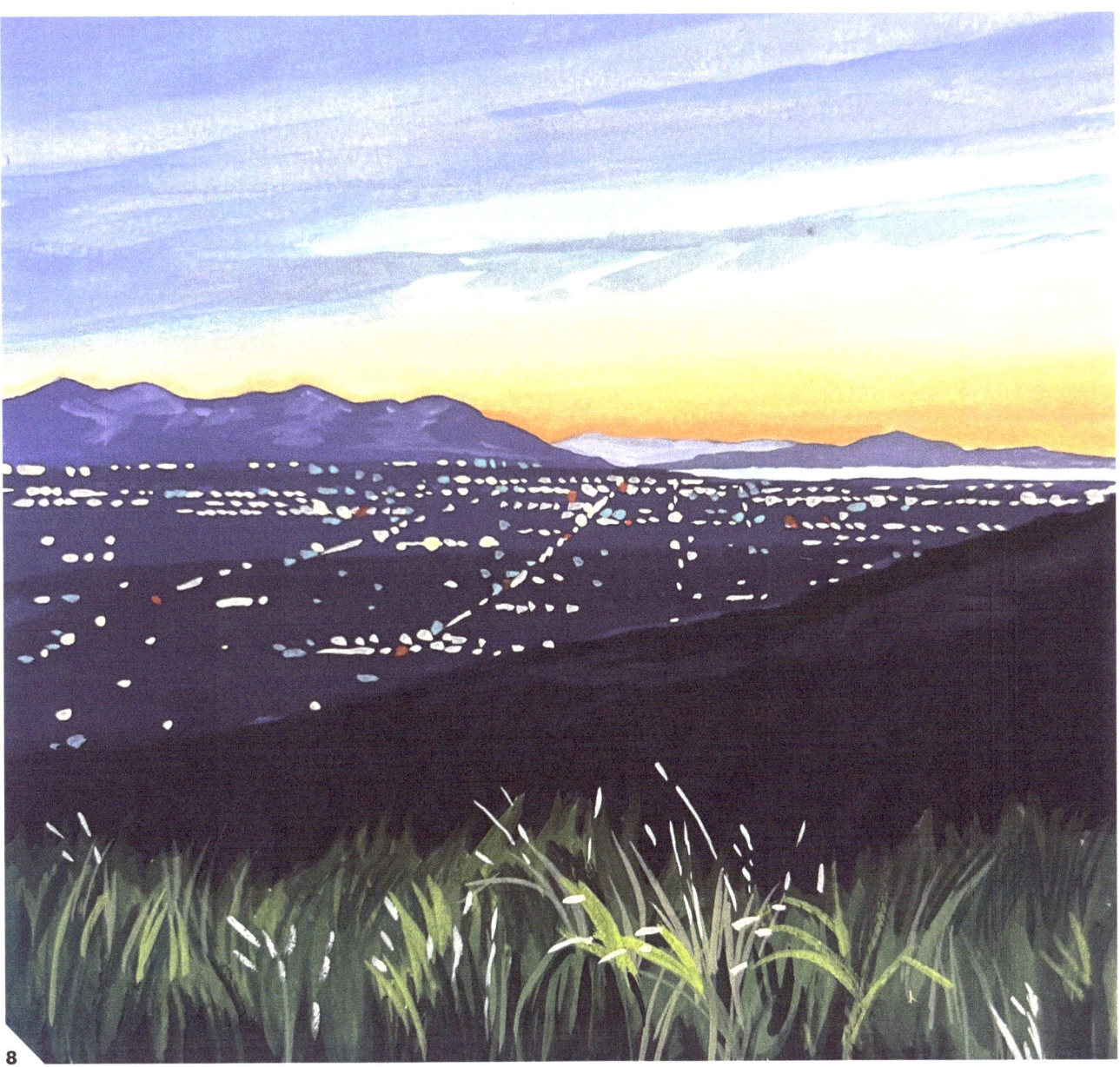

8

8 There are just a few very minute details to think about in this step, but even though they're small, they illustrate what a few well-placed colors can do to enhance the final painting.

Using a very small amount of red and turquoise, mixed to a nice creamy consistency, use the same technique as in the previous step, thoughtfully adding a few dots of color in the city lights. You can be a bit more generous with the turquoise dots, but try not to overdo it.

BRUSH: *No. 1 round*

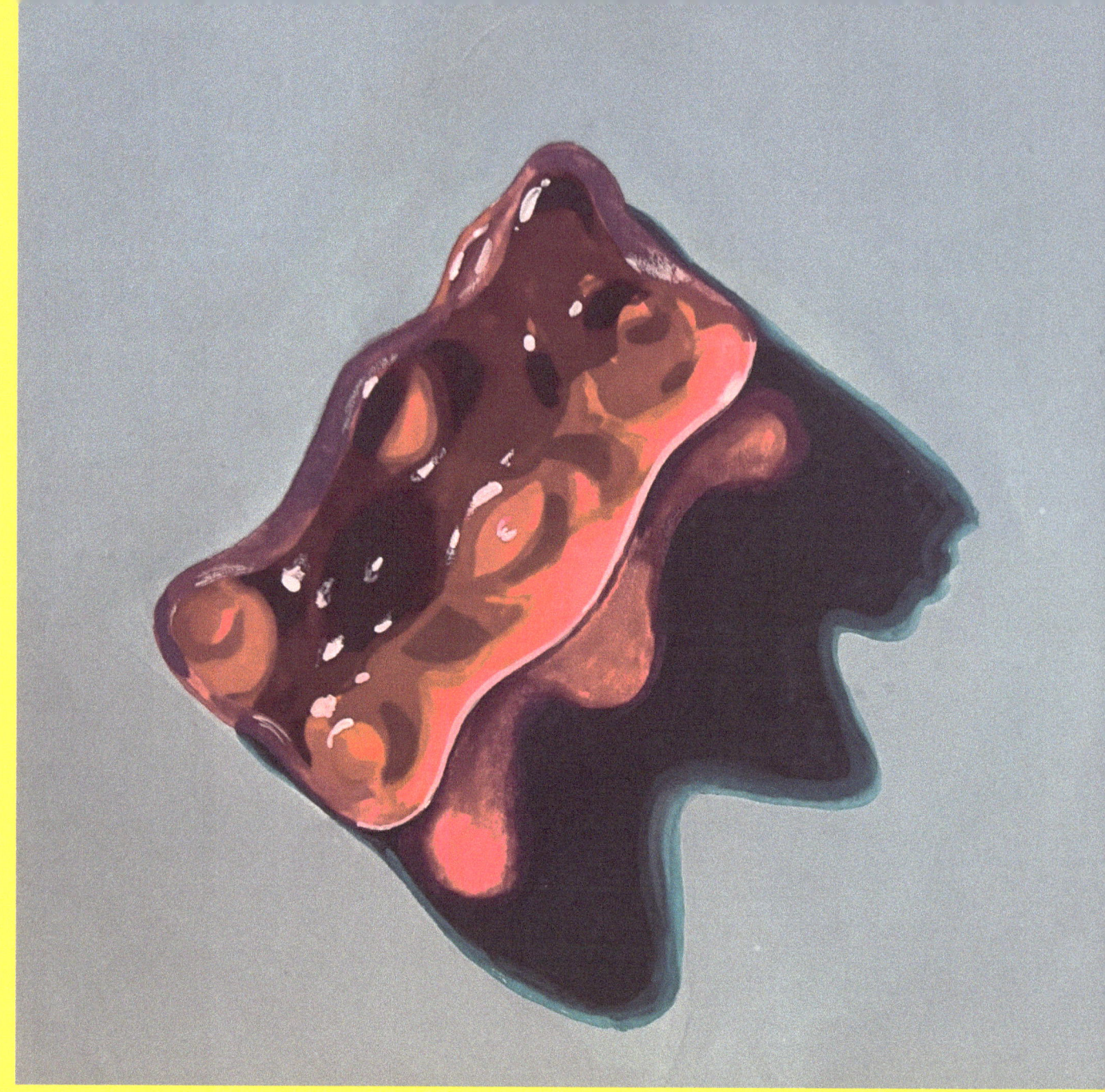

Painting Translucent Items

GUMMY BEAR

Have you ever come across a painting that seemed to glow? Often, the subject in the painting has a translucency that leads to this effect. It can feel a bit magical to create a painting that looks like it has its own light source, but as is true with any seemingly magical effect in art, it's simply a matter of technique. A few tricks, and you'll be painting items that appear to glow too.

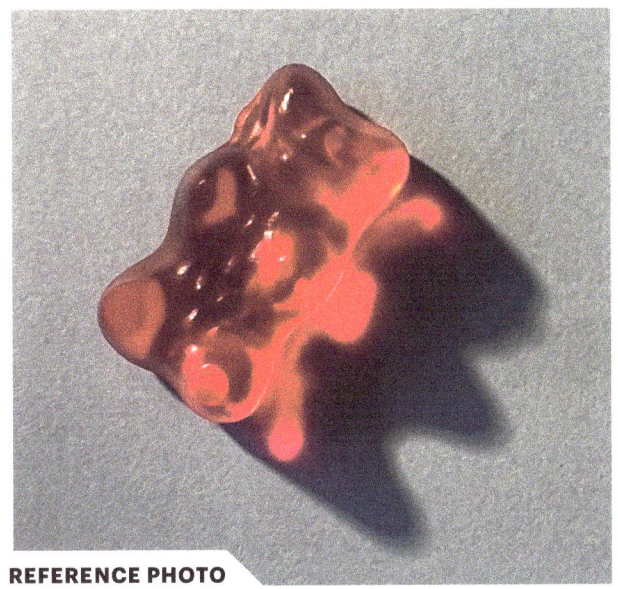

REFERENCE PHOTO

1 Being able to look at this object with an eye for shape will be very helpful in this project. A lot of the information about these shapes is figured out in the underdrawing stage.

Because the gummy bear is basically a rectangular cube, I find it easiest to first sketch the shape of a rectangle. You can then add the curves around this very basic shape. Think of the shadow in a similar way. It's also basically a rectangle of equal size.

When drawing in the details you want to consider while painting, concentrate on the places within both the gummy bear and the shadow where you see strong changes in value.

1

2 This is definitely the easiest step in the process. Remember to keep your paint the consistency of thick cream or milk. You want to make sure it's not so thick as to be unspreadable, but not too thin or you'll be stuck painting layer upon layer. Be sure to allow your background to dry completely between these layers, or the places where the paint is still wet will not accept another layer, making your painting streaky.

BRUSHES: *No. 6 or 8 filbert or flat*

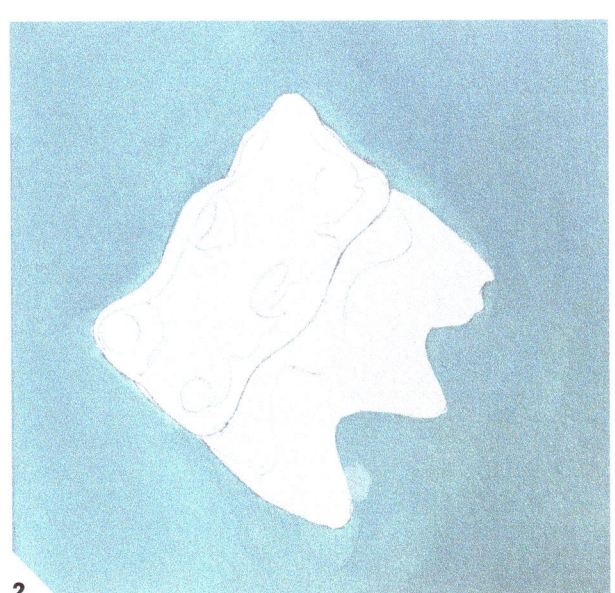

2

3 Make sure the brush you're using is nice and clean. Because you'll be painting pinks and reds, make sure the colors are nice and pure. Do not gray them down at all. Starting with the shadow, use a very bright pink. Opera pink is a great color to use and can be tinted with a bit of white.

The area on the far right side of the gummy bear is slightly darker than the pink in the shadow, but not much darker. Because you've already mapped out the shape in the underdrawing, filling in this shape should be really easy.

BRUSH: *No. 4 filbert or round*

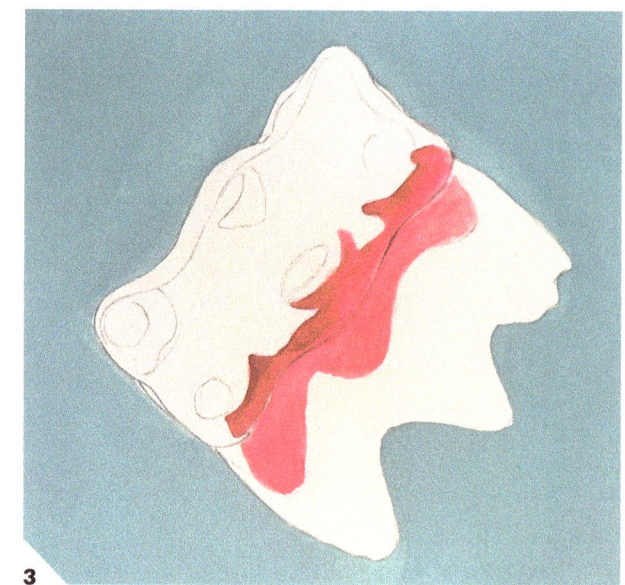

4 To make the pink reflection in the shadow really pop, use a dark color for the remaining shadow. The contrast between the pink and the very dark turquoise will help accentuate the feeling that light is moving through the transparent gummy bear.

Notice that there's also a very small amount of the darker shadow running along the very edge of the place where the gummy bear meets the shadow, and also extending slightly along the top and bottom of the candy.

After rinsing your brush, lightly blend some of the darker shadow color into portions of the pink reflection, leaving a few portions brighter than the rest. To finish off the shadow, blend a bit of darker turquoise along the outside of the shadow and then soften the lines to make the cast shadow less sharp.

BRUSHES: *No. 1 round and No. 4 filbert or round*

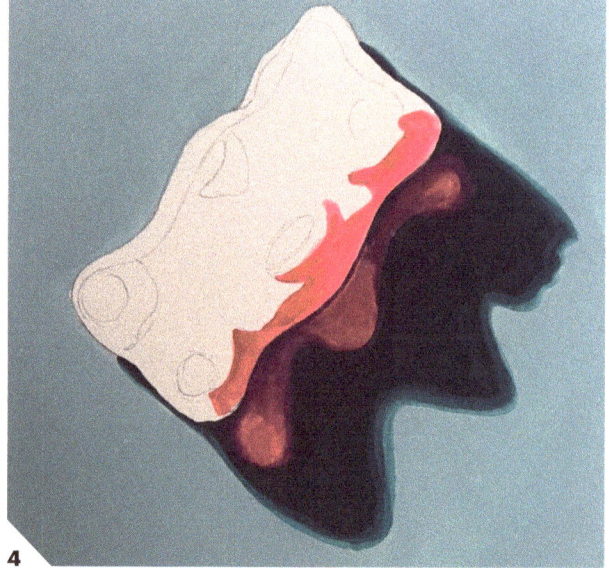

5 For this next step, try to observe the next two darker red colors in the reference photo. It can be helpful to limit yourself to trying to see only a few things at once. The only thing you need to currently paint are those midtone reds, the ones that would probably be about a 50 or 60 if changed to a grayscale.

BRUSHES: *No. 1 round and filbert*

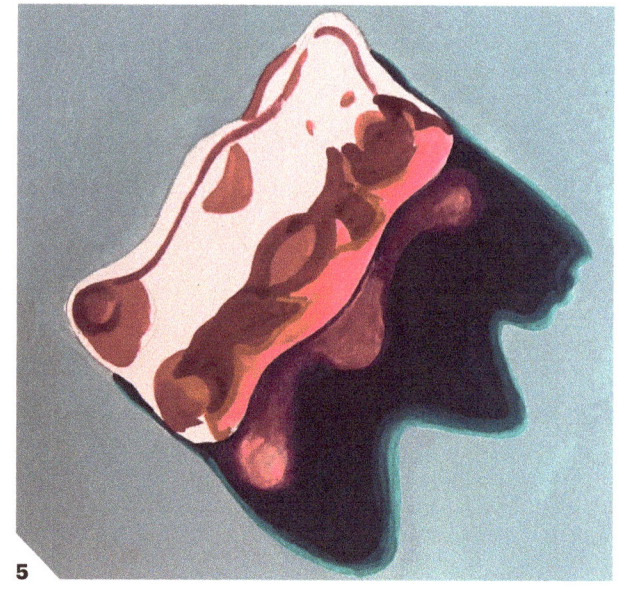

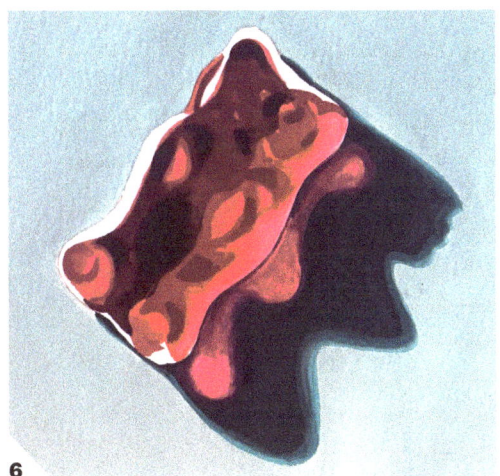

6

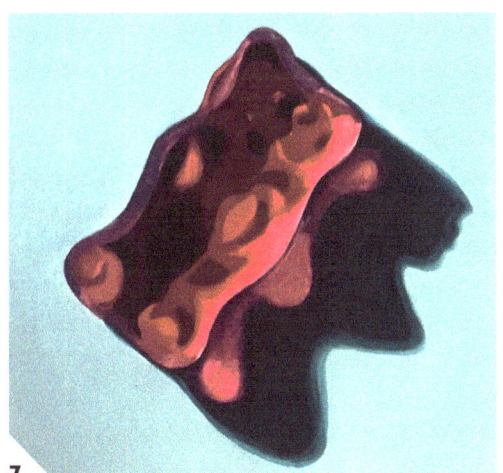

7

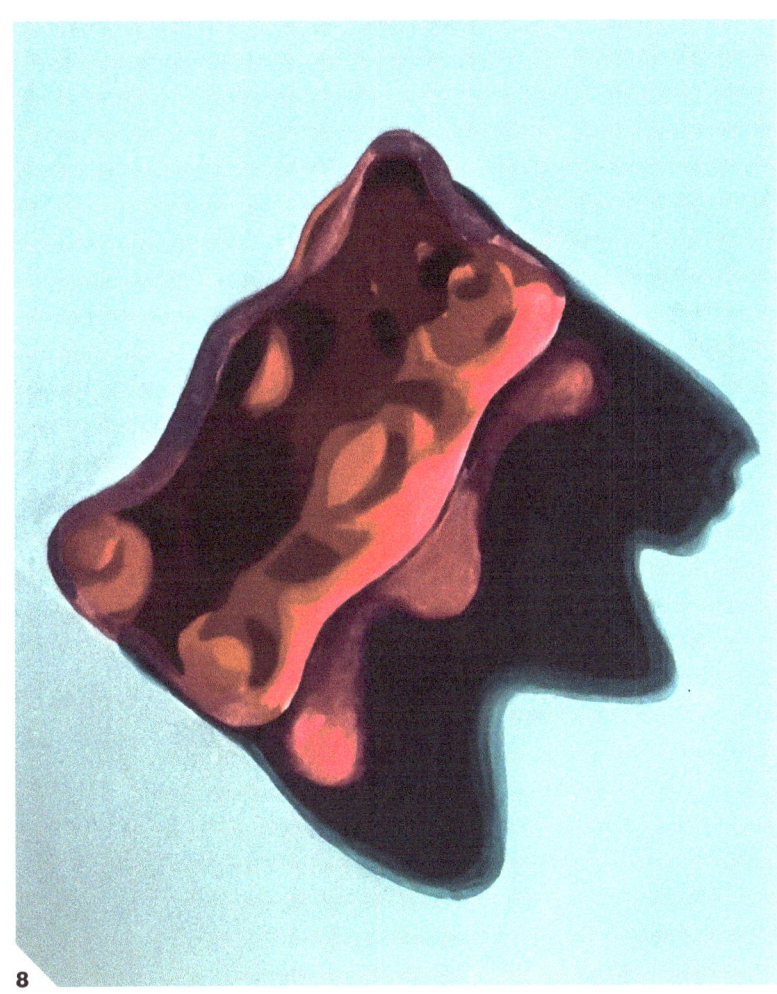

8

6 Imagine you're just working your way down the value scale, except instead of gray, you're using red. You've already added your light and middle values and for this step, you'll move on to those dark values. Remember, when making red darker you can add violet as well as black.

_____

BRUSHES: *No. 1 filbert or round and No. 4 filbert or round*

7 The remaining portions of the gummy bear that haven't been painted in yet are interesting because they are all located on the outside "walls" (for lack of a better word) of the candy. The sides of the gummy bear appear less intensely red as the parts of the candy looked straight down on. One of the easiest ways to paint this is to tone the red in these areas by adding gray to your pure hue. You don't need to add a lot of gray. A small amount will suffice.

_____

BRUSH: *No. 1 round*

8 By now you're probably as excited to add the highlights in the final steps as I am, because you know what a huge difference those final marks make. These highlights work to give the painting a final hit of dimension.

Besides the obvious highlights created from the direct light, there's also a fun highlight that runs along the bottom of the candy where it meets the shadowed edge. This additional highlight will give the candy the extra appearance of glowing.

_____

BRUSH: *No. 1 round*

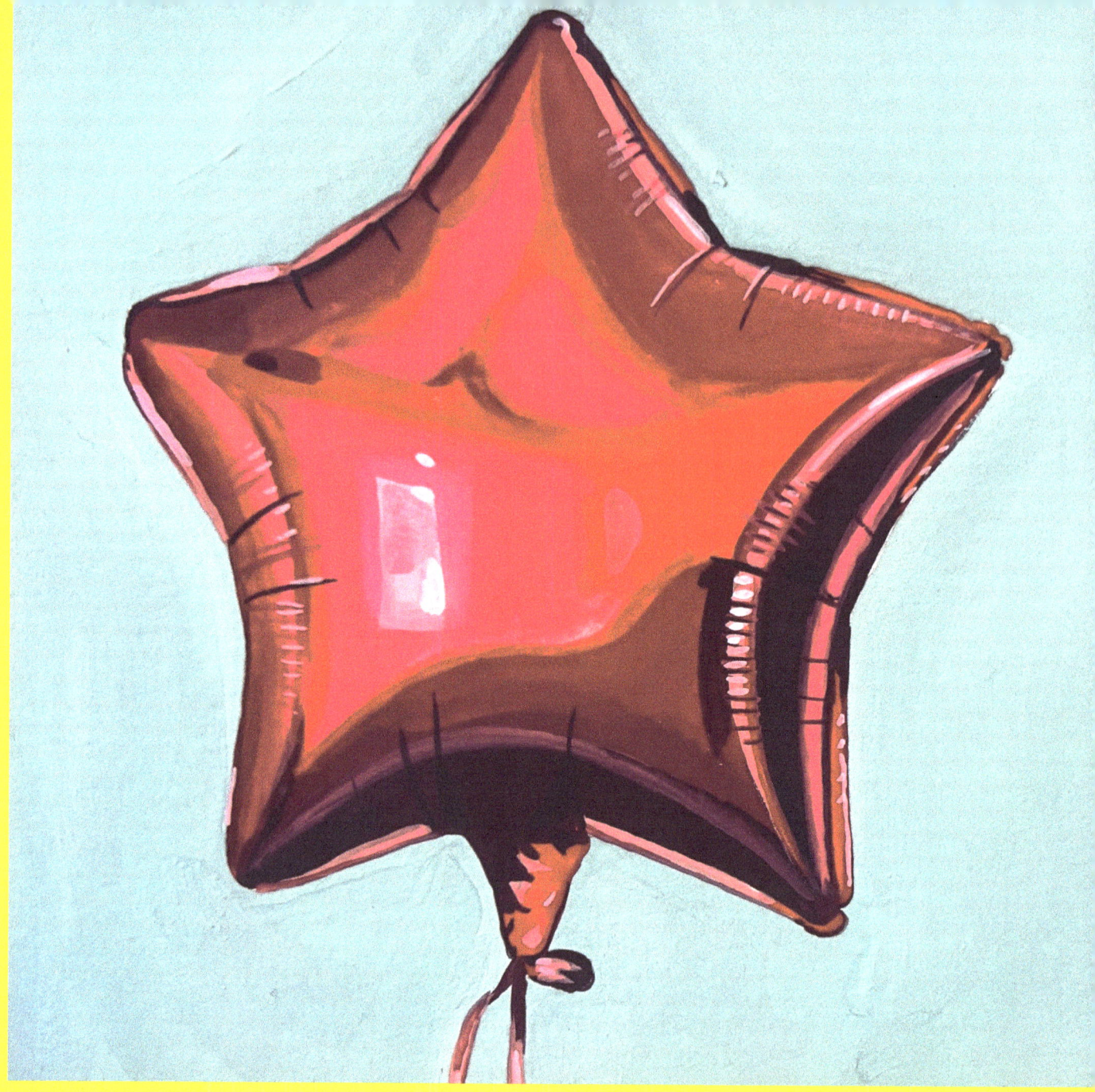

Painting Shiny Objects

BALLOON

Reflective surfaces can show up in all sorts of subject matter, whether it's an actual mirror, a wet road, or a glossy object. The metallic spoon that you painted earlier is also a good example of a shiny object; and in this lesson, you'll continue in that vein. Although this piece will have less of a mirror-like reflection, you'll be focusing on the places where light and dark do reflect in the surface of your object, but it won't translate color in the same way as metal. Because of this, it'll be a bit easier to focus on the gradations in the overall color of the object (in this case, the red of the balloon) without getting caught up in the colors being reflected.

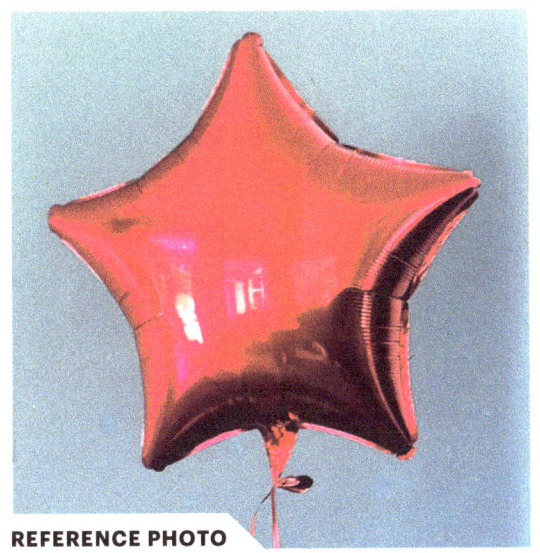

REFERENCE PHOTO

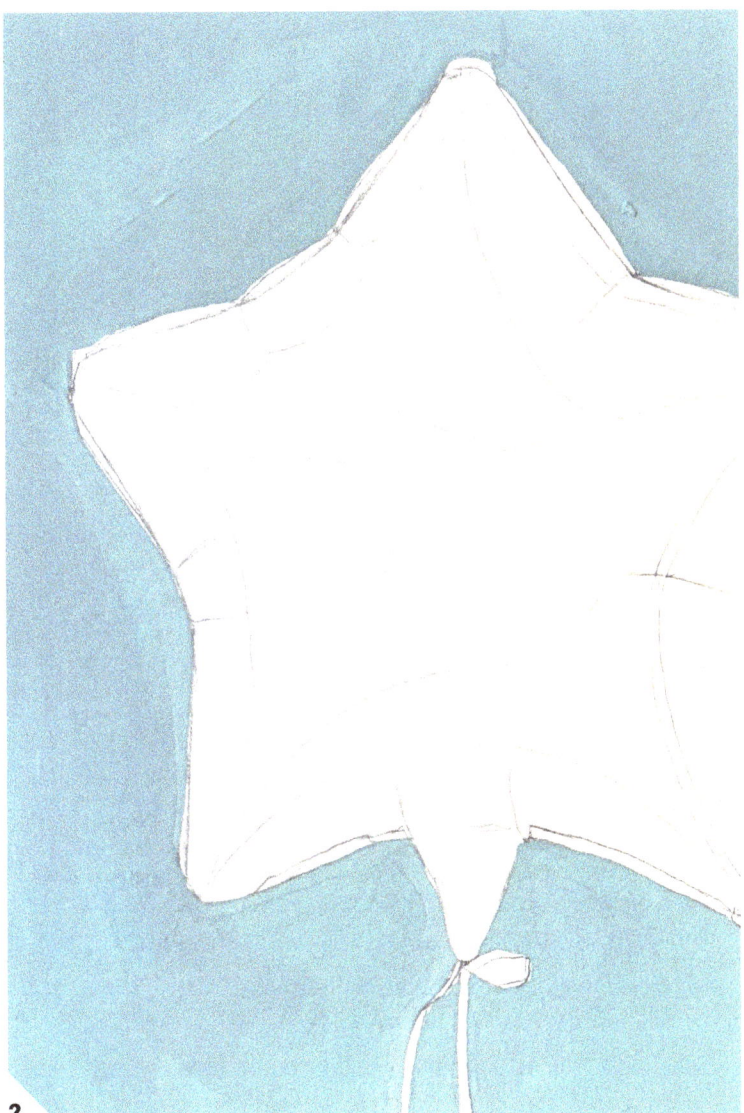

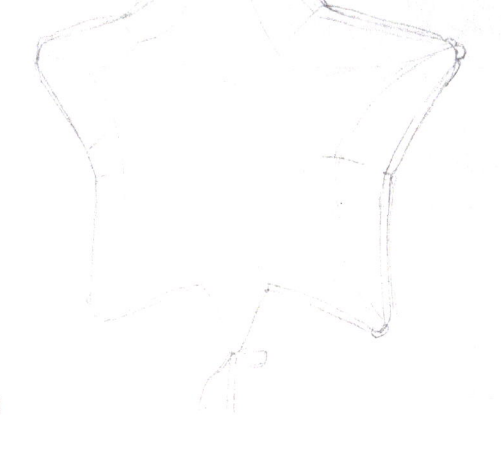

1

2

1 As you draw, proper placement of the balloon's five corners will be a good reference for the rest of your shapes. You'll notice when looking at the reference photo that the light and dark shapes reflected in the shiny surface mimic the shape of the balloon. As with the metal spoon, it's helpful to think of those light and dark shapes independently. Don't worry about making sense of what you see in the reflection. If you get the values correct, the image will read as realistic.

2 At this point, I hardly need to tell you how to get a good background color down. I'm guessing you could probably teach me a thing or two by now. But just in case you're beginning with this project, I'll explain. Mix a good amount of paint for the background color of your choice. Make sure you have enough paint mixed to cover the area in at least two coats so you don't have to remix and chance having to rematch the color exactly. Make sure your paint is mixed to a nice even, creamy consistency and use the biggest brush you feel comfortable using while still maintaining control.

BRUSHES: *No. 6 or 8 filbert or flat*

3 Starting with a very bright red-orange, paint the sections that correspond to this midrange red from the reference photo. Keep the hue very pure, making sure to not contaminate it with any other colors, tints, or shades. Because of the way the light shines on the balloon, the middle section extending up into the top left corner of the balloon has mostly mid- to light range of values, while the lower right corner is predominantly dark values.

Notice how the paint in this step looks a bit like a spiderweb on the left side of the painting.

BRUSHES: *No. 1 round and filbert and No. 4 filbert*

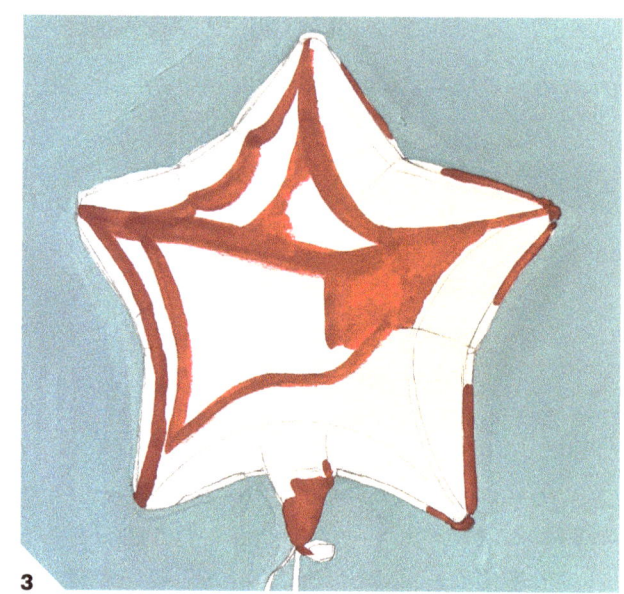

4 You'll step down a level or so in value with this next red. You might already have a cadmium red that works well for this section, or you can mix a bit of violet in with your bright red.

Moving out toward the edges of the balloon, fill in the areas along the outside of the top two sections, as well as the small section on the far left edge. You can darken the edges of a few of these sections if you want to (as I've done in my example).

BRUSHES: *No. 1 filbert or round and No. 4 filbert or flat*

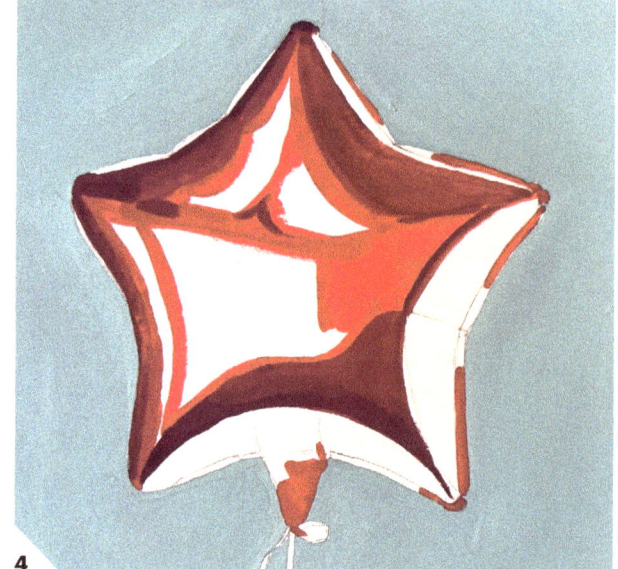

5 It's time to add those very dark values of red. We already discussed how they're predominantly located in the bottom and bottom right portions of the balloon, but if you look closely, there are a few other places where you can add dark strokes.

It may look like the dark values in this step are the same, but if possible, make the section on the bottom slightly less dark (more maroon) than the section on the right. This subtle difference will do a lot to make your painting feel more complex.

BRUSHES: *No. 1 round and No. 4 filbert or round*

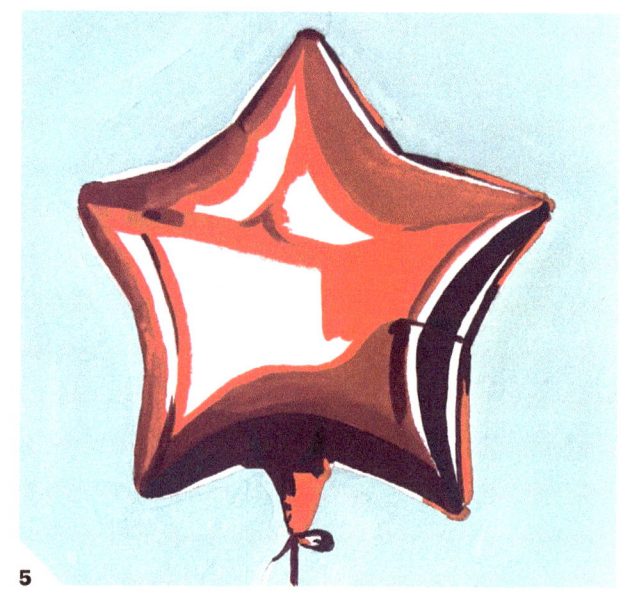

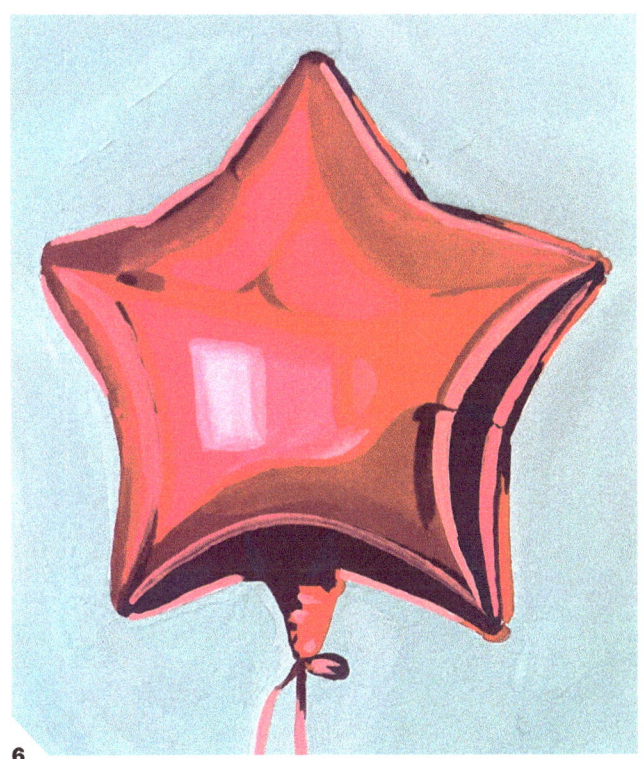

6

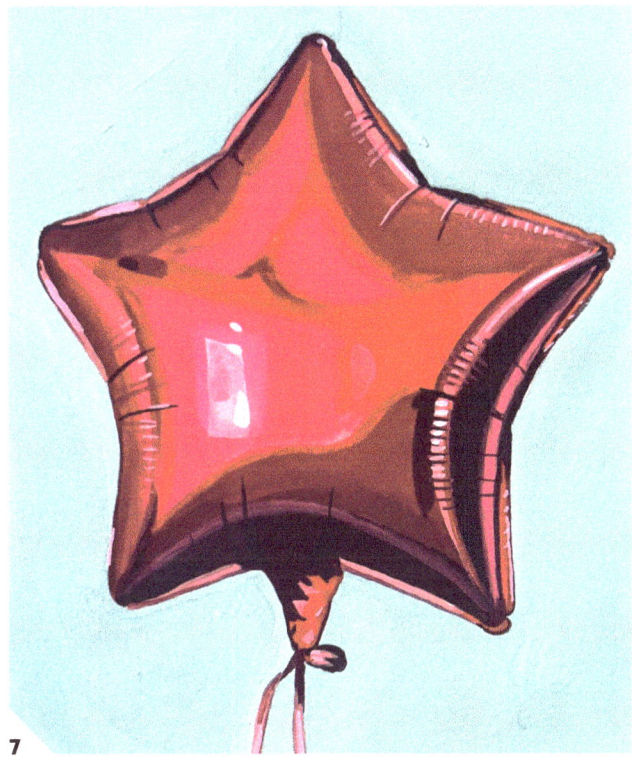

7

6 Up to this point you haven't added any tints to your colors, but in this step you'll paint a range of lighter "red" values. The only way to do this is to use a pre-mixed pink (like opera pink) or to add white, which will automatically turn your red into pink. Even though you'll paint almost as much pink onto this balloon as you did red, it's still going to read to the viewer as a very red object.

For the sections with the darkest pinks, I recommend using a premixed pink. You may choose to tone it down with a bit of red or orange, and even a bit of white, so it doesn't seem quite so neon.

Don't be afraid to mix many different pinks. Although most will be tinted colors (meaning you'll add at least a small amount of white), the reflected light along the bottom is less intense and can be toned down a bit with gray.

_____

BRUSHES: *No. 1 round and No. 4 filbert or flat*

7 It's time to add the detail! Normally these details entail mostly white highlights, but for this painting, you'll also add details in the shadows where the balloon bends and crinkles.

I almost always start with shadows, because the highlights often sit slightly on top of the shadow and will look a bit peculiar if they're added first.

Using your fine-tipped brush, use a small amount of paint to prevent accidentally creating a blob. It's also helpful to use a fairly light touch with these thin strokes. You don't have to press down at all. Beginning with those dark creases, work sparingly around your balloon. It's always easier to add more brushstrokes than to cover them up.

Finish off with the remaining highlights. Don't forget to add a few small marks in the center of the highlight in the middle of the balloon to make this area pop (no pun intended).

_____

BRUSH: *No. 1 round*

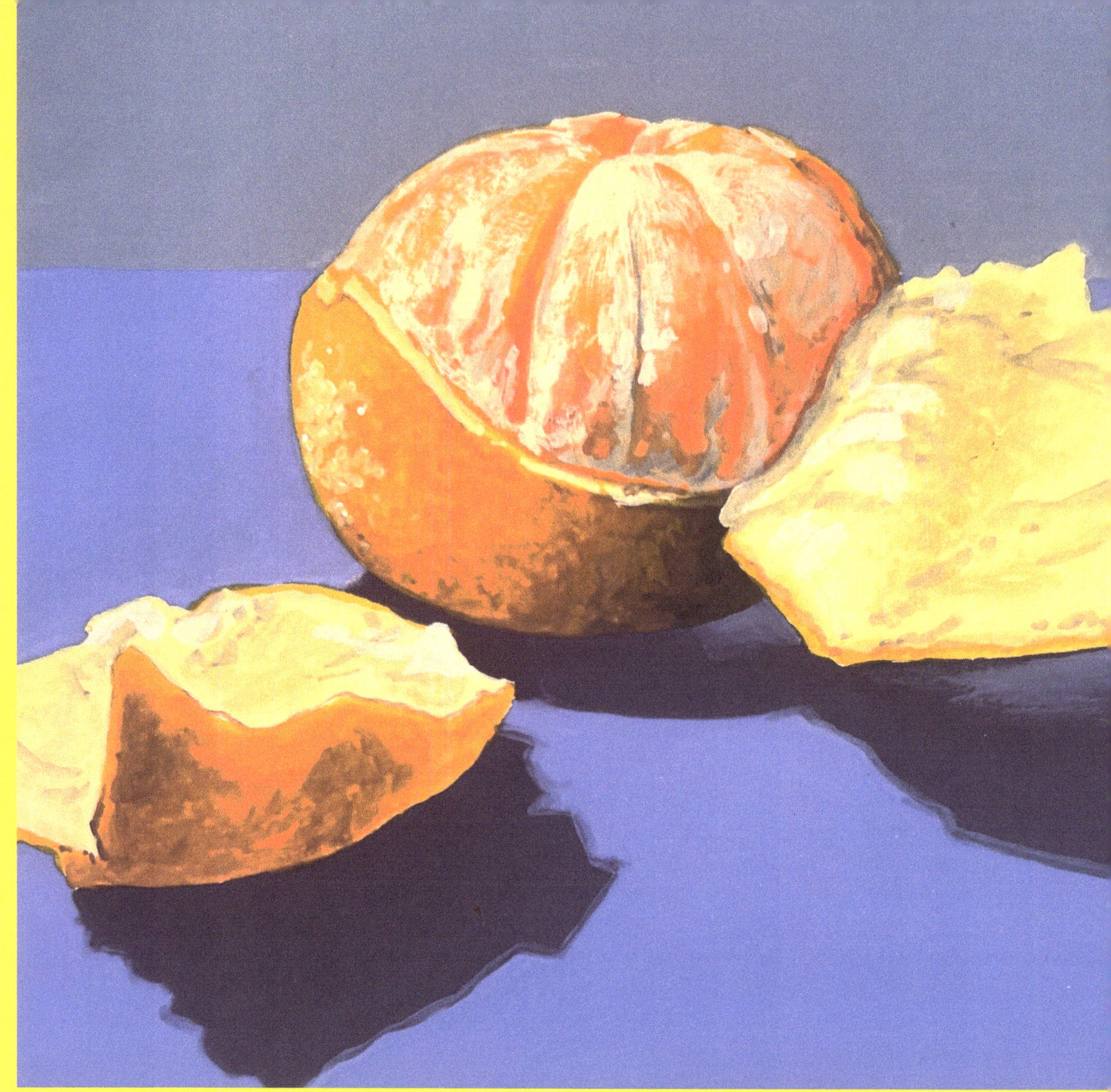

Painting Different Textures

ORANGE

The more you paint, the more you'll come across a variety of different textures in the objects you choose to recreate. Whether it's the bumpy skin of an orange with its flakey pith (like this project), the soft fur of a cat, or the rough bark of a tree, having a few helpful tools in your tool belt can help a lot.

The more texture an object has, the more likely you'll need to incorporate some layering into your process. Although drybrushing is certainly not the only technique you'll use when creating texture, I've found it's often quite helpful for a large variety of surfaces.

1 Begin by drawing your horizon line. Even though this isn't a landscape, you' still utilize some principles of perspective when drawing. This underdrawing is a bit more complex than some, so it might be helpful to lightly block in where you want the shapes to go.

When it comes to drawing the orange segments, it can be helpful to imagine the orange is a globe and the lines of the segments are actually the lines of longitude. You'll notice they follow the contour of the orange.

2 Choose which color you want for the background. You can see I chose to modify my colors a bit. Because orange and blue are complementary colors, I decided to go with a brighter hue of blue in my foreground than appears in the reference so the orange appears to pop off the page a bit more. For the background, I decided to tone that color and drop the value just a little bit so it appears to recede. You'll notice that for the shadow I also used blue, this time made darker by adding a bit of violet and black. All three of these analogous blues will help complement the complementary colors in the rest of the painting.

BRUSHES: *Nos. 4 and 6 filbert or flat*

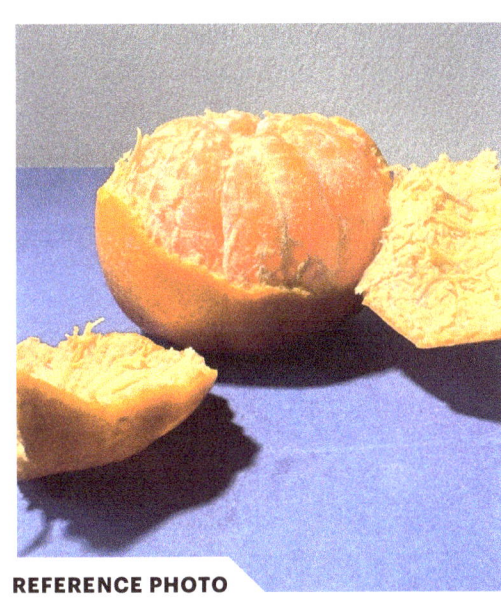

REFERENCE PHOTO

1

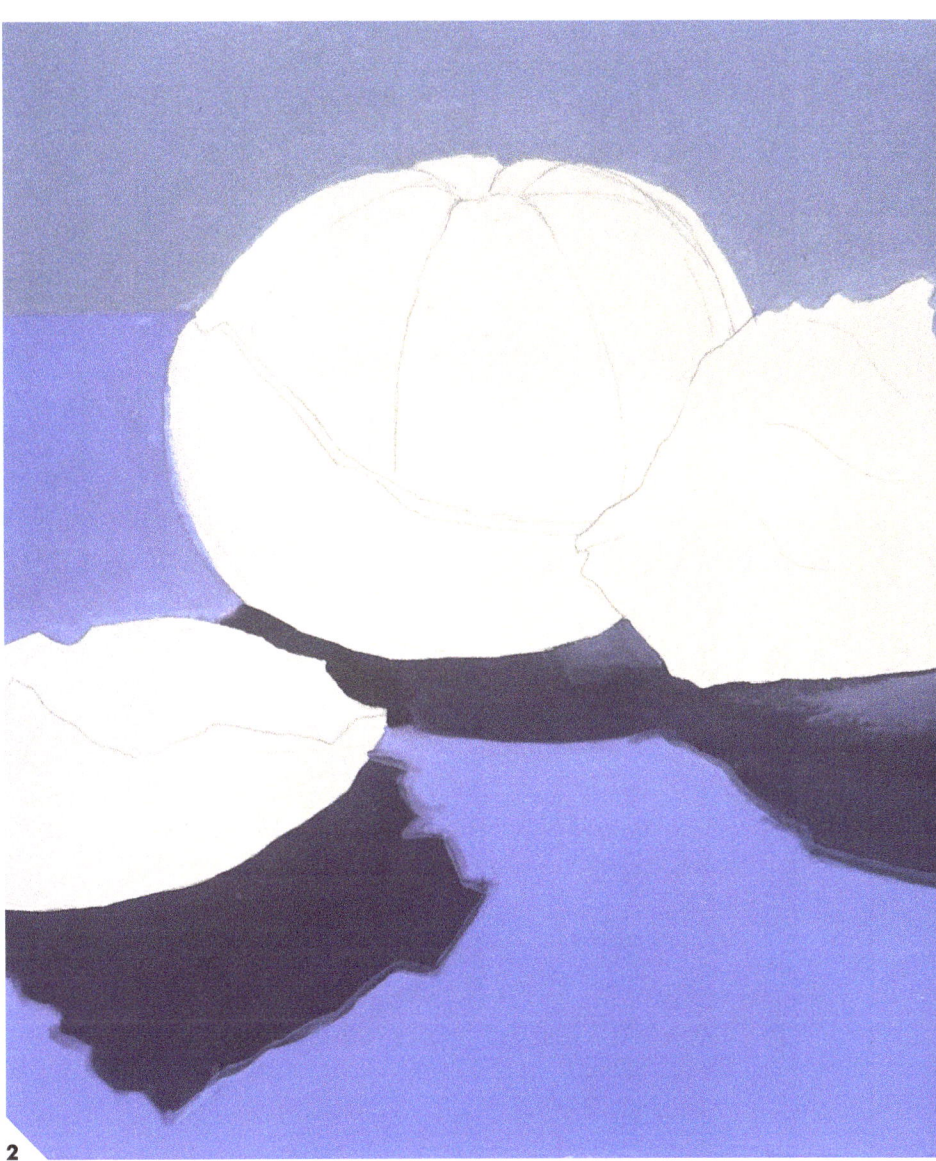

2

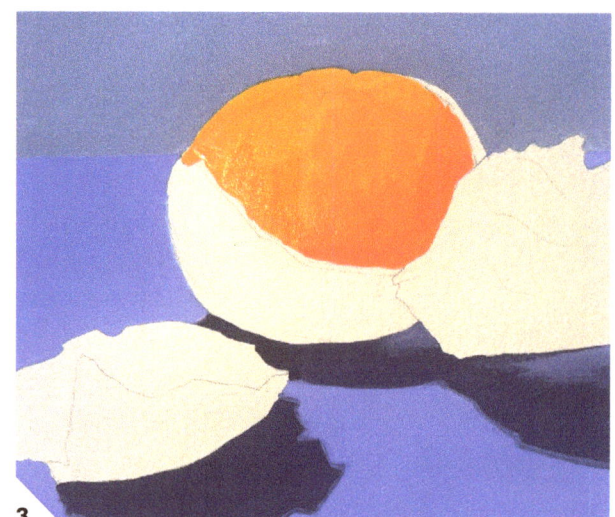

3

Make sure your brushes and water are clean when you begin working with your oranges. I recommend rinsing out your water and starting fresh. Because orange and blue are complementary colors, if you get any of the blue mixed into the orange it will gray it out very easily and one of the things that makes this painting interesting is the vivid hue of the orange.

Begin with your lightest orange. If you don't have one premixed, you'll want to add quite a bit of yellow, instead of white, to lighten it without tinting.

Working from left to right, gradually paint the orange segments, slowly darkening the orange as you move right. Here's another example of how you'll darken the orange by adding more red to your orange instead of adding black, because you want to keep the brightness and vibrancy of the color.

———————————

BRUSH: *No. 4 or 6 filbert*

4

Paint the outer skin of the orange in much the same way you painted the orange segments, with a gradient of light orange to dark orange. After that layer has dried, go in with the shadows, using a small round to stipple on small dots of darker orange. Beginning on the lightest side, use an orange slightly darker and more gray to paint the small indentations of the orange skin. Because the skin is a dimpled texture, your brushstrokes need to accentuate that texture as well. In much the same

way that you created the bright orange gradient, you'll now create a gradient of small dots with your dark orange. As you move to the darkest spot, the orange should actually be quite brown.

———————————

BRUSH: *Nos. 1 round and filbert and No. 4 filbert*

5

For the base layer of the skin's interior mix a pale buttery yellow to the consistency of milk. You don't want this layer to be too thick because you will be painting over it, but you also want it to be thick enough to sufficiently cover the paper. While painting this layer, use some of the buttery color to paint along the edge of the rind that's still attached to the orange. This section is important because it gives the rind depth as it covers the orange segments.

To give the interior of the skin a bit more texture, mix a tan that is slightly darker than the buttery yellow you just used. You don't want to add too much of this, as it mostly represents the shadows. Focus on the curved portion of the peel on the right-hand side. Adding this shadow will give it shape.

———————————

BRUSHES: *No. 1 round and No. 4 filbert*

6

Adding the dusty white pith to the individual orange segments is definitely my favorite part of this project. Not only does it give the segments a lot more dimension, but it's the part of the orange that makes it look the most realistic.

The white you'll use for this step shouldn't be pure white, but closer to an off-white. As you can probably tell by looking at the painting example for this step, you'll use drybrushing to achieve the effect of flakey pith. Be sure to start with a nearly dry brush before adding a small amount of creamy paint to the tip. Before you begin painting on your piece, drag your brush along your board or a paper towel to get off most of the paint. It's the individual brush-strokes that give this texture its believable effect. As you paint, pay close attention to where the light hits.

———————————

BRUSHES: *No. 1 round and No. 4 filbert*

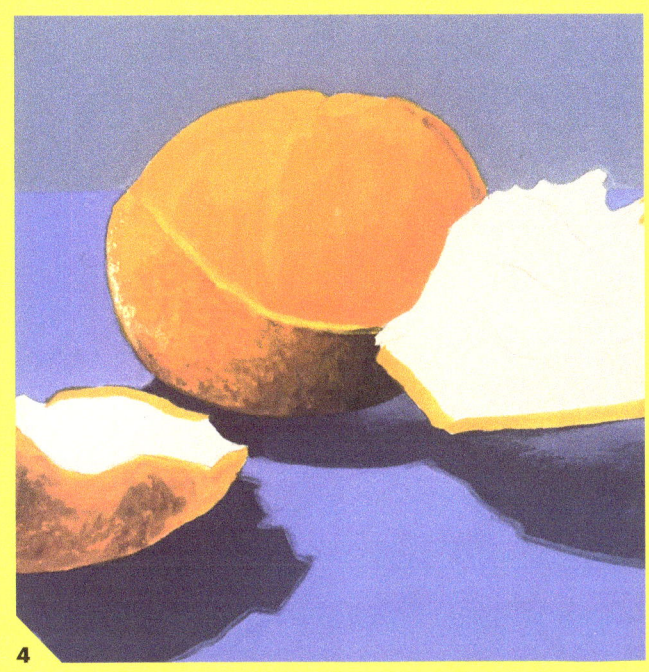

4

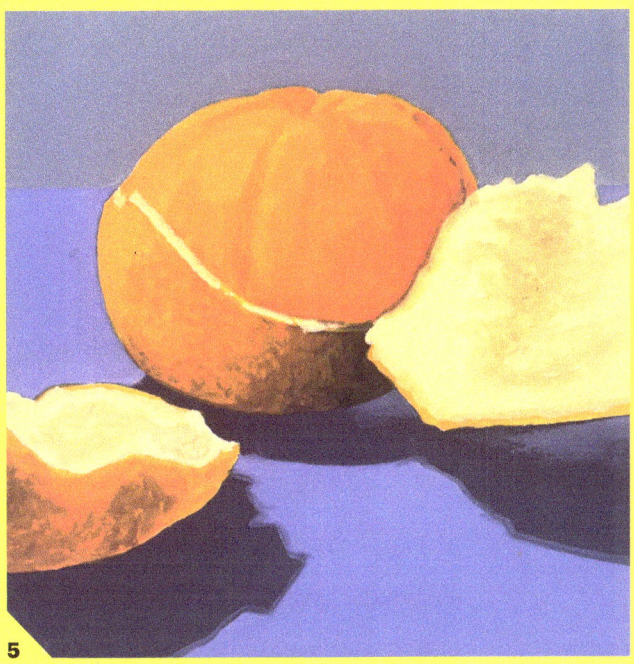

5

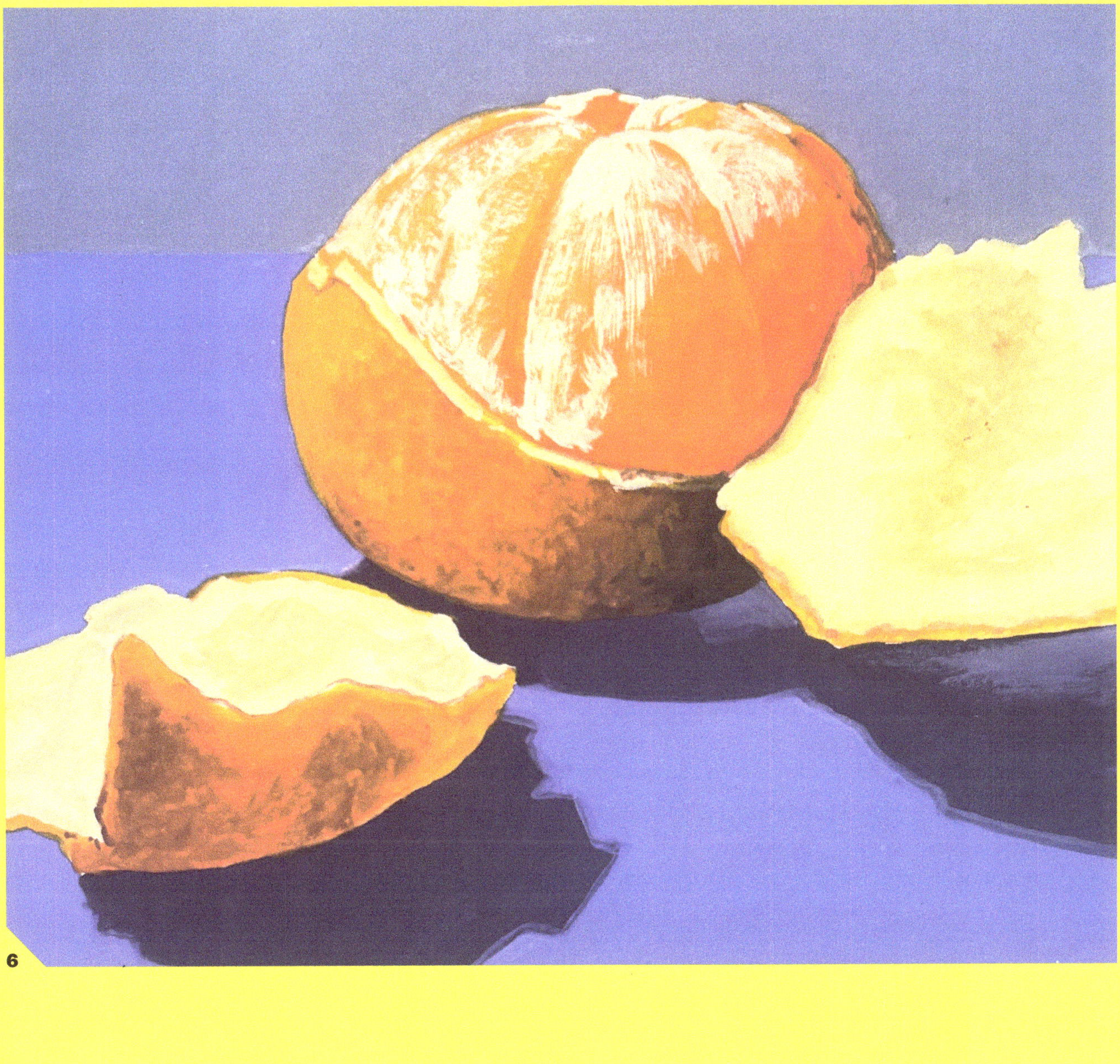

6

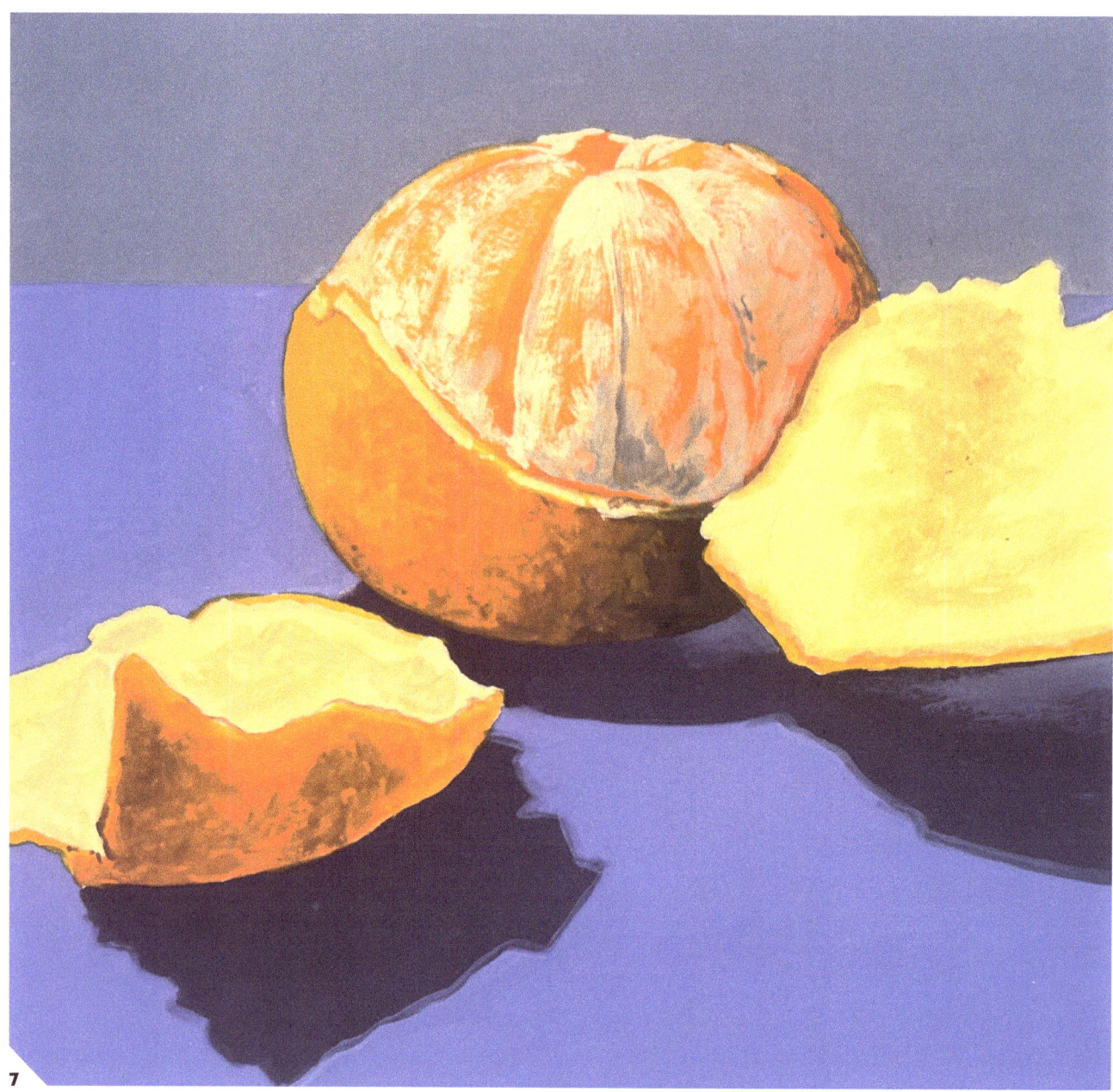

7

7 To create the correct tone for the shadowed pith on the right side of the orange, mix a midtone gray (about 30–40 percent) with a little bit of blue or lavender. In the same way you drybrushed the pith in the previous step, continue with the shadowed portion. Be sure to keep some of that orange showing through. You don't want to cover the base you worked so hard on. In fact, it's those bits of orange showing through that give the orange the effect of glowing a bit.

BRUSH: *No. 4 filbert*

8 The final step is your chance to add the tiny details you may have missed in the previous steps. Spend a bit of time on the shadows and highlights of the rind. You can also use some more stippling to add the highlights to the outside of the rind where the direct light hits.

BRUSH: *No. 1 round*

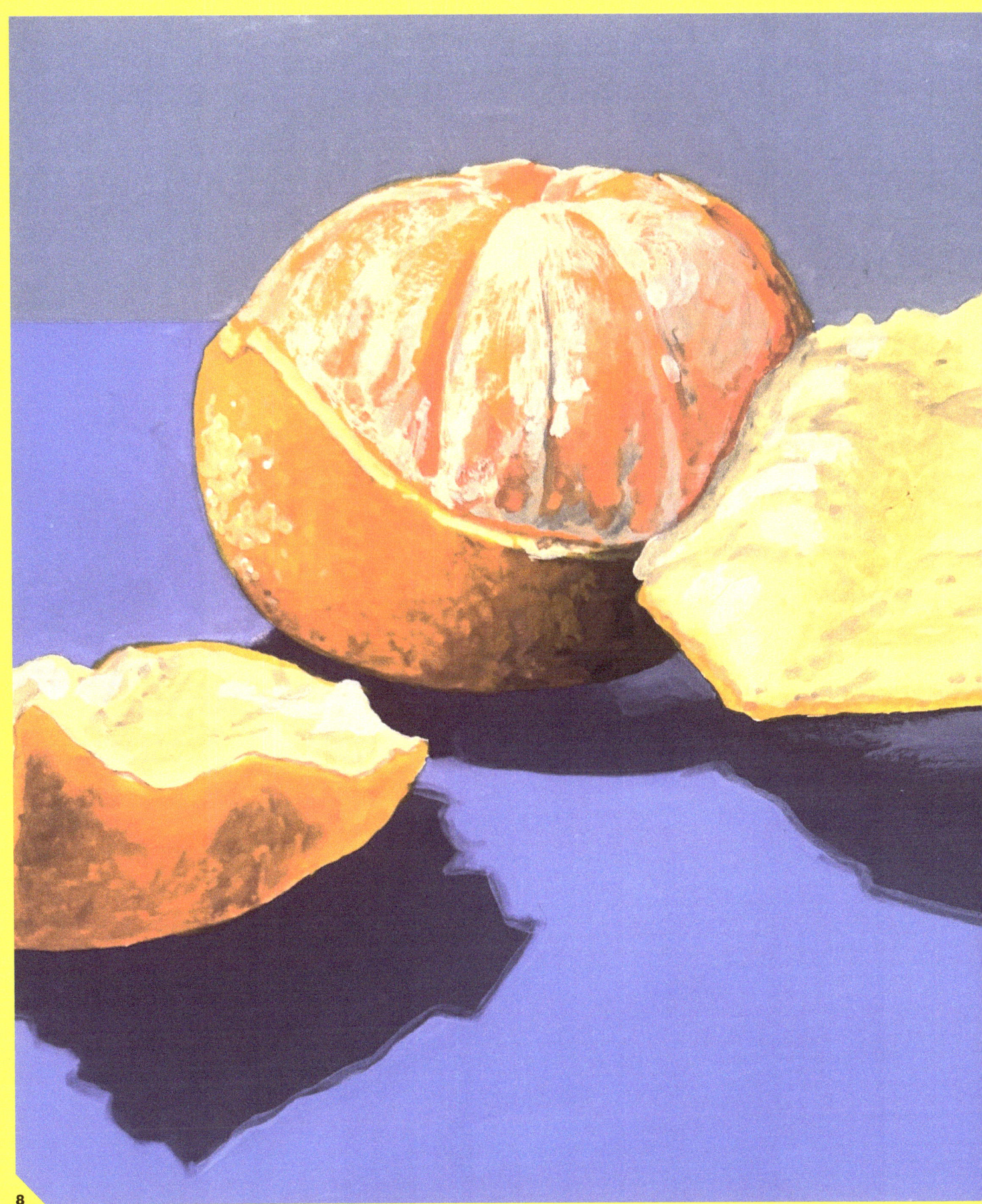

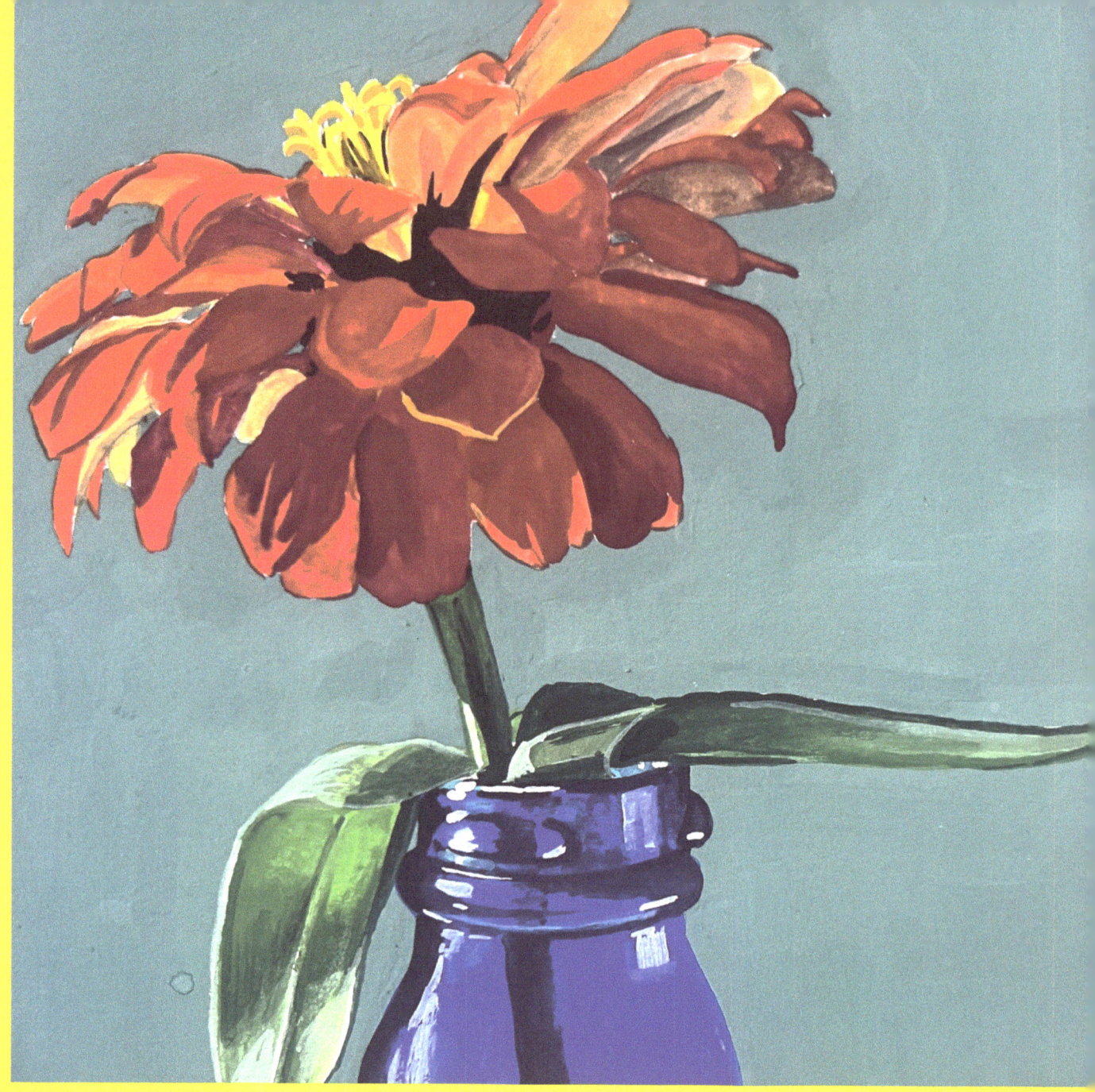

Painting Botanicals

FLOWER

There's such a wide range of subjects that falls into the category of botanicals. You might paint a still life with flowers (as in this project) or you might study a plant out in nature.

Because you'll focus on the closeup examination of leaves, stems, and petals, these paintings are often quite detailed, and there's the opportunity to get as intricate as you want. Feel free to make your painting more detailed or choose to simplify in ways I haven't. It's your painting, and the choice is yours.

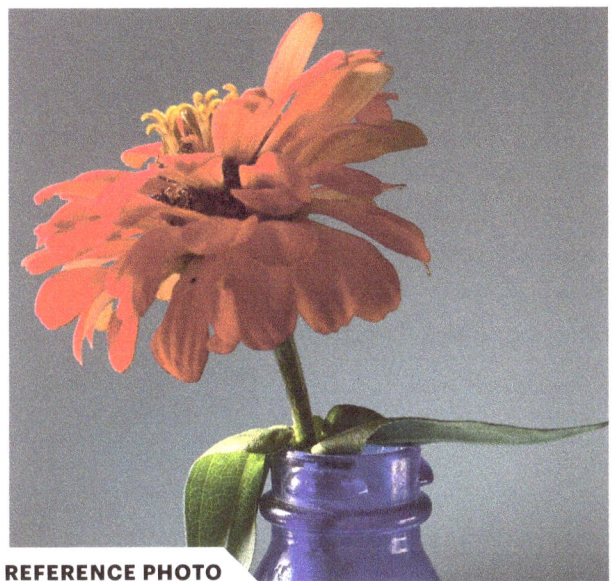

REFERENCE PHOTO

Tip

The drawing for this piece is a bit complicated, so you can choose to break it up into a drawing time and a painting time, or just do it all at once. If you're just going to do the drawing in this sitting, there's no need to wet your paints.

1

1 Because this is a detailed piece, I definitely suggest blocking out the placement of things lightly before you commit to darker lines. For example, a lightly sketched oval can represent the flower, a rectangle for the vase, and a couple long ovals for the leaves. Once these are sketched in with the correct proportions, you can get more detailed. As with any complicated drawing, look for shapes that can be simplified in your mind. The tips of the petals, for example, often have a very triangular shape you can modify more specifically.

2 Begin with the background color, making sure to get a nice even coat before moving on to the vase. You'll probably need to use a small brush to get into the tight crevices of the petals, as well as the small points in between the petals where the background shows through. Take your time here, because you want to avoid getting any of the greenish background color on the petals.

Moving on to the vase, start by adding the small sections of turquoise before painting in the predominant base of bright blue. You can leave the majority of the stem white for now, as you'll paint it in with a very dark blue on the next step.

BRUSHES: *No. 1 round and Nos. 4 and 6 filbert and flat*

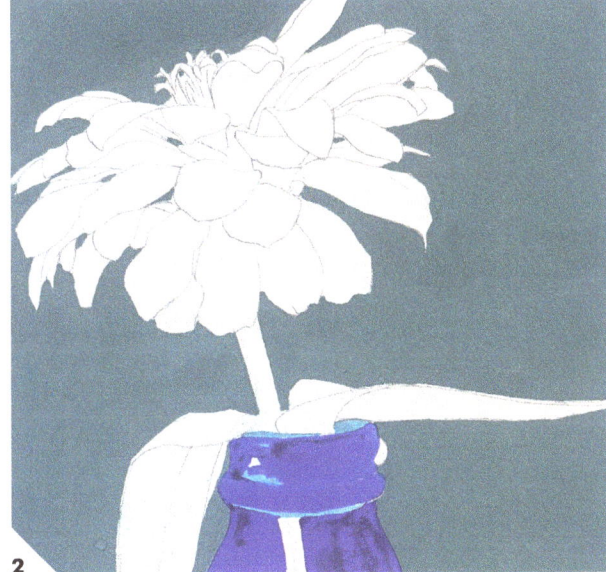

2

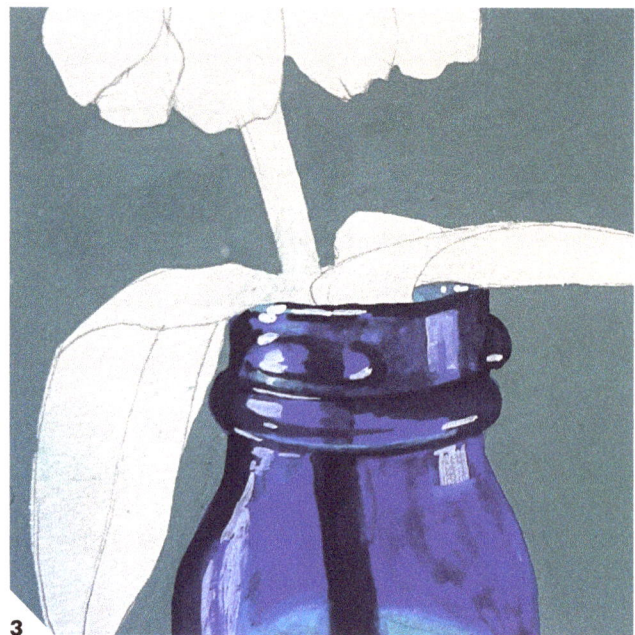

3

it lighter. Greens, especially light ones, can also be quite transparent and it's useful to put them directly onto the white of the paper.

As you study your reference photo, look for the subtle variations in the greens. Which places are brighter in hue? Which places look to be tinted or toned? I recommend starting with the places where the green seems the most vibrant and pure before moving on to the tinted or toned colors.

***

BRUSHES: *No. 1 round and No. 4 filbert or round*

3 Starting with a very dark blue, close to 90 percent on the grayscale, paint in both the flower's stem and the shadowed parts of the vase. This dark blue will help accentuate the shapes in the top of the glass jar, giving it dimension before you move on to the highlights.

I usually leave the highlights until the final step, but because this piece is so complex, it's easier to get the vase entirely finished before we move up to the flower. Use a very creamy white for these highlights, and wait until the blue of the vase is completely dry before applying the white to prevent unintended blending. For the larger sections of reflected light, use a bit of drybrushing to vary the opacity of the light.

***

BRUSHES: *No. 1 round and No. 4 filbert or round*

4 Knowing where to start when painting organic things like leaves can be a bit overwhelming. There's a large variety of colors, even in one leaf, depending how the light hits, and because of this, it can be easiest to break it down into bite-sized steps.

With green, I like starting light and working to dark. This is because it's always easier to make something darker, but much more difficult to make

5 Moving on from the light greens in the last step, begin working up to darker greens. Again, think about whether the green you're painting is shaded or toned. A lot of the darker greens in this piece will have gray added to them.

In the places where two colors meet, you can wait for the colors to dry and then come in with a damp brush to blend them or you can use a bit of dry-brushing to blend one color into the one next to it.

To finish this step, add a few highlights to key points on the leaves where the light hits them directly. This can help accentuate the edges of the leaves, as well as the veins.

***

BRUSHES: *No. 1 round and No. 4 filbert or round*

6 Because we're switching from blues and greens to oranges and reds, this is a good point to replace your dirty water with clean, fresh water and to make sure your brushes are clean as well.

Using a bright reddish-orange, paint in the lightest parts of the petals. For the most part, these are the petals on the upper and left-hand sides of the flower. But you will notice that it's mostly the top parts of the petals that catch the light. This is a helpful way to know which parts of the petals to paint during this step.

***

BRUSHES: *No. 1 round and No. 4 filbert*

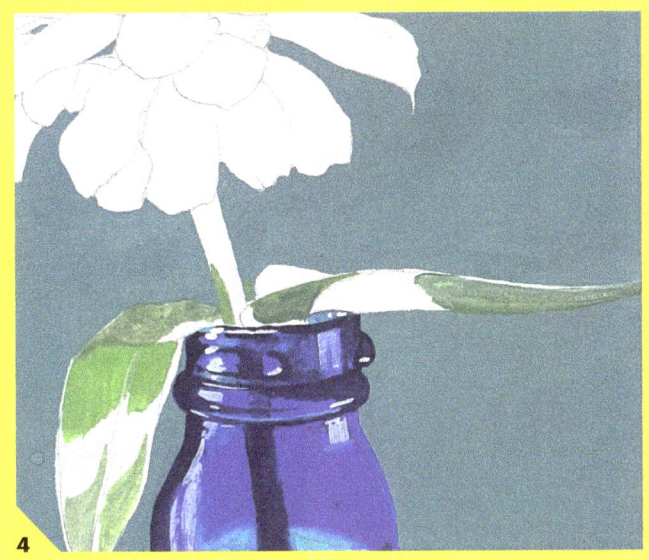

4

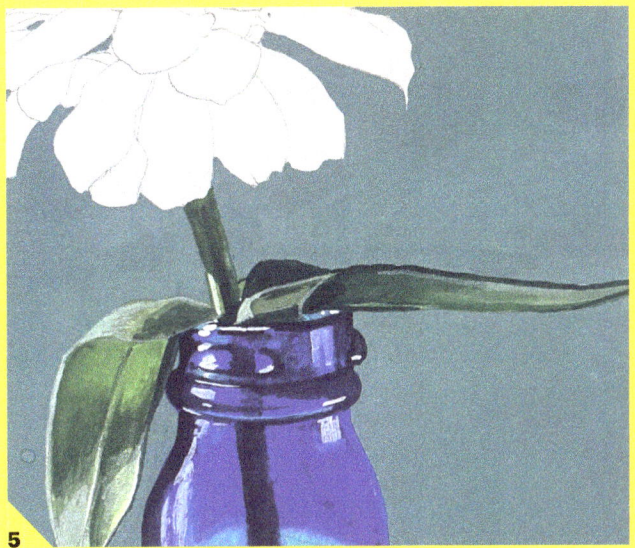

5

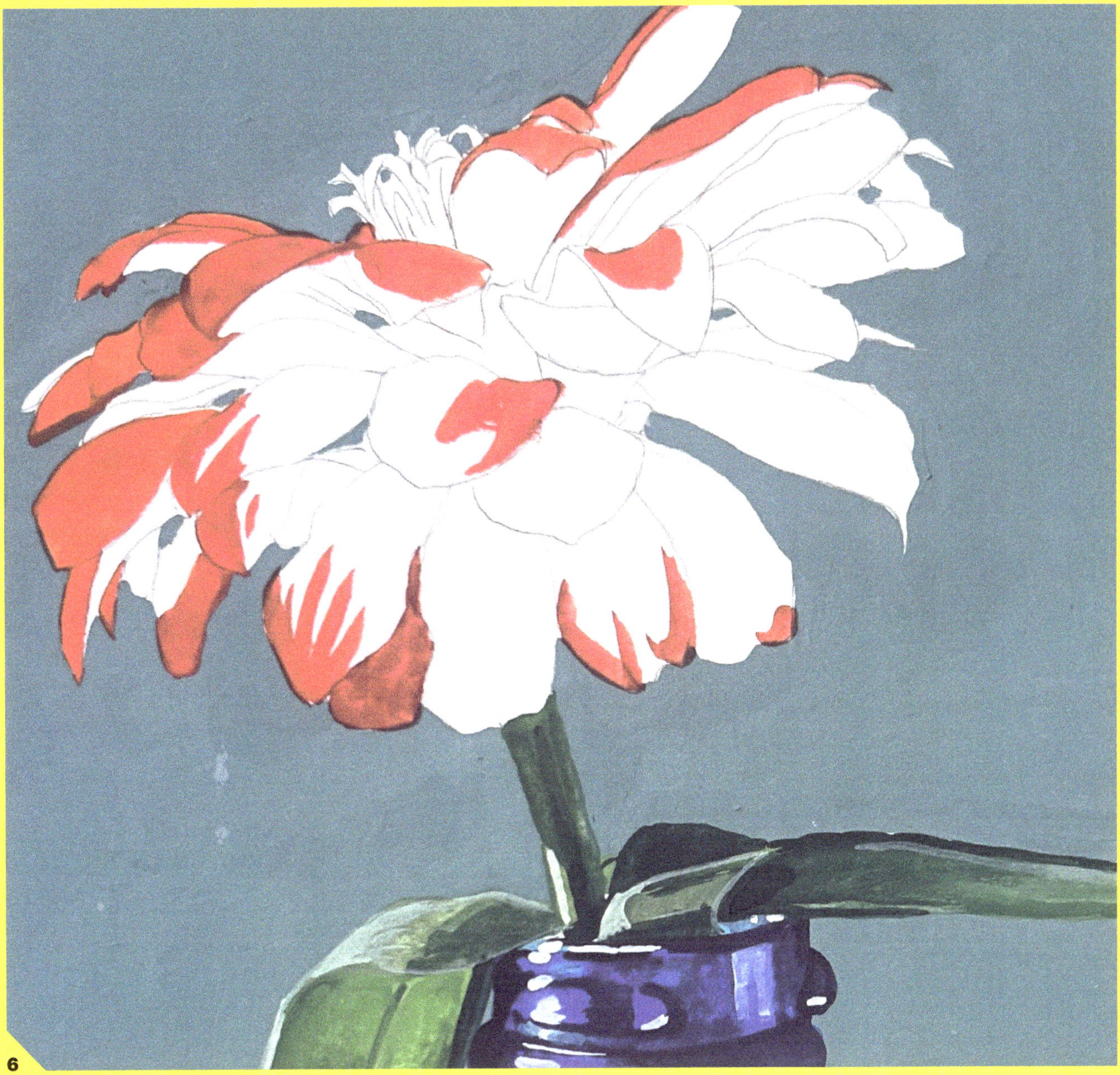

6

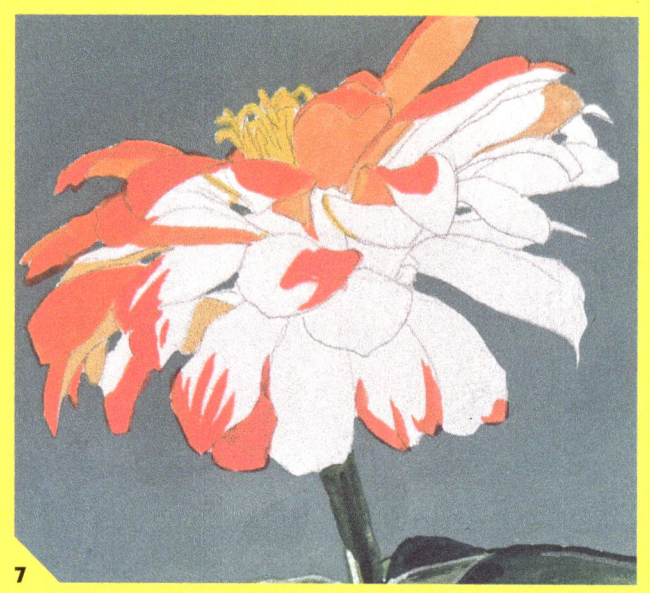

7

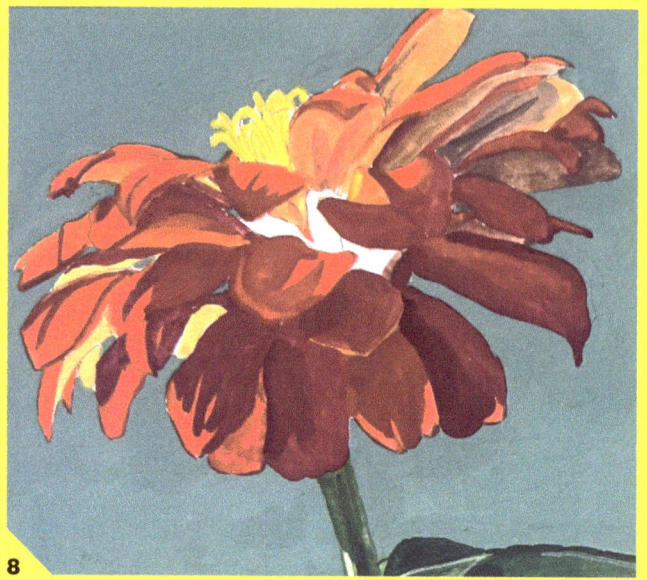

8

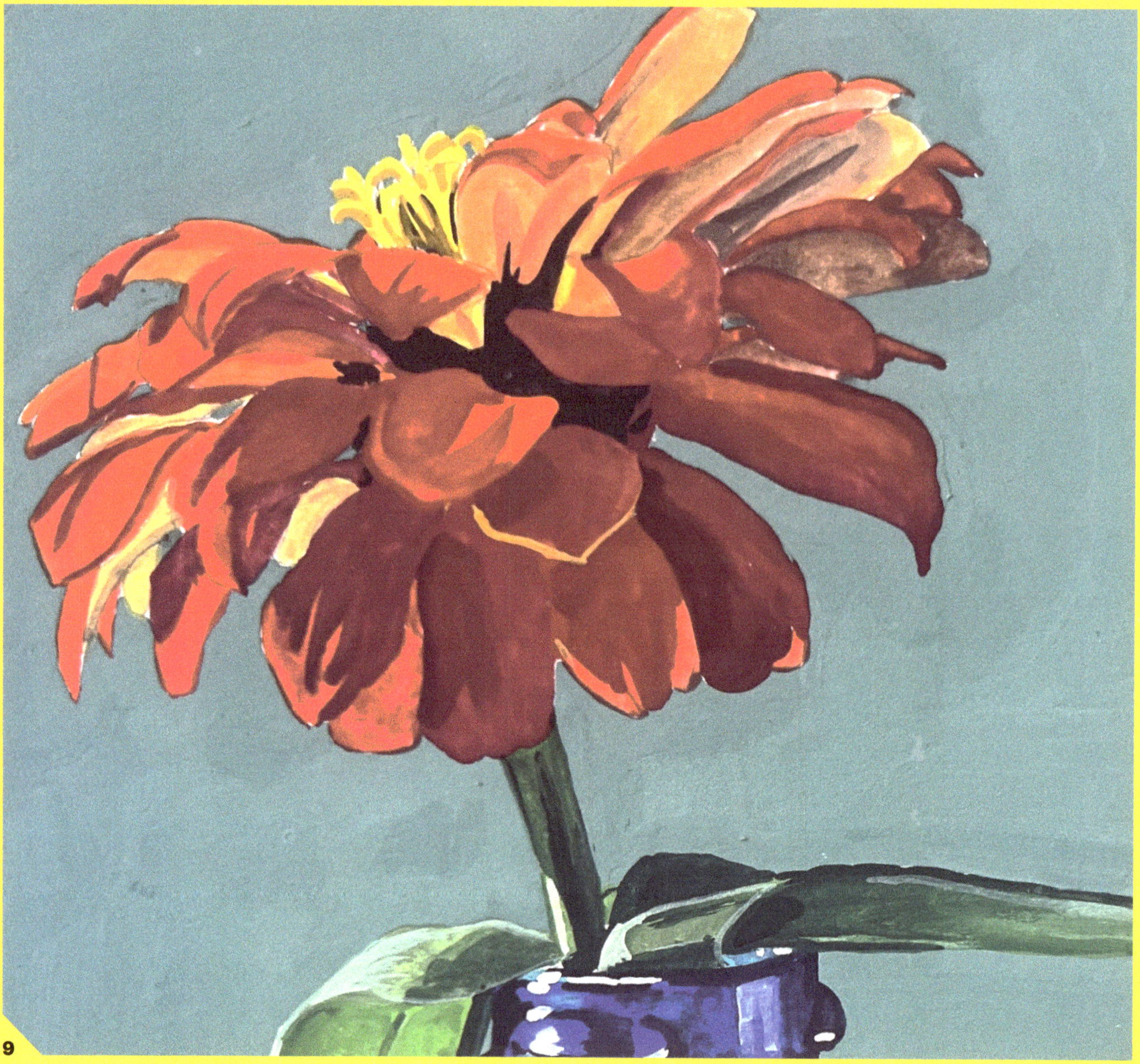

9

7 Continuing on with the portions of the flower most directly hit with light, you'll paint the bright yellow stamen, which are the tiny seeds at the center of the flower, and the orange undersides of the petals.

For the flower's stamen, use a bright yellow to cover everything. You'll come back in with a darker yellow in another step to add the shadows in this section.

The underside of the petals that are directly hit by light are an interesting color. They aren't brightly pigmented like the top of the petal but instead get a lot of their color from the light shining through the top of the leaf, making the bottom glow a bit.

———————————

BRUSHES: *No. 1 round and No. 4 round*

8 You'll use a couple of variations of dark red in this step, along with a toned version of the light orange from the previous step.

It might be easiest to begin with the toned orange, since you just used it. To achieve the correct value begin by adding just a little bit of gray. You'll notice that as you move down toward the bottom of the flower, the undersides of the petals get darker, meaning you'll add more gray to the orange.

Moving on to the dark red, there are parts of the petals you've already painted, which will also get a bit of this darker red. The only part you won't paint is the small section in the middle that has the darkest value.

———————————

BRUSHES: *No. 1 round and No. 4 filbert or round*

9 Unlike many of our previous paintings, in this piece, you'll add shadows for your final step. Remember I mentioned earlier that you'd be adding some darker yellow to the stamen? Now's the time. I used two different colors to achieve this. For the underside of the seeds, I used a few tiny dots of golden yellow to accentuate the bent shape of each of the tips of the stamen. Farther down, along the stems, I toned this darker yellow with a bit of gray.

The interior of the flower seen through some of the petals in this section can be painted a very dark brown. There may be a couple other points at the bases of the petals that you choose to add a bit of this dark brown to suggest the inside of the flower showing through.

Congratulations! You just completed the last project!

———————————

BRUSH: *No. 1 round*

About the Author

Kate Jarvik Birch is a full-time visual artist, author, playwright, and daydreamer. As a child she spent most of her time drawing girls in pretty dresses, horses, and dogs dressed as humans.

As an adult, her art has been featured worldwide in stores like Target, Pier One, and World Market, as well as in television series and major motion pictures such as *Transparent*, *Medium*, *Glee*, and *21 Jump Street*.

For the past five years, Kate has been working on her painting-a-day series, creating one small piece in gouache every day. Kate graduated with a degree in painting and drawing from the University of Utah in 2005 and lives and works in Salt Lake City, Utah.

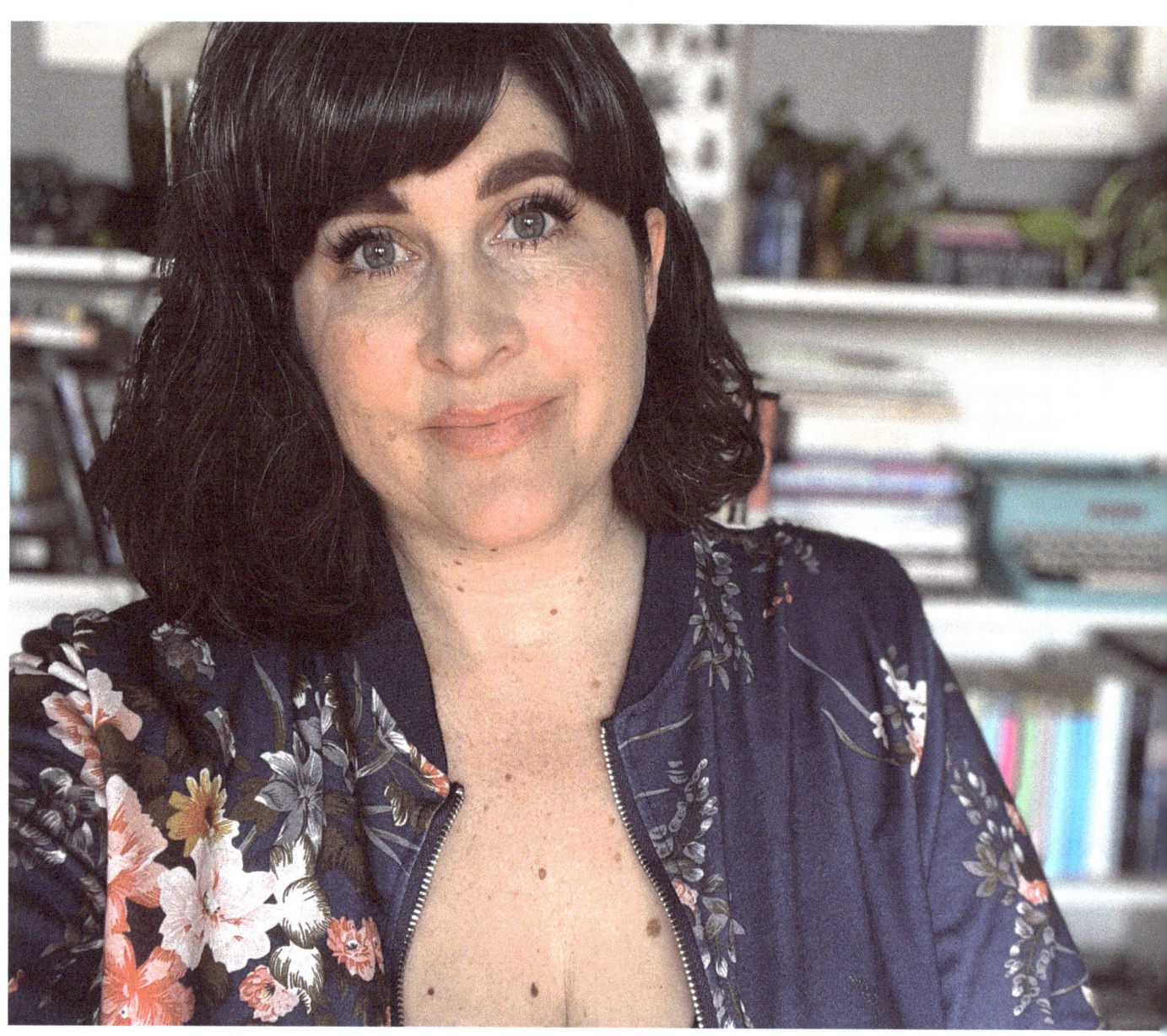

Index

www.ingramcontent.com/pod-product-compliance
Lightning Source LLC
Jackson TN
JSHW041120260725
88000JS00002B/2